UNDERGROUND
IN BERLIN

A young woman's
extraordinary tale of survival in
the heart of Nazi Germany

UNDERGROUND IN BERLIN

MARIE JALOWICZ SIMON

TRANSLATED BY ANTHEA BELL

WITH AN INTRODUCTION BY LISA APPIGNANESI
AND AN AFTERWORD BY HERMANN SIMON

ALFRED A. KNOPF CANADA

PUBLISHED BY ALFRED A. KNOPF CANADA

Originally published as *Untergetaucht. Eine junge Frau überlebt in Berlin 1940–1945* by S. Fischer Verlag GmbH, Frankfurt am Main.
Copyright © 2014 Hermann Simon and Irene Stratenwerth
English Translation Copyright © 2014 Anthea Bell
Published by arrangement with The Clerkenwell Press, an imprint of Profile Books, Ltd., United Kingdom

www.penguinrandomhouse.ca

Library and Archives Canada Cataloguing in Publication

Jalowicz Simon, Marie, 1922–1998
[Untergetaucht. English]
  Underground in Berlin : a young woman's extraordinary tale of survival in the heart of nazi germany / Marie Jalowicz Simon ; translated by Anthea Bell.

Translation of: Untergetaucht.
Issued in print and electronic formats.

ISBN 978-0-345-80969-8
eBook ISBN 978-0-345-80971-1

  1. Jalowicz Simon, Marie, 1922–1998. 2. Holocaust, Jewish (1939–1945)—
Germany—Berlin—Personal narratives. 3. Jews—Germany—Berlin—Biography.
4. Berlin (Germany)— Biography. 5. Berlin (Germany)—History—1918–1945.
I. Bell, Anthea, translator II. Title. III. Title: Untergetaucht. English

DS134.42.S54A3 2015   940.53'18092   C2014-906406-3

Cover design based on an original by Peter Dyer
Cover image: © Bert Hardy / Stringer / Getty Images
End papers: Map courtesy of S. Fischer Verlag
Printed and bound in the United States of America

10 9 8 7 6 5 4 3 2 1

Penguin
Random House
KNOPF CANADA

Contents

Introduction

Marie Jalowicz Simon, the extraordinary woman who narrates the wartime life recorded by her son in *Underground in Berlin*, was eleven years old when Hitler came to power in 1933. She was one of some 163,000 Berlin Jews, approximately a third of the total German Jewish population, which in turn was less than one per cent of the whole. Racist ideology doesn't need vast numbers to feed on. Feeling swamped needs no swamps.

By 1939, some 400 Nazi decrees later, the Jewish Berlin population had dwindled to 75,000. Laws had been put in place excluding Jews from the professions, public and business life, universities and state schools, and finally from unforced employment. Jews were stripped of assets, pensions and homes, compelled by the race laws of 1935 that made Jewishness a matter of lineage not religion, to declare themselves on ID cards and passports, and eventually on their clothes. After 9–10 November, 1938, *Kristallnacht*, the Night of Broken Glass, they were excluded from the very literature, theatres, concert halls, cinemas and sports venues that had so bound them to German culture. Eventually they were transported out of the country (on the only trains permitted them) and excluded from life itself. In May 1943, Berlin was declared *Judenrein* – cleansed and clear of its Jews.

But Marie Jalowicz was there. How this happened and how she managed to survive through the war years in Germany is the tale these vivid pages tell. They may be based on seventy-seven tapes of conversations she held with her son towards the end of what turned out to be a long postwar career as an academic in East Berlin, but they bear all the immediacy of the present tense.

Marie's mother, Betti, well-educated, vivacious died of cancer in 1938. Betti's brother, an orthodox and eccentric 'joke dealer', who lived with a gentile woman, followed her two months later, literally starving to death in protest at the Nazi prohibition on Kosher food provision. Marie's father, no longer able to practice as a lawyer, refused a visa to Palestine, lived an impoverished life with his daughter in bug-infested lodgings until he followed his wife in March 1941.

By this time Marie had already been working for some ten months – along with some 200 other Jewish women – as forced labour making armaments for Siemens at their Spandau plant. These were Rosie the Riveters with a vengeance! Their overseers were men, often enough Nazis. But a vibrant *esprit de corps* existed among the women. Solidarity, together with small acts of sabotage, made the long grind of daily life tolerable. Marie has a young person's curiosity about others and gets to know many on the shop floor. She also has a writer's relish for individual quirks and a marked ability to convey character with a telling detail.

Even though they may be anti-Semitic, the overseers bend a rule for her here and there and when she needs extra leave to cope with her father's death and funeral arrangements, it is granted. Soon after, since Jews can't leave a job, her superior fires her on her request. She wonders at this kindness of strangers, anti-Semites among them. She explains it to herself by noting that Berlin was not the provinces: its share of Communist and Social Democratic voters was far greater. Then, too, 'I realised that the same Aryan German who hated the rich Jew from the big house like poison … had nothing against starving young girls who worked hard, just as he worked hard himself.'

Her father dead, Marie has to find new lodgings. All around her relations and friends are being deported. She is pursued by official-dom to take up another forced labour post. But young woman that she is, she hungers for freedom rather more than for those essential ration coupons which come with registration and work. She starts wearing her Star of David only in the areas where she is known, then tears it off and hides it for long daily treks through the city. A threaded needle in her pocket allows her to sew it back as soon as she enters familiar terrain.

In June 1942, when the Gestapo come to arrest her at six in the morning, she manages to outwit them and leave the building in her petticoat. She has now gone to ground, or as the German title of this memoir has it, become *Untergetaucht* – submerged. U-boats was the name eventually given to those 1,700 Jews who managed somehow to survive the war under the surface of officialdom, to disappear, their identities changed and often changing, like their innumerable addresses and places of hiding.

When rules are made by madmen and torturers, justice lies in breaking them. It takes courage, cunning and occasionally a ruthless resilience that the young seem to be better at than the old. It also takes a great deal of the moral luck Marie has in spades to make it through the long, hungry war years, the bombing and the difficult aftermath.

I recognise that luck from my mother, whose wartime story I told in my family memoir, *Losing the Dead*. Living as a Jew under the Nazis was no business for shrinking violets or indeed for women who feel victimised by male attentions of the sexual kind. Linked to a fiancé, Marie escapes to Bulgaria. She enters into marriages of convenience, interprets a black eye as a feature that allows her to blend into the working class environment she moves in. She will do a great deal for food or lodging. This is not a time when anyone can be out on the streets during working hours. When the liberating Russians arrive, the sex act is no cause for immediate breakdown: rather, the proprietorial sign the soldier leaves on her door means she is bothered by no one else.

The fact that Marie emerges scathed but unbroken is a tribute to her great intelligence and inner resources.

This is a book which in its adventurous particularity as well as in its common experience sheds new light on a terrible time. Like Hans Fallada's *Alone in Berlin*, it throbs with the pulse of the backstreets of a world capital in peril. Here the working and criminal classes can be kinder than the educated elite who administer injustice.

But unlike Fallada, *Underground in Berlin* is testimony. It's also that rare thing – a wartime story from the woman's point of view. I couldn't put it down.

Lisa Appignanesi
December 2014

Prologue, 1942

It was freezing outside, and already dark. The bar was in Wassertor-strasse, part of the Kreuzberg district of Berlin where I had never been before. I entered the place, which was still entirely empty. Someone called 'Hello?' from a back room. Looking through the open doorway, I saw a woman sitting there mending a fur coat. She seemed very reluctant to abandon this occupation and shuffle through to the front room to see me.

Benno Heller had sent me here. He said I was to approach the only waitress in the bar, a woman called Felicitas. She was one of his patients. As a so-called 'half-Jew', she ought really to have been wearing the yellow star, but she was not. Heller, a gynaecologist, had already found me a place to stay now and then, but this time he had warned me: Felicitas is something of a crook. He had not been happy about giving me her address, but he didn't know anyone else who could help me.

A sense of terrible dread surfaced in me, a deep fear: everything in my situation and in this part of the city was strange to me. All the same, I brought myself to tell Felicitas, in a few words, why I had come.

She thought for a moment and then told me, in her thick Berlin accent, 'I know what. The rubber director ought to be here soon, he's always one of the first in the evening. He might be able to help.' Meanwhile, she told me to stand at the bar counter and act like any ordinary guest drinking a glass of beer.

Soon the 'rubber director' entered the bar. I was horrified. At a rough guess he was in his early fifties, and he walked with great difficulty. He moved as if his legs were made of rubber, and owed his nickname to his awkward gait and the fact that, as I learned later, he really was the director of a small company.

His way of communicating was like his odd walk, a kind of verbal mishmash, and he brought out what he meant to say only after various failed attempts. In order to be understood, he kept saying the same thing over and over again, hoping to get it out more clearly. Yet again I felt terribly anxious. A woman doctor among my circle of acquaintances had once told me about patients in the late stages of syphilis to whom she gave psychiatric treatment. She said that they walked as if their legs were made of rubber, and they could no longer articulate properly. For instance, they didn't say *Topflappen* [oven cloth] but *Topfappen*, and then corrected it to *Opfappen* – exactly as the man now before me spoke.

I couldn't hear what he and Felicitas were discussing, but afterwards I realised that she had sold me to him for fifteen marks. She wanted twenty, he offered ten, and they split the difference. Before I left the bar with him, Felicitas poured him another beer – he was a regular customer – and told me to go into the back room with her for a moment. There she told me the story she had served up to him: I was an old friend of hers, I had a husband at the front, and was living with my in-laws. My relationship with them, she told me, had become so unbearable that I had asked her to put me up somewhere, anywhere. She also confided, in an undertone, that Karl Galecki, the 'rubber director', was a Nazi whose fanaticism bordered on derangement.

Then we set off. It was so icy cold outside that it took our breath away. He offered me his arm; we did not say a word to each other.

The snow had frozen over and was glittering brightly. The moon was nearly full. I looked up at the sky: the Man in the Moon showed in gigantic proportions, a podgy face with a nasty grin. I felt desperately unhappy. Dogs can at least howl at the moon; I mustn't even do that.

Then I pulled myself together, thought of my parents and spoke to them silently in my mind. You needn't worry about me, I told them, not in the least, your upbringing has left a deep impression on me. What I'm going through now has not the faintest influence on my mind or my development. I have to survive it, that's all. The idea comforted me a little.

Marie Jalowicz in 1942, aged twenty.

The rubber director's home was not far from the bar, but he had such severe difficulty in walking that we made slow progress. Finally, we were outside a large building, with an arched entrance leading to a yard. The long, hut-like structure where he lived stood there, and a little further off was a second hut which was his workplace.

He ran the beam of a torch uncertainly over the door, looking for the keyhole – blackout restrictions were in force. I saw the nameplate beside the bell. Then I made my first mistake; to overcome my terrible fear I tried a touch of humour: I gave him a mock bow and said, 'Good evening, Herr Galezki.'

He stopped short. I was obviously the first person ever to have called him anything but 'Galekki'. But how was it that I knew the right way to pronounce a Polish 'c'? To explain that, I had to think up a lie quickly: a Herr Galecki used to live opposite us in my childhood, I said, a Pole who insisted on the proper pronunciation of his surname as 'Galezki'. The rubber director promptly insisted on more information: could this man be a relation of his, what was his job? And so on and so forth.

Then we went inside the hut. He lived here alone; his wife, he told me, stammering, had left him because she didn't want to live with a cripple. He had spent years of his life in hospitals and sanatoriums. And now, living here, he indulged in the passion that helped him to endure his loneliness: his fish. The walls of the long room were covered to left and right by aquariums. Here and there a gap between them left room for a piece of furniture, but on the whole the place was devoted to fish. I asked him how many he had. There were far more than he could count by now, an astonishingly wide variety of species.

Then he told me at length, and struggling again and again to get out the individual words, that he had his own fixed routine and wasn't going to change it. I reacted with great understanding. 'Why, of course you go to your regular bar every evening. We're joining forces, but we won't disturb one another,' I reassured him, adding, 'And of course you'll be eating your midday meal with your mother as usual.' We addressed each other by the informal *du* pronoun from the first, in the easy, spontaneous way of the bar-frequenting classes.

His bed stood at the back of the long hut where he lived, among the aquariums, and there was a sofa at the front on which I was to sleep. He showed me where to find a blanket, pillows and sheets.

Even without Felicitas, I would soon have realised that he was a fanatical Nazi. He proudly told me how, while he was in a sanatorium, he had made a matchstick model of Marienburg,* dedicating it to the Führer. He asked me to guess how many matchsticks he had used. I guessed some very high figure, but of course it was nothing like high enough. He happily corrected me, and showed me a couple of newspaper cuttings praising this little miracle, with pictures of it. I praised it too.

---

* *Translator's note:* Marienburg – a masterpiece of Gothic architecture now located in Malbork, in northern Poland.

Towards the far end of this curious dwelling a picture frame hung on the wall, containing another frame, an empty passe-partout consisting of two pieces of glass. Oh dear, I thought, maybe this was someone's way of portraying a void, or some such nonsense. When the empty item was being framed, a hair must have got stuck in it. It lay at a slant on the surface, and showed an interesting play of colour.

'Any idea what that is?' he asked me, pointing at it.

'No idea at all.' Even if I'd guessed, I would never have said so. Finally, he revealed the secret: he had acquired this item by complicated means and at some expense, as he told me, closing his eyes. It was a hair from the Führer's German shepherd.

'Goodness me,' I said, 'I'd never have ventured to suggest such a thing in case I hurt your feelings if I was wrong. Why, that's wonderful!'

Then he showed me the kitchen, and something that I hadn't expected in this crazy aquarium: a side door leading to a proper, normal bathroom.

After that we sat together for a while. I had become used to the strange jumble of words that he came up with, and I did not stare at him inquisitively, so he gradually cast off all inhibitions and gave his enthusiasm for Nazi ideology free rein. None the less, I was terribly afraid of betraying myself. I could keep myself from saying the wrong thing, but I didn't have all my physical reactions under control. For instance, he assured me that 'the Ewes, the Yoose, the Jews must all die'. I felt myself flushing red, jumped up, pointed to one of the aquariums and said, 'Oh, look, those fish are swimming in a different way now.' He clapped his hands in approval – I was a good observer of his darlings!

It was in fear and desperation that I made contact with those fish. I knew no *broche*, no Hebrew blessing for them, and I was not sure whether God existed at all. On the other hand, he was my reliable companion – *hakodaush boruch hu* – and I told him, 'You must take the *broche* as it comes to me. If you won't even let me have a *siddur*, a prayer book, or a reference book where I can look things up, it's no use expecting verbal perfection.'

I think God was reasonable himself, and saw my point. My improvised *broche* ran, 'Praise be to you, king of the world, *baure ha dogim*, who made the fish.' I also addressed the fish directly in my mind. I am in mortal danger, abandoned by everyone, I told them. You are innocent creatures, just like me. Please intercede for me, you silent fish, when human beings abandon me.

A little later, the rubber director announced, 'There's something I must tell you. This isn't easy for me, so I will keep it short.' With bowed head and tears in his eyes, he said he was afraid he must disappoint me: he was no longer capable of any kind of sexual relationship. I tried to react in a neutral, friendly manner, but I was overcome by such relief and jubilation that I couldn't sit still, and fled to the toilet.

It was the most sublime and edifying visit to the toilet of my life. I conjured up in my mind Friday evening prayers as I had so often heard them in the Old Synagogue, of course in an abbreviated version. I call on you, dear choirboys, to sing, I thought, and made them sing as I remembered it. Everything served to thank God for saving me from deadly danger.

I do not know, of course, just what Galecki really suffered from at the time, but I believed he was syphilitic, and if I had been obliged to share his bed I would indeed have felt myself to be in mortal danger. Once I knew that matters would not come to that, I felt deeply relieved, as if I had been set free. *Hashem li welau iro* – God is with me, I fear nothing, I recited silently before I returned to Galecki.

The rubber director's hut would really have been an ideal hiding place for me, if only the man hadn't been such an incorrigible Nazi.

ONE

I was to learn to assert myself

Childhood and Youth in Berlin

1

My parents had been married for eleven years when I was born on 4 April 1922. I was their first and only child, and my mother's late pregnancy was a great surprise to them both.

Hermann and Betti Jalowicz had both grown up in the Mitte district of Berlin, but in very different circumstances. My grandfather Bernhard Jalowicz dealt in job lots of cheap goods, a business based in Alte Schönhauser Strasse. He was a heavy drinker and beat his wife. His birth name had been Elijahu Meir Sachs, but after emigrating from Russia he had bought identity papers bearing the name Jalowicz from a widow in Calbe on the River Saale.

His sons went to school, gained their school-leaving certificates and studied at university. Besides studying law, my father participated in the Zionist sports movement. Jewish immigrants from Eastern Europe were considered physically degenerate, as a result of the cramped living conditions in ghettos and their pursuit of such traditional Jewish activities as selling their wares from door to door. The Zionist idea was to do away with this stigma, and encourage a new national Jewish frame of mind by means of healthy exercise in the fresh air. From time to time my father was the editor responsible for the supraregional journal of the Jewish gymnastics association.

My mother Betti was also active in the Bar Kokhba sports club. Her father was a grandson of the famous rabbi Akiva Eger, and thus belonged to the Jewish scholastic aristocracy. The prestige of his family background enabled him to marry into the Russian Jewish Wolkowyski family, who were very rich, and he invested his wife's substantial dowry in building up a large forwarding agency with offices on Alexanderplatz in Berlin.

My mother, the youngest of six siblings, had been born in 1885. She was a plump little woman whose intellect, wit and enormous

Hermann and Betti Jalowicz,
Marie's parents, around 1932.

vitality impressed everyone as soon as she opened her mouth. Her unusual combination of dark hair with blue eyes was an attractive feature in her; less attractive were her short, fat legs.

My father, at that time a good-looking young man with many girls chasing him, got to know Betti Eger for the first time on the telephone. He is said to have told her, 'I've heard so many delightful things about you; I suppose I'm sure to be disappointed when I meet you in person.' My mother immediately fell for that line; they did meet, and fell in love. In 1911 they were married in my mother's family home at 44 Rosenthaler Strasse. My Eger grandparents' large apartment lay opposite the newly built courtyard complex of the Hackesche Höfe in central Berlin.

In his early years practising as a lawyer, my father had gone into partnership with his colleagues Max Zirker and Julius Heilbrunn, who had their chambers in Alexanderstrasse. He had been to school with Zirker, who had grown stout since those days, but enjoyed social occasions as much as his partner Heilbrunn. Meanwhile, my father sat at his desk attending to the everyday work of the practice.

Angry resentment gradually built up in Betti Jalowicz. She felt that Zirker and Heilbrunn were unscrupulously exploiting her husband. 'Let's build up a practice of our own. We'll make it,' she kept telling my father, to encourage him. And a little while before the outbreak of the First World War the two of them did indeed move into their own premises, at 19a Prenzlauer Strasse, a few hundred metres from Alexanderplatz. That address was their living and working space rolled into one.

My mother devoted herself energetically to this legal practice. She had always been sorry that she couldn't take a school-leaving examination and embark on further studies herself. When her older brothers were studying jurisprudence, she secretly followed the course that they were taking. As a young woman she had been office manager in her brother Leo's large legal chambers, where she was not only in charge of all the staff but drafted whole documents herself. From the legal viewpoint, they were often so brilliantly written that nothing in the wording or punctuation of her drafts had to be changed.

My father was certainly interested in jurisprudence and the philosophy of law, but he hated the daily routine of a lawyer's life, and was useless as a businessman. He would sometimes leave the room when a client got on his nerves, slamming the door behind him and telling my mother, 'You go and deal with him; this is *your* practice.'

On the other hand, he loved to amuse a large social gathering with accounts of curious incidents from his working life. For instance, he told the tale of the client who, in great agitation, showed him a summons to appear in court on a certain day. 'Look at that, Dr Jalowicz, look at that!' he kept saying as he pointed to the date. Only when the client explained that it was Yom Kippur did my father understand the problem. 'It's Puderbeutel's doing!' the client lamented. Puderbeutel was the name of his adversary in the case concerned, and he was convinced that the villain had meant to hit him where it hurt by ensuring that he would have to offend against the Jewish holy day by appearing in court.

My father also liked to tell the story of the old Jewish woman who came to see him in order to ask whether a man is supposed to beat his wife. Even as she spoke she was beginning to remove her clothes to show him the evidence of conjugal violence. 'No, no, don't do that!' he had said, horrified.

His clients also included non-Jewish members of the working class, like the man who came to ask a question; he stammered, but my father made out, with difficulty, that the matter concerned someone whose gold teeth had been removed after he had died in hospital. With care and great tact, he asked which of the man's loved ones had been so shamefully mistreated. 'Doesn't have to be a loved one, does it?' inquired the man, annoyed. He was a pall-bearer, and wanted to lodge a complaint against the Virchow hospital, which was delivering corpses deprived of their gold teeth to the cemeteries. In the opinion of my father's client, it was the pall-bearers' right to supplement their meagre income by robbing the bodies themselves.

My grandparents on my mother's side had both died before I was born. After that, my aunt Grete took over the apartment at 44 Rosenthaler Strasse. She gave dinner parties there for the whole family circle on the major Jewish holidays, and every year our unforgettable Seder evenings took place in her huge dining room.

As far back as I can remember, my great-aunt Doris presided over the company, as the eldest member of the family. She always wore grey silk, with a ribbon round her neck, and the expression on her face reminded me of a bulldog. Doris Schapiro had once been a very rich woman, and had fled from Russia to Berlin before the revolution. Her daughter Sylvia Asarch, who had a similar story behind her, was always present at these gatherings as well.

There were not many children in the family – apart from me, only my cousins Kurt-Leo and Hanna-Ruth. That made Uncle Arthur all the more important to us. A very amusing man, and fond of children, Arthur was an extraordinary bundle of contradictions.

A family party at the summer house in Kaulsdorf in March 1932. Top row, from left: Herbert Eger, Sylvia Asarch, Mia Eger, Edith Lewin (a niece from Riga), Betti Jalowicz, Julius Lewin. Bottom row: Kurt-Leo Eger, Margarete (Grete) Eger, Marie Jalowicz. Front: Hanna-Ruth Eger, Hermann Jalowicz.

Even his outward appearance was unusual. The Egers were usually short and either fat or thin, but Arthur towered at least a head above them all. The others had nondescript dark hair; Arthur's was fiery red. He differed from the rest of the family in mindset as well, being both a communist and a passionately Orthodox Jew. He used to send his sister Grete, with whom he sometimes stayed, nearly crazy with his religious notions and practices. Professionally, Arthur traded in joke and novelty articles. For a while he had a shop in Münzstrasse, later he ran a market stall, but his projects regularly led to bankruptcy.

On Jewish holidays there was bound to be trouble with him. When everyone else had arrived at Rosenthaler Strasse after the religious service, and were waiting for the festive meal to be served, he invariably arrived last. At the time, family members used to say, 'Ah, well, Arthur's closing the *shul* again,' referring to the synagogue,

Picture postcard of Arthur Eger as a soldier in the First World War, 1915, left in the picture. The postcard reads: 'How well one could live if one were a millionaire and the war was over – apart from that, we're in good health. Regards from Arthur.'

and with a punning reference to *Schule*, school. He always met more acquaintances outside the synagogue and would talk to them for hours.

But when, on a Seder evening, he spoke of the exodus of the Jews from Egypt, he did so with such deep and serious feeling that he might have been there himself. And every time the standard liturgy continued after the meal, he looked a little paler, and announced with credible alarm, 'The Seder cannot go on; thieves have broken in and stolen the *afikaumon*.' The word meant a special piece of matzo that we children had hidden. If we brought it out, we were rewarded with something sweet – that was the custom.

Long before I went to school, Arthur tried to teach me the Hebrew alphabet. That, too, was in line with an old Jewish custom. My father used to tell me how, when he was a little boy sitting on his grandfather's lap, the old man had told him, 'My boy, now you are three years old, and I don't want you learning your German alphabet first and then our own sacred letters, but the other way round.'

However, Arthur's way of going about my lessons infuriated my mother. The first that he drew for me was ה, the Hebrew letter H. Arthur told me, 'Look at that, my child, that's H, and you say *hi*. Now repeat it: *hi*.'

Of course I showed it proudly to my parents. 'See that? It's a *hi*.'

'Where did you learn such nonsense?' they said at once. For pronouncing the letter *hi* instead of *hey* was an older usage, regarded as outmoded and inelegant, something that they did not want me to learn.

Arthur was constantly at odds with Aunt Grete. For instance, he liked to drink tea with a great many sugar lumps in it, which she thought wasteful. But whenever she protested, Arthur, adding lump after lump to his cup, quoted a silly advertising slogan claiming that the body needed sugar for nourishment:

Don't believe the folk who say that sugar is no good.
You need sugar every day as an essential food.

Sometimes he declaimed the rhyme like a small child reciting a verse and then getting stuck; at other times he assumed the manner of a ham actor. My stern, dour Aunt Grete kept begging him to stop it – until even she burst out laughing. By then he would have more than ten lumps of sugar in his tea.

When I was about ten years old, I saw him sitting at the table a day or so after Pessach, putting a piece of matzo on top of a piece of bread, and repeating over and over again, with a silly giggle, 'Chometz and matzo', leavened and unleavened bread. No sensible person would still be eating unleavened bread after the Pessach festival,* but he made a joke out of it. It was then I realised that

---

*Among the main features of Pessach is the ban on eating leavened bread (chamez, in Hebrew) or even having it in the house. However, no one eats matzo, unleavened bread, after those few days, although it is not forbidden. In the narrative read on the

Arthur was acting a part, only you never knew where his joking ended and he was serious again.

The apartment in Rosenthaler Strasse was also the scene of many family stories that were told only surreptitiously. One of them was about my aunt Ella, and happened when I was still a small child.

At the turn of the century she had been sent for a few months to Boldera near Riga, where one of the Wolkowyski family's country estates lay. She must have been a pretty, amusing young woman then, and it was high time for her to marry. In Riga she met Max Klaczko, and they married soon after that. It was only later that she realised he was a terrible psychopath, always grumbling and finding fault, a man who would make her life hell.

Ella and Max Klaczko once came to visit in Berlin, bringing their daughter Edit. While Ella was happy to be back in her familiar childhood surroundings in Rosenthaler Strasse, her husband went off on his own to see the city. One evening in the year 1926 he stayed out for a long time. When the family had begun worrying about him, the doorbell rang. A police officer stood there, and told Ella, with the usual set expression of sympathy, 'It is my sad duty to inform you that your husband has had a fatal accident in crossing the road near the Kaiser Wilhelm Memorial Church.'

The story goes that Ella uttered a cry of joy, flung her arms round the policeman and performed such a wild dance with him that he could hardly keep his footing. After that, he had to be paid handsomely to keep his mouth shut – while he kept assuring everyone that he was not corrupt. Even Uncle Arthur, who had been broke all his life, offered, 'Shall I contribute something? It's a tidy sum.'

A few days later, Ella Klaczko could feature as the perfect example of a grieving widow, not just to outward appearance but in her general attitude. And indeed, her situation was wretched;

Seder evening we are asked: 'Why is this night different from other nights? On other nights, we can eat leavened and unleavened bread (chamez and matzo), but on this night only unleavened bread.'

her husband left her his typewriter shop in Riga, and nothing else but debts. All Ella possessed were a few typewriters, with which she opened a typing and translation bureau in her apartment.

My mother often told me about the delicious things she had eaten when she, too, went to spend a few months on the Boldera estate. Sometimes we went to a Russian delicatessen in Charlottenburg. I always loved to go shopping for these good things. Particularly choice tea came in boxes with gold decoration and a strange inscription. 'Why is there a back-to-front R here?' My mother explained that it was a Я, pronounced 'ja', which means yes in German. So I got to know the Russian alphabet.

We sometimes bought sugared *klyukva*, cranberries, thickly covered in icing sugar. You nibbled them while drinking tea. Or *kil'ki* – sprats in oil – and grilled peas, with a slightly smoked flavour. I don't know whether all these things really tasted so good, or whether I was just enchanted by their exotic aspect. My mother told me how in her own childhood she could tell from the smell in the front hall of the apartment whether visitors from Russia had come. The smell of Russian leather given off by their heavy coats could be picked up even in the stairwell; it evoked that special, intense French perfume *Cuir de Russie*. She felt those odours were promising – they promised that soon there would be delicatessen to eat. Our relations from Riga also brought us special delicacies from there, for instance *kalkun*, stuffed turkey. My mother waxed enthusiastic because it reminded her of her childhood, and I liked the taste too.

Soon after my sixth birthday I began going to elementary school in Heinrich-Roller-Strasse. It was 1928, the time of mass unemployment. Many very poor people lived near the catchment area of this school. All the same, my parents did not want to send me to an exclusive private school. I was to learn the social environment there, along with its Berlin dialect, and learn also to assert myself in those surroundings. At the same time, however, they wanted to limit my contact with that world.

The first day at school; Marie Jalowicz in 1928, aged six.

For many years my father took me to school every day. Our morning walk together, and the good conversations we had, strengthened the bond between us. I was collected from school by my nanny, Levin. As soon as I got home I was stripped and washed from head to foot. My clothes were either put in with the laundry or hung up to air, and I wore a fresh set: apparently I had taken on the typical, musty smell of the school.

I skipped the third year. Even before 1933, my parents had a pressing sense of inner uneasiness, and wanted me to get through my schooling quickly. Like my mother and my aunts before me, I changed to the Sophien-Lyzeum elementary school. The three years that I spent there did not mould my character in any particular way. What impressed me most was the arrest of our mathematics teacher Frau Draeger.* This must have been in 1933; from my desk,

---

* Margarete Draeger was obliged to retire in 1933 because she had Jewish forebears. After several other activities, she became a forced labourer at Siemens in 1942, went

I saw her being prevented from entering the classroom. Two men in civilian clothes were standing outside the door. She was white as a sheet. A little later I heard the click of handcuffs. Of course I talked about this incident at home. 'Ask a few questions inconspicuously,' said my father, 'and try to find out who else saw it.' I did as he said, with the result that I was apparently the only child to have observed the scene.

---

underground before she was due to be deported, but was discovered in 1944 and sent to Auschwitz.

2

My mother was only fifty-three years old when she died, on 30 June 1938, of the cancer from which she had been suffering for a long time.* We spared our non-Jewish friends the dilemma of whether or not to attend a Jewish funeral by intentionally sending out the death announcements too late for them to come.

We were in a terrible situation. My father was earning almost nothing now, and he had run up debts everywhere. He had not been allowed to practise as a notary since 1933. His permit to run a legal practice was valid until September 1938, on the grounds of a regulation making an exception for Jewish 'frontline fighters' in the First World War. But when that date came, his career in the law ended. We had nothing left except for a small pension, and

---

*Marie Simon says no more about this event; only that one sentence. More about the death of Betti Jalowicz can be gathered from Hermann Jalowicz's diary. '5.5.38. Went with little Marie to see Betti. X-ray of her head. In great pain. <u>Very serious conversation with little Marie that night</u>. The child's calm is amazing. Before, however, she wept a great deal. 6.5.38, little Marie has been sleeping in Betti's bed since 4. May. 12.5.38, to see Betti with little Marie. Conversation with Dr Jakob. I felt ill in the hospital. – On foot with little Marie to the Gesundbrunnen underground station. Conversation very serious and moving. 31.5. Not a single peaceful night since she came home (the same as before she was in the hospital). [...] The prospects are gloomy. True, Betti does not talk as sadly as before, but her thoughts are sad. At the end of May she told me she could hardly bear the pain, we must not mourn her too much when she is gone, it would be a release for her. June 1938: a considerable deterioration in the last week of the month. [...] While Betti lies in pain on her deathbed, children are daubing slogans on the doors and windows of Jewish businesses. Later, other Jewish nameplates are defaced, for instance Jacobi's, Eger's, Michelsohn's and my own. [...] On Tuesday, 28.6, Dr Gorze urged me to take Betti to the hospital. Little Marie and I declined, since that was not Betti's wish and she is incurable. 30.6. At three-quarters to three, the nurse woke me, I woke little Marie. We sat quietly with Betti, I held her hand in mine, until at six in the morning her heart stopped beating.'

what I could earn by providing schoolchildren with extra coaching.

Aunt Grete had had to move out of Rosenthaler Strasse long ago, and was now living with Arthur in a small apartment in the same building as ours. She ran the typing bureau from it, keeping herself and her brother as best she could.

Arthur too died that summer, only two months after my mother. He literally starved to death. He was stricter than the most Orthodox of rabbis in observing the dietary rules, and among other things had eaten no meat at all since ritual slaughter was forbidden. I was present when one day Grete served meat all the same. Eyes flashing, he asked, 'How do we come to have something so good in this hovel?'

'It's the new kosher, you see,'* explained Grete. He pushed his plate away, saying, 'New kosher is *treife*.'

Because of his stomach ulcer, he had to go to hospital several times in the months before his death. 'His ulcer is not so bad in itself,' the doctors told Grete, 'he's ill because he refuses to take nourishment.' And it was no joke when he said that he wanted to sacrifice himself, but his answer to the political situation.†

The big apartment at 19a Prenzlauer Strasse was much too expensive for us now. We needed somewhere else to live, and found a place through a former client of my father's who was an opponent of the Nazis, and a faithful friend to us. Herr Weichert was so short-sighted that he was almost blind, and so hard of hearing that he was almost deaf, but he drove at breakneck speed through the city in a

---

* Under National Socialist law, animals had to be stunned before being slaughtered, which is contrary to Jewish ritual law. Becuase of this law, stunned animals were slaughtered by Jewish ritual butchers and the meat then called 'new kosher'. However, in the view of strict Orthodox Jews, such meat was considered *treife*, 'impure'.
† Arthur Eger left a short farewell letter to his girlfriend, Hilde Hauschild: 'A special farewell to you, dear Hilde. Forgive me! Thank you for the last time for all the joy you have given me. I could not reward you earlier, nor can I now. May God reward you and give you a happy life. Do not mourn or weep, I beg you. Yours beyond the grave. Arthur.'

little delivery van. One day he came to see us and said, 'I have just the thing for you.'

He had entirely misunderstood us, and thought we wanted to buy a small house, which would have been grotesque in view of our situation, for in the late summer of 1938 we not only had to give up our apartment, we also had to sell the plot of land on which our small summer house in Kaulsdorf in the Wuhlheide stood. My father and mother had bought it seven years before. The new owners were Hannchen and Emil Koch, acquaintances of my parents who came from Kaulsdorf and had previously rented our wooden house there.

But Herr Weichert had also misunderstood the people with whom he put us in touch: they didn't have a small house for sale at all, only sewing machines. Adolf and Margarete Waldmann, as Jews, had to give up the little ready-to-wear clothing business that they had run at 47 Prenzlauer Strasse, so there was a large room left empty at that address, and we moved into it.

Soon after my mother's death, Margarete Waldmann became my father's last great love. She was much younger than him, had a small son, and felt greatly honoured because my father adored her so much. He wrote verses to her, and even though we didn't have any money at all to spare, he spoiled her with presents of good things to eat. At the age of sixteen I could easily see that she was just toying with his affection. You didn't need either maturity or intelligence to work that out.

At the same time, there was the possibility of his contracting a marriage of convenience with a school headmistress called Dr Schiratzki, so that he could emigrate with her. The suggestion came from the Palestine Office.* You just marry her, I thought, and I'll never have anything to do with you again!

Outside the quota regulations, there was a chance that my father

---

*At the Palestine Office in Berlin, which had been set up in 1924 as a welfare institution, Zionist groups under the aegis of the Jewish Agency organised the emigration of German Jews to Palestine.

might be granted what was known as a veteran's certificate for Palestine, a permit for a deserving former soldier who was a member of the Zionist movement to emigrate there. The certificate would probably have covered me as well, and we would both have escaped from Germany. But then, in a rather dubious manner, it went to someone else, and the chance fell through.

The Waldmanns were also trying to emigrate. The only possibility was for them to go to Shanghai, and they planned to make the immensely long journey on the Trans-Siberian Railway. That woman tried to make my father believe that she was going to jump off the train at the last moment. 'My husband will leave with little Martin on the train, and then I'll be all yours,' she promised him. 'Don't believe her nonsense!' I protested. We had a terrible quarrel, and he almost won it. I was still too immature to recognise this ridiculously youthful love of his for what it was: a flame flickering for the last time before death.

The situation was becoming acute. If we didn't want to be turned out on the street, I thought, then I must do something – which meant making myself available to the woman's husband. I had some sexual experience already, and I thought: what does it matter? Let's get it over and done with.

In fact it happened only twice. Herr Waldmann and I went to the once very respectable King of Portugal Hotel, a Jewish-run establishment. And whom should I meet on the steps outside it but my gymnastics teacher? We smiled at each other. So she, too, was here with a man. And I was still a schoolgirl.

In the autumn of 1938, all Jews with Polish passports were expelled from Germany. Several boys in my class at the newly founded Jewish secondary school in Wilsnacker Strasse were affected. Most of these fellow-students of mine were natives of Berlin who had been born in the city or had arrived as babies. Now, all of a sudden, they had to leave. Our class reacted to the parting in a remarkably disciplined manner: for a while we kept silent, and then lessons went on. There was nothing to be said about what had happened.

The places formerly occupied by these classmates of ours were not left empty for long. The next thing to happen was that all Jewish students were expelled from non-Jewish schools, and crowded into our classrooms. More and more chairs were brought in, and many students had to write on their laps.

Our supervising teacher was one Professor Hübener, a specialist in the philology of modern languages. He had been in a relationship for years with our class teacher Fräulein Philippson, who was Jewish. He was not a very courageous man, and he clearly felt it uncomfortable to be in charge of this Jewish school. When he fell ill, the headmaster of another secondary school, Herr Schröder, was appointed to supervise the school-leaving examination, the *Abitur*. Reinhard Posnanski, a fellow-student who had previously been taught by Schröder, was horrified when he heard that. 'For God's sake,' he said, 'Schröder is an officer in the SS.'

We were all dreadfully afraid of him. When he marched into the classroom, all of us taking the exam gathered together, along with the teaching staff. In the sharpest of military tones Schröder barked, 'Posnanski! Come forward!' My classmate went white as a sheet, but the supervising teacher put out his hand and said, 'Greetings to you as my former pupil!' And that was all there was to it.

I had chosen German as my special subject, and in the oral examination I was given a poem in Middle High German to read aloud. When I had finished, Herr Schröder told me, 'That was really excellent! You look so young, yet you could have stepped into this room straight out of the Middle Ages.' Our teachers told us later that when it came to marking the exams, Schröder had insisted on giving them all a score higher than the original assessment, and in fact that was definitely a fair judgement of our achievements by comparison with those of non-Jewish schools. Apart from that, this was a difficult time. Most of my fellow students came from families who were doing all they could to be allowed to emigrate. The happy life usually enjoyed by young people who had just taken their school-leaving examination was not for us any more.

None the less, my father wanted to have dinner at Grete's

apartment in celebration of my exam results; there was no way of doing it in our own room. The Waldmanns were to be among the guests. 'If he dares to bring that tart into the house so soon after my dear sister's death, I'm not lifting a finger to help you!' declared my aunt. I was at my wits' end. I was still very inexperienced as a housekeeper, and now I had to cook dinner for a dozen people. Furthermore, of course there was no money.

In the end, exactly what I had predicted happened. My father took the Waldmanns to the station, the train began moving away, and Frau Waldmann did not jump out. At that moment my father was finally disillusioned. He collapsed completely, and from then on I just felt dreadfully sorry for him.

We moved out of the Waldmanns' apartment, and rented two little rooms from a family called Goldberg at 32 Landsberger Strasse. They meant well, but they were typical *petits bourgeois*, and frankly inquisitive. We couldn't put up with it in the long run. Frau Goldberg kept following me about, almost treading on my heels. The linoleum in the kitchen was always polished to a high gloss, and she would wail, 'Mind you don't let a drop of water fall on it!' We soon gave up using the kitchen at all, which saved us a few marks. We made tea for ourselves in our room with a kind of mini-boiler element.

Early in 1940 we moved again, this time to a horrible, bug-ridden room with a family called Ernsthal at 9 Prenzlauer Strasse. My father was in despair. He kept saying that he wished he could offer me a comfortable life, but there was nothing he could do for me. And for my part I kept telling him that none of that mattered to me.

TWO

Alone in the icy wastes
Forced Labour for Siemens

1

For hours on end we stood crammed together in a long, dark corridor. There was nothing we could do but wait. Of course we were terrified of what was going to happen now. We felt as if we had been placed in this humiliating situation on purpose.

In the spring of 1940, the Nazis had begun sending Jewish men and women to do forced labour in the armaments industry. In July I myself was ordered to go to the Central Administrative Office for Jews, the employment office on Fontanepromenade – commonly known as Harassment Promenade.

'I'm going out of my mind. I'm a heavy smoker, I have to smoke or I'll go mad, but I don't know if it's allowed,' groaned a man beside me. 'And if it's forbidden they'll strike us all dead.'

Young and naïve as I was at the age of eighteen, I replied, 'It's easy to find out. Just ask.'

At that moment someone shouted, 'Out of the way!' We squeezed even closer to the walls to right and left of us, to make room for the man who had given this order. I turned to him, speaking in a very friendly, civil tone. 'May I ask you a question? There's a gentleman here who isn't sure whether smoking is allowed.'

I had no idea that I was addressing Alfred Eschhaus in person, the head of this so-called Central Administrative Office and a notorious anti-Semite.

'You impudent Jewish riff-raff!' he immediately shouted back. After another furious cannonade of abuse, he went on his way.

But now some of the others moved towards me, threatening me with violence. A fat Yiddish-speaking woman who smelled unpleas-antly of moss snatched me away from them and clasped me to her wobbly bosom. 'Who's going to hit a Jewish child, then?' she said crossly. I could have burst into tears.

At this point a lady made her energetic way towards us. 'I'm sorry you're having such trouble here,' she said to me. 'Let me introduce myself: my name is Rödelsheimer.' I found out later that she was a musicologist. Of course I introduced myself in return. 'Well, Fräulein Jalowicz, you made a mistake,' she explained to me. 'You acted like a normal human being.' The incident taught me a lesson that would come in useful for the rest of my life: it is no use behaving normally in an abnormal situation. One has to adjust to it instead.

We were about 200 Jewish women and girls who began working at Siemens at the same time. Our workplace was very close to the entrance of the Werner Works in Spandau, so that we forced labourers did not have to assemble somewhere else, which was the usual way, to be led to work in a flock. We could arrive separately in the morning, collect a key to a locker where we left our coats, and then go to the work bench. The keyboard also served as a means of checking whether we had arrived for work on time.

We formed gangs of six, each gang supervised by a man who set our tools. Most of us worked standing at our lathes in a large factory hall. A few sat at tables in adjoining rooms.

I was in a gang working at the machines near the windows, so at least we could see whether the sun was shining outside, or whether it was raining or snowing. But it was like being screwed down firmly to our lathes all day long. There was no chance of stretching our legs now and then, even for a few seconds, because we used our hips to hold the slides of the lathes in place and move them. You were always getting new, blue bruises, while the old ones were still discoloured yellow and green. It would have been illegal not to provide protection for Aryan workers standing at lathes like that, but the exploitative Siemens management could save the firm the price of leather aprons.

We did hard physical work. Even worse, however, was the monotony of making the same movements all the time, along with the feeling that we were doing wrong in working for the German armaments industry.

Our gang's tool-setter was called Max Schultz, and he had worked for Siemens for many years. He was a devout Catholic, and lived in a residential area with allotment gardens in Lübars. He originally came from near Bromberg – 'It's called Bydgoszcz in Polish,' he told us. He was what people called a Water Polack, he came from Upper Silesia, and his mother tongue was a Polish dialect.

Max Schulz began every other sentence with the words, 'My priest says …' Not only did he go to the priest to make his confession, he held regular conversations with that cleric. 'My priest says that all men are brothers and sisters, and I must show you as much love as I can. My priest says the Nazis are the worst criminals in human history –' As time went on, he made such remarks as that last one more and more openly.

He had probably not been able to attend school for long. Max Schulz could read, but he had great difficulty in writing. That gave him trouble when it came to making out our pay slips; there was a special column where he had to enter the number of screws that each woman had made. Finally, he turned to me for help, which of course was strictly forbidden. I had to pack the forms up in grease-proof paper, wrap them in a floor cloth, and secretly take them to the toilet, where I filled them in before returning them to him.

Fluid ran over the metal we worked on our lathes to cool it, and we always had floor cloths with us to mop up the surplus. In between times we tucked them into the belts of the smocks we wore for work. They also provided a means of transport for everything that was forbidden in the factory hall. In the same way, we wrapped family photos and private messages in greaseproof paper and cellophane, and exchanged them with our tool-setters.

For all these men were curious about us. They liked to get a glimpse of our personal documents, or they questioned the supervisor of the factory hall about us. It intrigued them to find out whether a woman surnamed Cohn or Levi used to be a salesgirl, whether she lived in Reinickendorf or Wilmersdorf, whether or not she was married. Many of the women doing forced labour were equally curious about the tool-setters: where did such-and-such a man live, did he have a wife and children? Private contacts were strictly forbidden, and thus all the more intriguing.

My colleagues talked about the tool-setters much as school-children speak of their teachers. They were always saying, 'Ours said ...', or, 'Ours thinks ...', and positively competed to claim the tool-setter who was friendliest to Jews as their own. Something else that influenced the atmosphere was the fact that there were many extremely pretty girls and young women among us.

Most of the tool-setters behaved in a correct and friendly way to their charges, but one of them, a man by the name of Prahl, was an exception. He was a repellent psychopath – one of creation's mistakes, with a kind of steeple head* and a brutish, vacant face that always wore a grin. The problem wasn't his Nazi cast of mind, it was that he had no real cast of mind at all. He was a perverse character, a sadist. For a short time he had been in charge of first aid in the Siemens works, but he had to be removed from that post because of the delight with which he probed the wounds of injured colleagues – even Aryans. If he had to bandage small cuts and grazes, he did it so tightly that he cut off the circulation of his patient's blood.

There was a girl in Prahl's gang who had warts on her face and a deformed nose that made her look like a witch. He was always calling her names, and if her work didn't please him he would push her around so roughly that she was bruised all over. But obviously the supervisor of the factory hall had decreed that Jewish women were to be treated decently. Pushing and jostling them was a form of touching, touching could, in its turn, lead to communication and fellow-feeling, and anything of that nature was to be avoided.

When the factory supervisor heard about the bullying, the girl was moved to a gang with a less vindictive tool-setter, and instead of her a very pretty girl with magnificent breasts joined Prahl's gang. Her name was Katja, but I thought of her as the chestnut girl: she had beautiful brown eyes, and her hair was the colour of chestnuts

---

* *Translator's note*: The medical term for this condition is oxycephaly.

just fallen from the tree. Goodness knows what she might have become if she had survived.

Sometimes, with a file in my hand, I managed to go over and spend a minute with her. Or she would come over to me when her machine had been reset.

'I've always managed it with any other guy – so I wanted to see if I could do the same to Prahl,' she once told me. She went on to tell me, in her heavy Berlin accent, how she had been trying to arouse her tool-setter sexually, adding a wealth of indecorous detail. While he was adjusting her machine, she stood just behind him, breathing down his neck and pressing herself closer to him. The man had to beat a hasty retreat, or his trousers would have burst. Max Schulz went scarlet in the face when I told him this story.

Ruth Hirsch, Nora Schmilewicz and I worked in the same gang. We soon grew close to each other, because all three of us came from incomplete families, and we had all had sad experiences early in life.

Ruth Hirsch, with her many freckles and her strawberry-blonde hair, was very pretty and attractively youthful. When she had to do something that entailed moving the lever of her lathe slowly, she would gaze out of the window, daydreaming. 'I was just thinking how nice it was when we could pick up windfall apples and eat them,' she told me once, and then immediately apologised, because she saw how my mouth was watering. Unfortunately I couldn't hide my reactions.

She came from Memel in Lithuania. Hesitantly and shyly at first, she told us that she was an adopted child. With her twin brother, she had grown up in the care of a married couple who ran a small shoe-shop and had a little house and garden of their own. Her birth mother's name was Zilla Rostowski, and she used to work as a cook in a prosperous Jewish household. Her master had climbed up to her room one day and got her pregnant, but she couldn't keep her children; the twins were handed over to the childless Hirsch couple for adoption.

Ruth was a very simple soul, but that made no difference to

our friendship. I liked her quiet, naïve, shy way of telling her stories. Her brother had emigrated, and she herself had moved with her parents to Berlin, where the three of them shared a horrible furnished room. Her adoptive mother had severe heart trouble. When Ruth came home in the evening after ten hours of hard work in the factory, she would begin cleaning the family apartment. She thought nothing of that, and merely accepted it as her fate. All she minded was the way that her father was constantly complaining and finding fault.

Ruth Hirsch was the best worker in our gang at the factory. She was bright enough to understand the work, and very good at carrying it out, but not intelligent enough to hate it. She often said, 'How nice it would be if we had normal wages, not the reduced wage for Jews. Then we could train properly and become qualified lathe operators.'

Her best and happiest time had been when she had a job as a maid with a Jewish husband and wife, both of them doctors. Full of enthusiasm, she told me that once, when her employers went away for some time, they left the whole apartment to her. Ruth kept precise records in an octavo notebook of what she did every day, what she bought when she went shopping, what she ate, and so on. However, she didn't have enough work, so she decided to surprise the two doctors. Her mistress had said the parquet flooring was getting so dark that its surface would have to be stripped.

So Ruth set to work on that. She got some metal filings and used them to strip down the surface of the wooden parquet. While she was working on it she ate nothing but dry bread, to save her employers money. When they came home, she had stripped down all the floors in the front rooms, and showed them her touching notebook, where she had entered everything she did in a childish hand, with many spelling mistakes. She brought the notebook to show us, and in the breaks at work she read aloud from it in a sing-song voice, like a child who has only just learned the whole alphabet: her entries began with the date, then went on, 'A piece of bread for breakfast. From nine to ten, scraped down parkit.' The afternoon was also spent scraping down the 'parkit', and the same again in the evening.

When her mistress had seen the results, she said, 'Here's some money – now, you go straight out and buy a whole litre of milk and the ingredients to make chocolate blancmange with vanilla sauce, and then you're to eat it all yourself. You're half starved.'

I heard Ruth Hirsch tell this story, inconsequential in itself, at least ten times, and I never tired of it. It was Ruth's greatest experience and the high point of her life: the tale of how she was told to make a whole blancmange with plenty of sauce and eat it all by herself.

What would have become of her if she had survived? She had such touching charm, in her shy, simple way, that she was one of the dead whom I mourned for many years. For the figure of millions of dead means nothing much to anyone. We cling to the image of a single face, and for me it was the face of Ruth Hirsch.

The first name of my other neighbour at the bench of lathes was really Anna. Her parents were Russian, and had called her Nyura when she was little. As that pet name wasn't known in Berlin, it became Nora. She signed her name that way as well: Nora Schmilewicz.

Nora too was a very pretty girl; in fact a voluptuous beauty. Whenever I looked at her I was reminded of the women who modelled for Rubens. She might have become very fat in time, but she didn't live long enough for that.

She was startlingly beautiful in her own way, with deep black hair, expressive black eyes, a lovely mouth and unusually regular, white teeth. But she suffered from something I had not seen in any of the other women doing forced labour: she had swollen legs as a result of oedema caused by malnutrition. A Jewish doctor – he couldn't call himself a doctor any more, only a man who treated Jews – had told her, 'What you need can't be bought in a pharmacy, only in food shops, and only in peacetime at that. There's nothing I can do for you.'

As the daughter of well-to-do Russians, Nora was much better educated than Ruth. Her mother had died very young, and her widowed father had a non-Jewish housekeeper, known to Nora as Auntie. But now her father, too, was dead.

Nora still lived in her parents' large apartment in Urbanstrasse. She lived in one large room, where all the furniture from her parents' household was stored. A Jewish family was accommodated in each of the other rooms.

'Auntie' still played a large part in Nora's life. There was a strange love–hate relationship between them. Auntie must have been a highly strung, hysterical woman. Sometimes she called Nora her child, and gave her food, at other times she scolded her in the most vulgar language.

She had a key to the Urbanstrasse apartment, and now and then she turned up in Nora's room in the middle of the night. When the girl woke, sensing that there was someone standing beside her bed, Auntie might smother her with kisses, declaring, 'You are all I have; you are my lover's child, so you're my child too.' Or then again, she might let fly with a wildly anti-Semitic tirade of abuse. Nora suffered a good deal from this woman.

Nora and I were once invited to Ruth's home on her birthday. Her father had been skilfully exiled to the kitchen, where we politely wished him a good day. He muttered and scolded and called us names, but only to himself. Ruth's mother, overweight and sick as she was, sat beside him and didn't say anything.

'It's very cramped at home,' Ruth had warned us in advance. Indeed, it was terrible. Cupboards were stacked on top of each other in a tiny room with a very high ceiling, and those three people lived there. The only space was a narrow pathway through the middle of the room.

Apart from us, a woman who seemed to be a cousin had come. A gramophone was brought out, the kind with a horn, and we played records of ancient hit songs on it. I remember one record that I didn't know at all, typical honky-tonky 1920s stuff, songs about: 'Records, black matzos we call them, everyone knows them, everyone has them, records are the latest thing,' … and so on.

All of it is imprinted on my memory like a scene from a film. The raucous gramophone, the embarrassingly Yiddish hit songs, and the terrible birthday coffee party. The cousin was very ugly, with extremely fat legs, and had no inhibitions at all. As she danced she raised her skirt right up. It was so grotesque, and the whole atmosphere so awful that I thought: there ought to be some way to capture this for later.

Nora and I glanced swiftly at each other, and then looked away again. After two hours we said goodbye. Ruth's tour de force had been to bake a cake, using potatoes. She didn't really mean to tell us how furious her father had been, but it slipped out. He had been deprived of potatoes for the sake of that cake. Like good girls, we said what a lovely party it had been, and left.

Hand in hand, Nora and I went down the streets in silence. After a while we exchanged glances again, and quickly, with very few words, we agreed that we wouldn't tell anyone else about the party. Not a word about the wretched background; Ruth's so-called parents; the barely edible potato cake; the music and the fat cousin hopping about. I said, 'Someone ought to make a film showing how a Jewish girl's birthday party changes from year to year. First there's Ruth with her non-Jewish women neighbours, in the family's own house, and the garden with all the children. And then things get worse every year: first the Christian children don't come to the birthday party, and in the end all we see is the Hirsch family in their emergency quarters in Berlin.'

'Are you feeling all right? Who on earth would make a film about Ruth's birthday?' asked Nora.

So I told her that after these terrible times, other days would come, and we ought to tell posterity what was happening now. She stood still, and replied, 'Yes, I see what you mean, and you're right. You must make that film. You're going to be the only one of us to survive; Ruth and I won't.'

2

It was hard to leave our apartment in the dark in autumn and winter to go to Spandau, and then come back in the evening when it was dark again. When I finally got home, worn out by my many hours at work and the long journey, my lonely father would be waiting for me: half-starved as he was, he had been with me all day in his thoughts.

He often took his meals at Danziger's Diner in Königstrasse. He had a few acquaintances there, and found a little entertainment talking to other Jewish widowers and similar lonely people. He frequently talked to a lawyer from south Germany whose Aryan wife had left him. This man had once been extremely prosperous and well-known.

For a meal at Danziger's you had to hand over a five-gram or ten-gram fat coupon, and you would need a magnifying glass to search for a globule of fat on your plate. It was the same with coupons for fifty or a hundred grams of meat. All the restaurants cheated their customers at the time – and in particular, of course, they cheated Jews who had to depend on such establishments.

Danziger's served the most meagre fare imaginable. What the place called soup was pure salted water without any other ingredients in it. The main dish consisted of a piece of meat visible only under a microscope, a nasty substitute for gravy and two potatoes. Dessert was a concoction of water and artificial sweetener.

The boss, Paula Danziger, had severe heart trouble. She was unnaturally fat, and had blue lips and elephantine legs. My father was warned, several times, that her daughter worked with the Gestapo. This young woman, Ruth, who was also very fat and had a face covered with spots, tried flirting with all the male customers at the diner. And they all obliged her, paying her compliments and laughing at her jokes, because, without exception, they were terrified of this Jewish informer.

Every day my father brought one of those horrible lunches home for me, to be heated up in the evening, and I was so unspeakably hungry that I ate it. Of course it tasted disgusting, and I never felt full after eating it, but at least it was something to put in my mouth.

He often had the gas lit in the kitchen before I came home. As soon as he heard my key in the door, he put the pan on the gas flame so that I could have some of the hot, thin soup at once. Then we sat together for a while, and I told him about my day of forced labour.

'What's going on here? They're queuing up at your workbench,' asked Edith Rödelsheimer one day, as she passed me during a break. Three or four girls were waiting in line to talk to me.

I had met the musicologist again soon after I began working for Siemens, and we were both glad to see one another. After I had behaved so naïvely at the Fontanepromenade employment office that she had to rescue me from disaster, her influence gave me a great advantage: now I was the one to whom others turned for advice. Most of my colleagues came from a background very different from mine; few of them had any higher education. Now I heard my companions telling me, 'There's another girl who has her school-leaving certificate working in the next room. I simply must introduce you to each other.'

I had learned to adjust to an abnormal situation and come to terms with it. But again and again I was beside myself with rebellious feelings, crying out silently for liberty. One way that I tried to give the immeasurable horror and monotony of my existence at Siemens some kind of meaning was by getting to know as many of my companions as possible, and finding out all I could about their individual lives.

In our breaks at work, I was always going round to collect stories of their impressions and experiences. Many of my colleagues didn't like that. 'Why do you go paying so much attention to those girls

*Hermann Jalowicz aged
sixty-two, in Berlin in 1939.*

all the time?' they asked. 'We belong together, and it's not so nice anywhere else as in our room.'

'I know, but I have to get to know everyone,' I would reply.

So I was pleased when the supervisor walked through the hall one very cold winter's day asking for volunteers to shovel snow. Freedom from using my hips to operate the lathe. Freedom from the workshop, out into the wonderful, fresh, snowy air! There were not many other volunteers. Most of the women doing forced labour came from poor backgrounds, and thought it was better to do a job that they had learned at one of the lathes than to clear snow.

Unfortunately it took us little more than an hour to clear the path all the way to the entrance of the works, but it was wonderful! Of course Edith Rödelsheimer was another who had volunteered, and once again she introduced me to other women. We got on very well. I met a very nice nursery-school teacher from the hall next to ours. She was a good-looking young married woman, with two children. 'You're a young mother, so why do you have to work here?'

I asked her. She told me that her own mother had been allowed to look after the children instead of her, and they both preferred that arrangement. She herself enjoyed being with other people, whereas her children's chatter got on her nerves, while her mother hated working on the factory floor.

Another woman who interested me very much was Betti Riesenfeld; at over forty, she was an old lady from my point of view at that time. I knew her slightly from meeting her at a golden-wedding anniversary party in the well-respected Jewish Wolff family. She was tiny but well-proportioned, with snow-white hair, a fringe, and a pert snub nose – an unmarried bourgeois Jewish woman.

She worked as a quality controller at Siemens. In the broad gangway down the middle of the factory hall stood a table with a stool placed on it. Riesenfeld sat on this stool, with a container beside her in which finished items were placed; she had to measure every single screw. Any that did not match the prescribed norm were thrown out as rejects.

Fräulein Riesenfeld, who had an education at a girls' secondary school for the humanities behind her, followed by training as an office worker and a household shared with her mother, was now, so to speak, enthroned above us, and visibly enjoyed her superior status. When anyone came over to her this tiny creature called down from on high, 'Hand it up, and let's see if everything's all right.' At the end of every working day, she stood at the door as we all filed past her separately, and said, 'See you bright and early tomorrow!'

When our tool-setter Max Schulz bent over Ruth's machine we could all see that not only were they were very like each other, they looked almost identical: the same shape of nose, the same hair colour, the same complexion. It was positively uncanny. Max Schulz was at least forty, while Ruth wasn't twenty yet, but even people in other gangs noticed it. 'Your tool-setter and that girl look like identical twins. I've never seen such a similarity before.' I usually replied, ironically, 'I expect it comes of the racial difference between them.'

This striking phenomenon corresponded to something very

personal. Ruth was Schulz's great love. Not just a passing fancy, but his great love. And Schulz was Ruth's first and, because she was not fated to live much longer, her only love.

To a man like Schulz, such feelings denoted profound conflict. As I knew from his shy confidences, he had a wife whom he found unpleasant, malicious and demanding. That was one of the things that sent him to confess to his priest every week. 'My priest says that love is good,' he told us, 'and I must love you all.' But I could guess what he really meant.

There was a second phenomenon of this kind at Siemens, and I discussed it with Edith Rödelsheimer, but only once. When we were talking about the similarity between Max Schulz and Ruth Hirsch, she said, 'Nature has even allowed herself two such games, and everyone with the slightest intelligence here has noticed it.'

I knew who she meant: Schönfeld the SS man and me. Our supervisor sat in a separate glazed compartment in the factory workshop. He was clever enough to know how to employ us so that production would go on without a hitch. He had the same grey-green eyes as I did, the same shape of nose and mouth, the same teeth. We might have been twins.

Glancing at the man, I thought that I was looking in the mirror. It was terrible. We had both noticed it, and each of us knew that the other was also aware of it. Nature had indulged in a whim whose meaning we did not understand.

One Sunday I was on the way to Alexanderplatz Station with my father. I saw Schönfeld coming towards us on the steps up to the station, with about half a dozen other uniformed SS men. It would have been wrong to exchange any greeting, but I looked him full in the face as I passed him. His upper body literally gave way as he cast down his eyes, deeply ashamed, and blushed.

Although our wages were pitifully small, we adopted a piecework rate. Now and then the timekeeper came into the factory hall, trying to look inconspicuous, and checked the speed of our work. However, we were always ready for him. There was a warning system in all departments of Siemens, letting workers know in advance that the timekeeper was on the way, so that no one would lower the rate for the job, which was poor enough anyway, by working with excessive zeal. We also made sure that jobs were fairly shared out, so that everyone got the basic wage.

That mattered much more to the others than to me. I couldn't really feel either glad of what we called 'roast pork' – a productive job that paid well – or resentful when the job was too difficult for us to meet the piecework rate.

Matters improved when I discovered that there was a saboteurs' ring at Siemens. Those members of my gang who were not too stupid or unsuitable in character for it were gradually drawn into the ring, and that made it far easier to bear the mind-destroying tedium of the work. Exercising unobtrusive sabotage meant going to the farthest limit of what was permissible. In addition, you had to know all about the tolerance values of the product we were making, and the workers in all the different parts of the factory had to co-operate. The real achievement consisted in setting up these links.

To take one example: a nut had a tolerance of a fraction of a millimetre. The internal thread could be only a certain size, no larger than x and no smaller than y. Within those limits – and this called for great precision – you cut the internal thread of the nut as narrow as possible. And in another department of Siemens, the part that was to be screwed into this nut was cut as wide as possible, and consequently would not fit. The separate parts passed their separate quality controls without any objection, because they had been made to fit within the scope of tolerance. It was only when they were put together that they refused to fit and were thrown out as rejects. Ruth Hirsch was the best saboteur of us all, because she worked like a precision tool herself to achieve that tiny fraction of a millimetre.

This sabotage ring worked extremely well, and was never exposed. Not only did Max Schulz belong to it, so did another tool-setter called Hermann: a strong-minded intellectual who had been a Social Democrat before 1933, when the National Socialists came to power, and who had attended adult evening classes. After the war, he intended to take the *Abitur*, the school-leaving certificate, and thus qualify to study at university. Hermann was a radical anti-Nazi, and a leader in ideological discussions. It was also Hermann who protected us from the sadistic Prahl when the latter was appointed first-aid man to our department. 'For heaven's sake – that could mean physical contact between an Aryan and a Jewish woman!' Hermann pointed out. 'Surely it's racially disgraceful for Herr Prahl to bandage the finger of a woman like that?'

As a means of conveying such ideas to the supervisor Schönfeld, we made use of one Herr Schön, another curious figure among the tool-setters. He was in his early fifties, extremely thin, and also vain; he thought himself handsome, and was always asking the young girls in our gang, 'Don't you think I'm good-looking?' Every few minutes he would take out a pocket mirror in order to examine a bald patch surrounded by a wreath of grey hair. 'My hair still looks good,' he would say, 'even if there isn't much of it left.' Everyone laughed at him, Jews and non-Jews alike. He was stupid enough to have thought that if he joined the National Socialist party wonderful privileges, including money and property, would come his way, and he would no longer have to work hard in a poorly paid job. None of that, however, had happened.

Schulz and Hermann took him in hand, cautiously discussed matters with him, and they gradually succeeded in their aim: Schön became an anti-Nazi. He was even thought worthy to join the sabotage ring. 'I understand it all now,' he declared firmly. 'The Nazis are criminals. My parents and grandparents were always decent folk. I don't want to be a member of a criminal organisation!' It was explained to him, however, that he would do better to stay in the Party, so that he could get access to internal information from the Nazi cell in the Siemens works, and to a certain extent even influence that cell. Here, of course, Schulz and Hermann had to take his stupidity into account, and they flattered his vanity to very good effect.

Indoctrination in racial policy was his strong point; the stupid questions he asked, taking the nonsensical and pseudo-scientific contradictions of Nazi racial doctrine as his target, were provocative.

He himself wasn't bright enough to have come up with them, but the questions were devised by Hermann, precisely phrased and then handed in writing to Herr Schön, who learned them by heart.

By the normal laws to protect workers, only men could work at the really large machines. At Siemens, however, particularly tall Jewish women had to use them. We called these women 'the giantesses', and the machine parts they made were so large that they had to use a special tool – a hand threading die – to cut threads inside the nuts. After a while the women's wrists hurt so badly that they could hardly bear it.

The tool-setter of this gang was called Stakowski, in reality Scrzsowki or something like that – a complicated Polish name, anyway. Stakowski was a Nazi and wore the Party symbol on his working clothes. Otherwise he was correctly behaved, not uncivil, but he never said anything personal to the women workers. In a friendly enough tone he told them what to do, but without a joke, a smile, or any remark that was not to do with the job.

That changed when Stakowski took a management course that entailed a great deal of theory. To the amazement of the women in his gang, it turned out that he knew one of them had studied mathematics. He spoke to her diffidently: 'You're a mathematician, and I have difficulty with maths myself.' Then – by dint of much going back and forth with notes wrapped in floor cloths – he asked her questions, and she wrote down the answers in the toilet. The ice was broken. To show his gratitude, he even brought sandwiches to work for her, an absolute delicacy at the time. She thought she must be dreaming, it couldn't be real, because like all of us she was terribly hungry.

Gradually, Stakowski extended this personal contact to the entire gang, and in turn he was drawn into the card games played by Schulz, Schön and Hermann. They met him regularly in the Aryans' toilet and brought their influence to bear on him. From being a fanatical Nazi he slowly changed to being a harmless fellow-traveller, and that meant a good deal.

Our tool-setters often disappeared to the toilet for hours. Sometimes they even included Prahl in the card games, so as not to leave the brute in isolation. Of course, we showed solidarity with each other. If a machine broke down and had to be reset, if a cutting tool had to be sharpened or replaced, we would unobtrusively ask one or other of the tool-setters for help. We knew exactly who was friends with whom, and where we could turn.

Our experiences of these men, who were employed on a regular basis at Siemens, were so good that I often wondered how the dreadful persecution of the Jews could have come about. The men we met here were not really anti-Semitic, they were perfectly nice.

Of course, that wasn't true everywhere. First, Berlin was different from the provinces. Secondly, I came into contact only with a certain section of society. And thirdly, I realised that the same Aryan German who hated the rich Jew from the big house like poison – maybe he thought the Jew had once defrauded him over the sale of a plot of land, maybe he fervently wished the man out of the way so that he himself could appropriate the Jew's living-room carpet – that same Aryan German had nothing against starving young girls who worked hard, just as he worked hard himself.

We forced labourers had our own meeting place in the toilet too, since Aryan men could not enter this room, which was reserved for Jewish women. Small social occasions were sometimes held there; a woman who had really wanted to go on stage as a soubrette did a comic dance for us, while we sang a hit of the time and clapped our hands. And Else Gottschalk, one of my few academically educated colleagues, gave lectures on Spanish literature – in fact, she gave them specially for me.

She was an outsider on the factory floor, because on principle she addressed everyone by the formal *Sie* pronoun. 'We mustn't descend to the level of our enemies,' she said. 'After all, our background is not that of factory workers.' She was regarded as ridiculous for the way she distanced herself from the others, and I laughed at her myself. Secretly, however, I thought she was right, and was happy to be in contact with this forty-year-old working in the giantesses' gang.

On her side, our friendship soon became a stormy one. She would often put her arm round my shoulders, commanding, 'You will have breakfast with me!' She advised me against contact with many of our colleagues. 'They're not your sort.'

Unfortunately she was also madly jealous. She couldn't stand Edith Rödelsheimer because she saw that I respected and admired her. Edith had a tiny nose set well away from her upper lip, so that when she was talking you saw that she had huge teeth. Her skin was covered with dense, fair down and she wore impressive dark horn-rimmed glasses because she was short-sighted. 'I warn you, Fräulein Jalowicz, Rödelsheimer is a witch!' my new friend informed me. 'You can tell from that tiny nose.'

Else Gottschalk was an Aryan convert to Judaism. Her father had been very briefly and very passionately married to a Jewish woman who died young. When he married again he had insisted on his second wife converting too. This marriage produced several daughters who were brought up in the Jewish faith but then went their separate ways. One had married a Jew and emigrated to America. Another had married a high-ranking officer and turned her back on Judaism. Else Gottschalk had never married. Before 1933 she intended to leave the Jewish community because she had become an atheist. After the Nazis came to power, however, she proclaimed herself Jewish loud and clear, and went back to regular attendance at synagogue out of a sense of solidarity.

I was once invited to her home. She lived in a large, handsome apartment block in Wilmersdorf, with a lift shaft surrounded by metal grilles. As I entered the stairwell I was aware of a very characteristic smell – the unmistakable mixed aromas of good coffee and floor polish. So such people still exist, I thought: people who make proper coffee and use good quality polish on their floors.

Else Gottschalk lived quietly alone with her father. That was a link between us. I had imagined the well-educated gentleman, of whom she had told me so much, as tall and with a mane of white hair. Instead I was facing a small, bald-headed man. She had a habit of placing her hand on that head quite often, and he always reacted by saying, 'Don't do that!'

When we were drinking ersatz coffee she said, 'Well, Papa' – she stressed the second syllable, Papá – 'as you'll see, I didn't promise more than I could perform. Fräulein Jalowicz can imitate that primitive tool-setter who comes from the Bromberg area so brilliantly that she has me in tears of laughter. We don't have much to laugh about these days, but you'd enjoy the performance too. May I ask for a sample of your art, Fräulein Jalowicz?'

Flattered, I laughed and stood up. But then I suddenly thought better of it, and said, 'No, I'd rather not. I don't want to make fun of that simple, friendly anti-Nazi.' I knew exactly what I was expected to perform: Max Schulz in his wooden clogs, dancing the polka on the factory floor and singing a comic love song in his thick Berlin accent.

Here the bald little man with the intellectual face stood up too, and said, 'No, Else, you didn't promise me too much. I congratulate you on your friendship. You have made friends with an unusually valuable human being. Allow me, dear young lady, to express my own approval of the liking my daughter feels for you.' At the end of this little speech he announced, 'And now let me show you my holy of holies.'

He opened the door at the end of the corridor. It led into a small room lined with tall and very dusty bookshelves. There were cobwebs everywhere, and the atmosphere was strangely magical. Herr Gottschalk had clearly spared neither trouble nor expense to fill this room with all the editions of Goethe's *Faust* that he could find, and all the critical works on that famous drama. He was a great admirer of Goethe, and spent his leisure time researching the character and history of Faust.

We left our ersatz coffee to get cold. And as we stood in that remarkable, dusty atmosphere among the spiders' webs, he took individual volumes off the shelves and talked about them. I was fascinated and enchanted.

At last it was time to go. We were already out in the hall when he said, 'Oh, and I have something else very precious to show you.' He took a Chinese translation of *Faust* off the shelf and said, 'This is a great comfort to me: Germany has betrayed her own German culture, but *Faust* will live on in China.'

3

My visit to Nora Schmilewicz was hardly necessary; her room in Urbanstrasse looked exactly as she had described it to me. I had arranged to visit her one Saturday afternoon and had bought her a few flowers, but by mistake I left them at home.

I had almost reached the station when I realised. I ran back and unlocked the door, calling out, 'I forgot my flowers.' I knew that Hannchen [Johanna] Koch was visiting us, as she did every Saturday.

'Please don't go out,' my father had asked me before I left.

'I'm here every Saturday when she comes, and I sit with you two for hours and hours,' I had replied. These visits were a real torment. My parents had known Hannchen and Emil Koch, who lived in what had once been our little summer house in Kaulsdorf, for many years. He was a firefighter and she worked in a laundry – they were simple folk, but anti-Nazis who had never dropped their acquaintanceship with us.

Since my mother's death, Hannchen had been to see us every Saturday. She would sit all day in our cramped room, ostensibly out of readiness to help and neighbourly love. In reality, however, it was up to us to entertain her. We often actually planned a programme in advance, deciding who could say what, and when. 'That subject could last one of us half an hour, and then the other can join in the conversation,' we calculated. The fact that Hannchen's main interest in visiting us was my father had not escaped anyone we knew, including her husband.

Now, when I came back to the apartment, the door to our room was bolted on the inside. 'Open the door; I forgot my flowers,' I called.

The door opened, and my father's bare arm handed the bunch of flowers through the crack in the doorway. 'Did you have to do that?' he asked very sharply.

*Johanna and Emil Koch on their
wedding day in 1929.*

He was still furious when I got home in the evening. 'Fancy delivering me up to that woman! Was it worth your while exposing me to such danger when I don't even like her? She disgusts me!' It was the only time I heard him deliver such an outburst on that subject.

A few months later, on 18 March 1941, my father died. He must have guessed that it was coming. A few days before his death the notes in the diary that he kept, finally, in five-pfennig octavo notebooks, were headed, 'Like being on the high seas.' He must have been feeling as if he were seasick. He had lain down for a moment, he wrote, he had felt so dizzy, and then it had passed over. But he had realised that this was a case of life or death.

I was not at home when he died. For the first time since I began to do forced labour, I had taken time off sick, as a result of meeting the Jewish doctor Helene Gutherz. When she and I were exchanging a few words on Alexanderplatz Station, she said at once, 'What a cough you have! I'll write you a certificate to be away from work. We all need a few days of rest now and then.'

I gratefully accepted. What she didn't say was that she herself badly needed the fee for the medical certificate; she had hardly any sources of income left.

On that day, 18 March 1941, I had an appointment to see the Siemens doctor first thing in the morning. Frau Koch had said she was coming to visit us in the morning, and I assumed that I would be home at midday. My father and I were going to take her to lunch at Danziger's, to show her the place – although non-Jews never usually went to such cafés.

When I was coming down the steps at Alexanderplatz Station, I saw Frau Koch standing there. She was white as a sheet. 'Have you been waiting here long?' I asked in surprise.

'About an hour,' she replied. She wanted to prepare me for her news, but she went about it very clumsily. 'Your *Vaddi*,' she kept saying – she meant *Vati*, short for 'father', but she annoyed me, because it sounded affected and did not reflect her real Berlin dialect. 'I don't like the look of your *Vaddi*,' she said.

'What do you mean?'

'Your *Vaddi* isn't very well.' She went on talking to me like this until we reached 9 Prenzlauer Strasse. Then Aunt Grete came to meet me in the front hall.

'Your father is sick. Your father is very sick. It's hopeless. He's dead,' she stammered. She really did break the news in that order. Curiously enough, the word 'hopeless' shook me more than that final, 'He's dead.'

At this point, summoned by telegram, Emil Koch and my aunt Sylvia Asarch, Doris Schapiro's daughter, arrived. None of the family, more particularly my father, had liked Sylvia very much; she was considered demanding and spoiled, and decades after her flight from Russia she still put on the airs of a rich estate owner.

Frau Koch burst into fits of convulsive weeping. Her husband stood there stiffly. It was clear to him that everyone knew his wife was so grief-stricken because the love of her life was dead.

Sylvia, with her wide experience of life, understood the situation very quickly. It was she who now looked after Emil: she took his head in her hands and rocked it gently back and forth, all the time saying, in her Russian way, 'There, there, there. You are a remarkable man! A truly unique man!' He had an unusual wife, she added, a brilliant wife, made in the mould of the great film stars, and he loved her, even with her love for others – she kept talking to him, paying such silly compliments again and again, meanwhile leaving on his fireman's uniform a dusting of the face powder she always wore, which was a shade of pale lilac. Her performance finally enabled him to mourn for his friend too, and after all, there was really no reason for him to feel jealous now.

When they had all gone again, Grete and I set to work doing all that still had to be done. We were able to get the death announcements printed free by a former client of my father's, and we took them to the main post office late that same evening. Aunt Grete was very short-sighted, and did not feel safe on her feet in the darkened streets. I had to support her to keep her from stumbling and falling. As I guided her home, while she clutched my arm, I thought: this is the story of my life, propping up other people. No one props *me* up.

A surprisingly large number of mourners came to the funeral. A representative of the Palestine Office spent five minutes churning out standard phrases about 'the funeral of a veteran', without ever saying anything personal about my father. I felt like slapping the man's face and telling him to stop it. For I had realised that there was something wrong when my father had been deprived of his chance of emigrating to Palestine.

'I don't want to die in this pernicious country,' he had told me. That was also the reason for not buying a plot for his grave. 'Why bother when we're going to emigrate? That would just be throwing money away.' The fact was, however, that he wouldn't have had a penny to spare for it. So now I couldn't have him buried next to my mother. Instead, he lay in a plot right at the back of the Weissensee cemetery, by the wall.

'Misfortune will befall the man who hardens his heart' – that message from Rabbi Singermann's funeral oration was mainly meant for me. Or at least, that was what I felt. Singermann knew me very well. He was literally addressing my conscience.

Until the funeral I had been reasonably calm and composed. Only after it did I collapse, dissolving in tears. This sudden loss was terrible for me, and so was the sense of being entirely alone. I was crying out in the street when my old schoolfriend Leni Riemer's mother came towards me. 'Frau Riemer, Frau Riemer! My father has suddenly died!' I sobbed.

'Yes, yes,' she said, walking on. Then she turned and said with no emotion in her voice at all, 'May God console you.' It made me realise that most people were egotistic, concerned only with themselves, and more so than ever in these times. I had to pull myself together to face the outside world and grow up in a hurry.

A few days after my father's death I had a terrible, very intense anxiety dream. We were both running along a paved road with pursuers behind us. I made good progress, but my father, running beside me, stepped on a lime-twig. He was wearing felt slippers, items of footwear that in real life he had never possessed. Every two or three steps one of his slippers stuck to the ground, so that he had to stop. Whenever that happened I freed the slipper again. He put it on, went a few more steps, I ran ahead – and the same thing happened all over again. 'Run, my child. I can't. I'm stuck here, you can see I am. Just run for it!' he begged me.

'No!' I said. 'I'll never let you down, never!'

This dream was repeated again and again. At last I woke up, and suddenly I felt certain that my father had died to leave me free to go my own way. So that I would be able to live, so that I must and would live, because that was what he had wanted.

I got my doctor, Dr Gutherz, to write me another sick note. Soon after that I was summoned to see the works doctor at Siemens again. I briefly told him what had happened since my last visit to him, and how I had found my father dead at home. 'The most I can do is write you another sick note to cover the next ten to fourteen days,' he said. For wartime, that was an astonishingly long period to take off work.

But I badly needed the time to settle my affairs. They included the matter of the small pension that my father had from his position as a notary. This was paid to Jews only in exceptional circumstances, if they had fought at the front in the Great War and had no other income: eighty marks a month, personally allotted by the President of the Berlin Superior Court of Justice.* We had met our basic expenses – rent, electric light, and so on – out of this sum. It was a privilege that we never discussed with anyone.

I went to the Superior Court of Justice with the money order that had come by post. I was going to offer to return the money, but at the same time ask whether I might go on receiving the pension. As I could hardly demand to see the President himself, I said at reception that I would like to speak to the President of the Superior Court's secretary – in person.

That young lady probably felt much honoured. She was blonde, slim, and wore her hair in what was called a Hitler knot. I stood two metres away from her desk, holding the money, and explained, 'I'm an honest woman. I'm sure no one would have noticed if I'd kept it.' And very briefly, I described my situation.

'Oh no!' 'Oh God!' 'Oh, I'm so sorry for you!' 'Oh, please don't stand in that military position,' she said, much affected. She was wearing an ivory necklace, and chewed on it in embarrassment now and then. Then she said, 'You wait here a moment. I'll go in and win the boss over!'

Two minutes later she came out again, beaming, and said, 'You'll go on getting the pension. But there's no legal basis for it, and it would be disastrous to create such a precedent. So you mustn't mention it to a soul.'

I thanked her fervently, and of course I promised to keep my mouth shut. I thought to myself: not only are our enemies prejudiced against us, we have prejudices of our own against all non-Jews.

---

*From 1933 to 1942, this position was held by Heinrich Hölscher.

This young lady was so helpful and sympathetic. Why must we be such total strangers to each other?

I had been so impressed by her habit of chewing her necklace that I went into Woolworth's and spent fifty pfennigs on the cheapest necklace in the store, incredibly ugly and raspberry-red. I wanted it to put it in my mouth; it was like a compulsion. When my friend Irene Scherhey saw it she asked, 'Are you crazy? What a frightful necklace! I've never seen you wear anything like that before.'

'Oh, well,' I said, 'I must have left it lying around somewhere.' And then I threw it away.

I went back to forced labour after those weeks off. Some things had changed. Edith Rödelsheimer, who had been working for a while as wages clerk, could no longer hold that elevated position because she was Jewish. In her place, one Fräulein Lorenz, an uneducated worker from another department, was given the job. She might find reading and writing difficult, but she was Aryan. And Edith Rödelsheimer the musicologist had to operate a stamping machine, a job that would normally have been done by an automaton. The unbalanced physical activity hurt her arms terribly, but she was glad that she wasn't required to be more attentive in any other way. In her mind she was singing her way through whole operatic scores from A to Z.

Soon after my return I had a long conversation with our supervisor, Schönfeld the SS man. I went off to his cubicle so that he could inspect a screw I had made: he had to certify that the machine was correctly set and that its product passed muster before I could begin making a prescribed number of parts.

'So you've been certified off sick?' he asked as he held up the screw to the light. There was concern in his voice. Of course we were under observation from where he sat in his glass box with a view of the whole workshop. 'My father died,' I replied. He looked at me with great intensity and sympathy, and condoled with me silently. He could not reach out a hand to me, but our mere eye contact did not escape the notice of my colleagues outside.

I plucked up my courage. 'I want to leave this job,' I said. 'But as I'm doing forced labour I can't give notice.'

'Why do you want to leave us?'

'I want to save myself.'

'But I don't think that's a good idea. You'll be sent to some other workplace, and you won't find such pleasant colleagues anywhere else. I chose my best tool-setter for the nicest girls.' He really did seem to be concerned for me. 'What will you do on your own?' he went on. 'Out there you'll be alone in the icy wastes.'

'That's where I want to be, and I want to be alone. Because I can see where all this is going. They'll deport us, and that will be the end for all of us,' I said. He nodded his head briefly; the movement was barely visible. 'We won't be safe from deportation for ever as armaments workers,' I went on.

'Very well,' he said at last. 'I'll fix it. We'll fire you for sickness. God bless you, and I wish you luck on your way through those icy wastes.'

Those were the last words we exchanged. Outside, I was asked, 'You've been talking to Schönfeld for hours. And he held something up to the light as if it were a Christmas tree bauble. What was all that about?'

I told them, 'There was something funny about the part I'd made.' I even remember, to this day, that it was a brass screw.

And then a miracle happened: Else Gottschalk, my academically educated friend from the giantesses' gang, got a permit to emigrate to America. She was going on one of the very last ships to leave before the trap finally snapped shut.

When she had all her papers, she came to the factory one last time, no longer in the overall she wore as typical work clothing, but in a pale, elegant dust-coat and a very ladylike hat. She walked through the whole workshop to hand in her key at the cloakroom, saying goodbye to a few of her acquaintances, and to her tool-setter. She did not shake hands with him, of course. He was the man with the party symbol on his overalls.

On the return journey she walked through our workshop again, without looking to right or left. Or rather, she did not exactly walk; she strode, a proud and free figure, all the way down the long aisle. We all stopped working for a moment and looked as she passed by. I don't think anyone begrudged her that prospect of liberty. But I never saw so many concentrated glances of yearning again.

Then the door opened, she was outside, and I thought: unforgettable! Two hundred women were thinking, with immeasurable longing, of just one word: freedom! It was a chorus that rang out louder, and without a single sound, than the most deafening of Nazi propaganda.

4

Soon after sitting Shivah, the week of mourning after my father's death, Georg Ernsthal, from whom we rented the room, was given notice to vacate the apartment. Jewish tenants were being turned out on the street everywhere now, and we had no protection. So I had to look for somewhere else to live, and that was getting more difficult all the time.

Finally I found accommodation with a Jewish family at 26 Schmidstrasse, a slum area in the northern part of Kreuzberg, on the border of the Berlin-Mitte district. Siegfried and Franziska Jacobsohn had two very nice adolescent children, Hilde and Werner. The furnished room that I rented from them, however, was a sad joke. It was as thin as a small towel, and gloomy, because the street was so narrow that the sun never shone in. All the concentrated misery of my situation was expressed by this room. The furnishing I found there consisted of a tiny table, a chair, a huge crate meant for furniture removals, and a piano with no strings that barred access to the room next door, which was also rented out.

At first Frau Jacobsohn had even wanted money for the fact that this room was 'partly furnished'. However, I successfully resisted this demand. I wrote out an agreement covering a page in my notebook and showed it to my guardian, the lawyer Moritz Jacoby. A former partner of my father's, he could not stop laughing when he looked at this agreement, which was as comprehensive as if I were trying to sell or rent something worth millions.

Then, with the help of Aunt Grete, who was working unpaid for the Jewish Community, I got hold of the furniture I needed. As well as a bed there was a cylinder desk, as it was known: a writing desk with a cylindrical semi-circular drawer that could be closed. I locked my few foodstuffs in this desk; unfortunately, that was necessary because Frau Jacobsohn was envious if, for instance, I bought sausage with my few meat coupons.

'But Frau Jacobsohn, you get meat for yours,' I pointed out.

'Yes, but sausage … my children are so hungry!' I could understand her, but it was unedifying. All the same, we gradually became friends, and often had long conversations. I had plenty of time now that I was no longer going to work for Siemens every day.

It was only money that I lacked. I was not earning anything, and the pension received by me instead of my father covered my rent and electricity, but not much more. I was so impoverished that I sold my coal coupons in order to buy food. It was horribly cold in winter, but I had decided to go cold and hungry and simply sleep through mealtimes rather than waste my strength doing forced labour.

Aunt Grete was among the first to receive a deportation order in the autumn of 1941. The days before she was taken away were bad. A woman I knew advised me to go with her, saying that we young people must look after our older relations in the concentration camp. Even then, however, instinct told me that all who went there were going to their deaths.

Aunt Grete herself wondered whether we shouldn't stick together. 'Won't you come with me voluntarily? Sooner or later everyone will have to go.'

It was very difficult for me to say no. I felt I was being hardhearted. I could hardly say, 'You can't save yourself. But I am going to do everything imaginable to survive.' All the same, that was what I thought.

Grete was a terribly prickly character, but at heart she had been the kindest and most generous of our family. After my grandfather's early death, she had continued to run his haulage company with great enterprise and energy. Then, when it went bust during the First World War, she had made her living teaching shorthand and typing and had built up a secretarial and duplication business. She had worked hard to keep not only herself but Uncle Arthur too. After my mother's death my father and I were often her guests. I always took it for granted that she would look after us all, although my thanks left something to be desired.

We spent the last days before her deportation sitting together all the time. Hour by hour, she tore up old photographs that she could not take with her, but didn't want to leave behind. It was at this time that she told me, 'I loved you more than your mother did, but I was never fated to find a husband and have a child.' And she confessed something else to me: 'I have loved one man all my life. He was popular with all the women, and he certainly did not return my feelings. He was your father.' I did not let her see how much this information shook me.

One of her many customers who was also a personal friend of Aunt Grete's was Herr Hidde. He ran a radio repairs workshop on Alexanderplatz. Because he was tall as a giant, immensely fat and heavily built, you expected his voice to be a deep bass, but it was a high falsetto.

Of course Hidde was an anti-Nazi. When Aunt Grete received her deportation order, he said, 'Eger, I give you my word of honour: if they try to take you away, then that's the end of my workshop. You did all the office stuff for me, I can't manage it on my own, and I don't want other people meddling. Can't the two of us emigrate to the North Pole? I'll catch whales and you can cook them in kosher sauce.'

'Stop talking nonsense, Hidde,' replied Aunt Grete. 'This is deadly serious.'

These last conversations before her deportation were deeply tragic, but at the same time comic. With a tearful expression on her face she kept telling me, 'On the day they come to take me away, I shall leave a letter for you under the doormat.' At least ten times, she told me not to forget the letter under the mat.

I felt unspeakably sorry for her, and I would so much have liked to help, but I couldn't bear it any more. I was even a little relieved when it was over. Her apartment was sealed, and I retrieved the letter from under the doormat. In her best handwriting she had written that our family had always been honest and upright people, and I must remain honest and upright too. She asked for God's blessing on me, and so on and so forth. My goodness, I thought; so much fuss about that letter.

I read it three times and then tore up the sheet of paper. When I was on my way back from Prenzlauer Strasse to Schmidstrasse, I was ashamed of myself. I felt that I had not grieved enough over Aunt Grete's farewell.

Desperate people are drawn to the water, or so I imagined, anyway. At nineteen years old I was still very naïve. So I went down to the River Spree, leaned over the rail of the bridge, and groaned dramatically. Whereupon a silly woman wearing a hat with a feather in it passed by, looked at me, looked at the Star of David on my clothing and announced, 'Oh well, go on, then. It doesn't matter.' A Nazi woman didn't need to show any support for a Jew. At this point a light dawned on me. Stop being so dramatic, I told myself. I was never going to indulge in such artificial spectacles again.

A few days later I was crossing Alexanderplatz and saw that Hidde had been as good as his word. His workshop was closed. A large notice in the display window said, 'Business closed until the final victory, for want of spare parts.' This phrasing was obviously intended to be taken as sarcasm, and passers by stopped, grinned and enjoyed the joke.

When I next passed that way, the notice had gone again. I stood outside the shop for a moment, looking round undecidedly. A man spoke to me. 'Wondering where the notice is, are you?' he asked. 'The Party came and said he had to take it out of the window. They accused him of wanting to take the piss out of Germany.'

'Oh, I really can't imagine that,' I said.

In October 1941, Grete was deported to Litzmannstadt. That was the name the Nazis had given to the Polish city of Łódź. After that, I had only a single sign of life from her. I twice sent her ten marks, which was a fortune for me in my circumstances at that time. The first time I got a confirmation that she had received the money, signed by Grete herself. After than I heard no more. There was already a rumour circulating that money sent in that way would never end up in the hands of the intended recipients.

As for Grete, she had meant me to inherit all that she possessed. In the Prenzlauer Strasse apartment, she had kept a collection of wonderful heirlooms from old Russia, above all porcelain and glass items. Of course I never saw any of them again.

Schönfeld, our supervisor at the Siemens works, had warned me that I would be sent to do forced labour again. I could get a medical certificate to cover ten or fourteen days off work, but the employment agency was soon summoning me again.

I simply ignored the first letter, an extraordinarily bold response to the authorities, who counted on all citizens to knuckle under to such demands in their fear of the law. Then I got a card bearing the words 'Second Demand'. I took it to the agency and said, 'This is funny! It says Second Demand here, but I never had a first one.'

I was sent to a spinning mill, a small business with what was described as a Jewish department. Before starting work, for some reason or other we had to have a gynaecological examination. An elderly gynaecologist who had a practice of his own in Wühlischstrasse had made an appointment for all of us women and girls to attend at the same time, and kept us waiting for hours. Here I saw the seventeen-year-old twins Hannelore and Rosmarie Herzfeld, whom I knew slightly. They were two years younger than me, were shy and respectful and treated me like an aunt. They even bobbed me a little curtsey.

When the first Jewish woman was called in, there was a difficulty in examining her. The doctor came into the waiting room and asked, 'Do you all have such full bladders that I can't get past them?' We told him, 'We can't go to the toilet – there's only one for patients here, and we don't know where the Jews' toilet is.'

He snapped at us in vulgar terms. 'You idiots, piss is piss and shit is shit! It's the same for all human beings. Now go off and have a pee one by one.'

Then it was the twins' turn. He came out of the room where he was examining us and called, 'A very interesting case, identical twins, both of them virgins, seventeen years old. You must all come and see this!' His wife and four or five other ladies in good silk dresses – they were having a coffee party – came to see the show. So did a workman, bending his head and kneading his cap in his hand with sheer embarrassment because he felt so awkward.

Work in the spinning mill was terrible. I was put on the night shift, and had to go to work down streets in pitch darkness. I kept stumbling or even falling over in the dark, and the factory hall where we worked was itself very poorly lit.

We women workers stood many metres apart in front of a long wall where I had to keep fitting new spindles and switching the machinery on. The first time I did it, the thread broke at once. The forewoman shouted, 'That's verging on sabotage, you stupid cow!'

After a few days I went to the office and told one of the younger members of office staff there, 'I really am trying to do my best, but I have a nervous illness and the threads keep breaking. You'll have nothing but trouble with me.' At that moment the forewoman came in and began shouting at me. 'We ought to throw this Jewish sow out, stupid creature, she's not even worth spitting at!' When she had done something or other in the office she left the room. I told the other staff member, 'Yes, please do throw me out. You see, I can't give notice.'

'I didn't know that,' said the girl on the office staff. 'Right, then we'll fire you. The forewoman said you were incapable of working.' She immediately made out my papers and, in friendly tones, wished me good luck.

But of course the employment agency got in touch again. I received another demand, and once again I didn't respond. Then the second came, and I thought that when the third card arrived I would have to go. But it didn't turn out like that.

Until recently my neighbour in the next room of the Jacobsohns' house had been Harry Kaplan, a waiter who played the trumpet. When he was taken away for deportation, I had simply gone to bed and pulled the covers over my head in unspeakable fear and desperation. The doorbell rang again while I was alone in the house. The postman had a registered letter for Herr Kaplan. I said, 'He isn't here. He's been taken away.'

'Oh, then I know what I have to write: gone east, no known address,' said the postman, an elderly man. 'And I have something else too; there's supposed to be a Fräulein Jalowicz living here.' I recognised the envelope at once; it was another summons from the labour exchange.

'Then you'd better put the same on it. Gone east, no known address,' I said quickly.

And so my name was eradicated from the employment agency's card index because I had the impertinence to tell the authorities that I had already been deported.

5

I often met Ruth and Nora at the weekend. We went for walks together, and they told me the latest news from the Siemens works. For instance, I learned about the reaction of the tool-setters there when, in 1941, a police decree announced that all Jews must wear a yellow star in public.

Schulz and Hermann had of course been indignant. Even Stakowski, the Nazi, thought poorly of the idea, and two men called Strahl and Bedurcke, whom I always used to confuse with each other, regarding them as convinced Nazis and far from bright, had been heard saying, 'We're ruled by criminals!' One of them had family out in the country, and sometimes brought the girls in Siemens sandwiches from then on.

I gradually developed a particular plan for my walks with Ruth and Nora. I wanted to take the opportunity of exploring the city of Berlin and getting to know its population thoroughly. My two friends were not very keen on joining in my game of sociological experimentation, but they did it for my sake. Nora worked out the routes to various places in the city, all of them a long way from our point of departure. There were various stages where I was going to ask a policeman the way.

I went along the streets with my two dazzlingly beautiful friends one each side of me. Many of the older people stared at the three of us and said, 'What a shame. Fancy those lovely girls having to wear the Jewish star!'

The policemen were happy to talk to us, too. 'Well, my lovelies?' they would ask.

Then I introduced myself exactly as the law stipulated: 'I am a Jewess, place of registration Berlin, registration number so-and-so. May I ask a question?'

'What?' the policeman would say in a broad Berlin dialect. 'What did you want? What's that you say?'

'The law says we have to identify ourselves like that. With a place of registration, a registration number, and pointing out that we're Jewish. And then, if you allow us, we can ask a question.'

'You mean there's a law like that? Well, I'll be blowed if I ever heard the like of it!' Only the younger officers had enough self-control to avoid showing clearly how surprised and repelled they felt. The older men shook their heads. 'Come on, there's no such thing. What was it you said again?'

'I am a Jewess, place of registration Berlin, registration number so-and-so.'

'And saying all that stuff is supposed to be the law?'

This taught me that not even the police force knew about all the legal regulations and petty acts of harassment that beset us as Jews. Ordinary citizens knew even less about them. The average German housewife was interested in finding out where she could get half a kilo of tomatoes on the black market at not too exorbitant a price, and would burst into tears if her soup was burned. She might or might not have anti-Semitic clichés in her head, but she was not aware of the oppressive regulation of Jews. That gave me an insight into the facts that proved to be important in my later life underground.

The question that I asked the policeman after this preliminary skirmish ran: 'Can you tell me how to get from here to X Street?'

I had always chosen a destination kilometres away. 'That's a long way off. You'll have to go by public transport,' was the reply.

'We can't, we're not allowed to use public transport except going to and from work on weekdays.'*

'I don't believe it!'

'It's so, it really is the law.'

---

*On 24 March 1942, the Reich Ministry of the Interior also banned Jews from using transport within the city centre of Berlin; only journeys of over seven kilometres to work were allowed.

'Well, if you can't use transport then you'll have to walk. But good heavens, it's such a long way!'

The street map of the city was unfolded, and it was clear at once that our way passed through the governmental district. Nora had worked it all out that way in advance.

'We're not allowed to go along those streets. Jews are forbidden there,' I explained. We were prohibited from setting foot not only in cinemas and theatres, but also in streets and squares in that part of the city.

'You mean you can't go by that route? Then it will be even further.'

Here we got the policeman to work out a long way round, we thanked him politely, and walked away. The whole scene was repeated a little later somewhere else.

'Oh, come on!' said one of these police officers, and he wasn't even an old one. 'You're three nice girls, no one would know you were anything else just from looking at you. Take that bloody star off, hop on the underground and there you are!' That was the most forceful answer we received, and it had a very encouraging and reassuring effect on us.

This game mattered a great deal to me, for it taught me to appear self-confident even when I was facing those of whom we genuinely lived in constant fear. It was to help me all the time I was living through the Nazi period.

Yet again and again I realised that any small infringement of the rules could put me in mortal danger. There was shopping, for instance; Jews could go into shops only at a certain time late in the afternoon, when everything was already sold out. However, I often went there in the morning; after all, I had nothing else to do.

Once, when I was strolling down Schmidstrasse with my Jewish star on display, carrying a net shopping-bag, a small, hunchbacked man with a sallow complexion came towards me. 'Stop!' he said, taking an official pass out of his pocket. 'Ministry of Food! You must know that Jews aren't allowed to go shopping except in the afternoon. I'm having you arrested!'

That would have been disastrous, and I wasn't holding anything useful – not even a bottle, or I could have cracked him over the head with it and then taken to my heels. My heart was racing. I took two or three steps back, so that he wouldn't notice how agitated I was, and said, 'I'm working shifts. I'm on the night shift.'

'Indeed?' he said. 'Let's see your identity card.'

'I don't have it on me.'

'Then I'm arresting you.'

Instinctively I let my knees give way a little, hunched my upper body and put back my head, so that I could look up at him. 'Oh, it's so kind of you to point that out! I didn't think, I mean I never knew I had to have my identity card on me at all times. It's really nice of you to tell me, because if I hadn't met such a kind official I might really have been in trouble.'

A conflict of feelings showed in the man's expression: he didn't know whether to be pleased or angry, spit at me or put his arm round me. He hesitated for a moment, then wagged an admonishing finger and said, 'Well, you know now. So mind you have that identity card on you next time!'

I had survived that encounter. Once again, I had been lucky. But I went straight home and made up my mind not to go about wearing the wretched star all the time any more.

I knew where to find what we called the transit buildings. Using them in summer was no problem; if you wore a lightweight jacket with the star on it, you just disappeared into a corridor in one of these buildings, took off your jacket, and left the house by a different exit without it. In winter, of course, that didn't work.

My friend Irene Scherhey's mother taught us how to sew on a star so that you could rip it off with a single movement, and then sew it on again at lightning speed later, using a ready-threaded needle hidden somewhere in the lining of your coat. From then on I walked around the area where I lived with the star duly displayed on my clothes, but loosely attached to them. Ten minutes later I was a free woman, without a star. On the way back I restored my appearance to suit the rules.

Merely covering up the star could have terrible consequences.

I witnessed such a scene in Neue Schönhauser Strasse. 'Stop!' two men in civilian clothes ordered an old man just a few steps ahead of me. Then I heard the click of handcuffs. The old man, who did look very Jewish, had neither ventured to go out without his star nor to wear it openly as the regulations required. Instead, he had been holding a briefcase pressed so close to his body that half the star was covered. That was reason enough to have him arrested and taken away.

In the winter of 1941–1942 the threat of danger settled round my neck like a noose and kept tightening. Fear had me in its clutches. I wanted to save myself, but I had no idea how.

I often had nothing to do all day. Then I would go all over the city, visiting even people I hardly knew to find out all that I could. I constantly heard bad news: someone had been taken away here, someone else had just had his deportation order there. I was so starving and desperate that I would do a little relaxation exercise in the stairway of a building before I rang the doorbell of whoever I was going to visit. If the door was opened I would say quickly, 'I'm so sorry, I don't want to keep you, but I simply couldn't pass by without looking in to ask how you are.' Usually I had some entertaining bit of news ready, a little gossip to cheer up my intended host, and if I was in luck I would get a cup of ersatz coffee and a biscuit, or some other small thing to eat.

One day I went into the Konditorei Dobrin. This café had once been among the smartest in Berlin. You went to Dobrin's in Königstrasse after a shopping expedition on Saturday afternoon. There was still a branch of it, not quite so fashionable, on the Hackescher Markt; the customers there were now exclusively Jewish. I had heard that there was a little diversion to be found in this branch of the café, and you could get a cup of ersatz coffee for a few pfennigs.

I went in alone, as indeed I went everywhere on my own. When I opened the door, I was looking at a room full of men in ski caps. I had a great dislike of that kind of headgear: its basic shape was like the SA cap, and at the same time it had become part of the uniform of the now despised Jews. The earflaps of the cap could be tied up with a thin string like a kind of shoelace. With these little bows on top of them, the ski caps looked so silly that I felt like knocking them off the heads of the Jewish workers and crying, 'Do something, why don't you? Don't go about in uniform, all of you wearing the same sheep's clothing!' Unfortunately they were no wolves in the sheep's clothing, only the meekest of sheep.

I sat down, ordered and drank my ersatz coffee. And suddenly I found myself in the grip of anger. I had a feeling that the Gestapo might march into this pigsty at any moment. The word 'pigsty' really did come into my head, and I looked at the floor in embarrassment – however, it was properly swept and polished. What I had noticed was not outward dirt, but the inner filth of this ersatz-coffee society.

A man who had kept his ski cap on bellowed to another one, right across several tables, 'Heard this one? There's this apartment where a different Jewish family lives in each room, and there's this twelve-year-old girl reading a book. So she asks her father, "Papa, what's a comet?"

'So Papa says, "A comet is a star with a long tail."

'Then the girl says, "Uncle Rosenthal in the next room is a comet."'*

Roars of laughter. I felt nauseated. At that moment I decided that whatever happened to these people, it wasn't going to happen to me. I wouldn't go along with them.

A man who didn't wear a ski cap was sitting close to me. There was a hat hanging on the coat-stand near him. I said to him, 'Do you mind my asking if that is your hat?'

'Yes, it is,' he said. 'That's an odd question.'

'May I ask you a favour? Would you escort me out of this café, just as far as the street?'

He looked at me as if I had gone mad, and so I had in a way: mad with fear and revulsion. I put my few coins for the ersatz coffee on

---

* *Translator's note*: In German the word *Schwanz* = tail, of an animal or in this case a comet, is also a slang term for the penis.

the table, with a tip, and he escorted me to the door. I felt a need to be accompanied safely out, and I was glad once I was back in the street again.

How often had my father quoted from *Pirkei Owaus – Sayings of the Fathers* – 'Do not separate yourself from the community!' But what I had just seen, downgraded and in the process of dissolution, condemned to death, was no longer my community. I wanted no part of it.

6

Toni Kirschstein was one of the few people with whom I still had regular contact in the spring of 1942. I had first met her on a Sunday walk with my father. As we were passing the Jewish Cultural League's theatre in Kommandantenstrasse, a matinée cinema showing had just come to an end. Members of the audience were spilling out into the street.

'Hello!' A lady with fair, curly hair and a pretty face greeted us as she left the cinema.

The Eger family had known Dr Antonie Kirschstein for many years. She was married to a school friend of my uncle Herbert. This man, Felix Kirschstein, had never learned any useful professional skills, but liked the good life. Young Antonie, who came with a large dowry, was just the thing for him. He married her, but was consistently unfaithful to his wife for years. By the time I met her they had long been divorced.

Toni Kirschstein was anything but the ideal of the good, domestic little woman. After completing her training as an opera singer, she had made a name for herself as an expert neurologist and psychiatrist. When she smiled she was beautiful; dimples showed in her cheeks, and you could see her regular teeth. But as soon as she stood up it was obvious that she had severe difficulty in walking. She had congenital dislocation of both hips and walked with what is known as a duck gait; she would push one leg out in front of her in a wide arc, then bring up the other behind it.

When we met outside the cinema, she was arm in arm with a man whom she introduced by saying, 'Meet Pope Leo XXII.' The man's first name was Leo, and as she herself remarked, he was the twenty-second man with whom she had had an amorous relationship. She was entirely uninhibited in showing off about the number of men she had slept with.

I was immediately fascinated by her. My parents were not prudes, but I cannot imagine that my mother would have liked to be acquainted with Toni Kirschstein in the old days. However, my mother was no longer alive, and the crazy time in which we were living meant that people drew closer together and set less store on the traditional conventions. So we stood outside the cinema for a while, talking, until Toni Kirschstein said, 'We can't put down roots here, but I live quite close.' In fact it was in Neue Jakobstrasse, and she told us to drop in and see her as soon as possible, so that we could chat in more comfort, adding that she could always spare a cup of ersatz coffee, and that was the beginning of the friendship.

Later on, it was she who had helped me to find my room with the Jacobsohns. She herself had to give up her own apartment, and moved with her son, who was slightly younger than me, to the apartment of a distinguished old lady near Sophie-Charlotte-Platz who sublet part of it to her. This landlady of hers had once been very rich. Her husband had travelled all over the world, bringing home valuable hand-made objects. Toni Kirschstein, who was no longer allowed to practise as a doctor, didn't have a penny, and she quite often abstracted something from the cabinet of travel souvenirs and sold it on the black market. When her landlady noticed, she would screech, 'This is outrageous! You're a thief!'

'What else am I to do, you silly old bat?' Toni would snap back. I was once present at one of these quarrels. It was terrible. Her lax morals were one side of Toni Kirschstein, her great generosity another; she would share her last piece of bread with her son and me.

A sociable circle regularly met at her place, and I was happy to be part of it. That was how I came to know Dr Ludwig Dahlheim, an elderly gentleman from a highly assimilated Jewish family. He had rather affected manners, and often mentioned having been a pupil at the elite Königliche Wilhelm grammar school, popularly known as 'the patent-leather-boots academy'. His wife Thea, née Toller, was a niece of the famous dramatist Ernst Toller. The Dahlheims also had Ludwig's sister living with them; she was known as Hildchen, and was severely mentally handicapped. The Dahlheim family had always been ashamed of her, kept her hidden away and sometimes actually locked her in her room.

Once, however, when they had a very distinguished aristocratic visitor, things went wrong. A communicating door had been left unlocked, it suddenly opened, Hildchen came in and went over to a valuable figurine of a dog standing on the mantelpiece. She made a deep curtsey, laughed in her weak-minded way and said, 'The lion won't hurt little children. The lion is a German animal!' and with that the secret was out.

When Ludwig's sister Eva told me this story she added, 'So now Hilde uses the living room with the rest of us and isn't hidden away any more. The Nazis have taken everything away from us, not just our possessions and our native land, our lives as well. But oddly enough that's a kind of liberation; they've released us from idiotic conventions.'

One day a letter for me arrived at Schmidstrasse. I looked in surprise at the sender's name: Blei. He was a judge in the district court, and I did not know him personally, but my father had often mentioned him. In rather elaborate handwriting, and with old Franconian courtesy, he told me why he was getting in touch. 'A girl like you, of a very respectable family, ought not to be on friendly terms with someone who not only has no basic morality left at all, but is positively criminal, and is doing her best to conspire with our worst enemies in order to support herself.'

It was put in such a way that I understood what he meant, but the censor did not: Toni Kirschstein had connections with the Gestapo. That was not entirely unknown to me. Someone else had warned me; Recha Frankenstein, my mother's cousin, had told me that Dr Kirschstein had applied to be a Gestapo agent. Her offer, however, had not been accepted, because that nefarious institution took no one with a physical handicap.

And finally, Toni Kirschstein herself had told me that she had set an informer on me. Crazy as she was, she had warned me of the man in the next breath, saying that this Dr Spiegel was a con man and a lunatic.

He did indeed turn up one evening at my room in Schmidstrasse, telling me straight out that we would be seeing a great deal of each other, and I was to tell him about everyone I knew. Then he had tried to impress me by all kinds of silly psychological tricks. He had claimed to have supernatural powers, asked me to think of a number between one and ten, and he would tell me what number it was. That worked several dozen times until I decided to set a trap for him. So I did not think of any particular number, only the plain and emphatic word 'Arsehole!' He promptly replied, 'I don't know what you were thinking of, but it wasn't a number between one and ten. You can't cheat me!'

I knew how this trick worked – from Toni Kirschstein herself. She had told me that when you were thinking intensively of a word, you pronounced it in your mind, and so long as you had only a few words available – as in the case of numbers between one and ten – your involuntary movements in the region of the larynx could easily be interpreted.

Spiegel tried other experiments with me. He stared hard at me, and pretended my father was speaking to me through him. Here pride in my education came to my aid. 'My father would never have used the kind of language in which his office staff spoke,' I said, 'but you probably don't even know the difference.'

At this point he lost interest in me. 'It's getting late, so I'll be off now,' he said. I knew I couldn't afford to make an enemy of the man, so I promised to inform him of anything special that I might notice anywhere.

Before I tore up Judge Blei's letter, I learned some phrases in it by heart. Alone in my furnished room at the Jacobsohns' apartment, I talked out loud to myself. I imagined what my parents would have said in this situation: 'We feel sorry for this deeply unhappy woman, whom Fate has mistreated so badly. But she is depraved, and the loss of all moral principle cannot be approved. We must withdraw from her society.'

With much labour and several drafts, I wrote an answer to Judge Blei thanking him for his well-intended warning. I explained that it would not be wise of me to let the lady in question know that I intended to break off my contact with her. I could only drop the acquaintance, I said, carefully and gradually.

But a few days later the whole thing took a sensational turn. Toni Kirschstein's cheerful social occasions had steadily declined to a vulgar and indeed semi-criminal level. I was regarded as a great humorist among her friends, and had the reputation of being scintillating in society – something that, of course, I enjoyed.

That evening Toni Kirschstein told her guests that she had a great surprise for us. 'We'll put the light out and then have fun – any man with any girl, any girl with any man.' She was proposing what we would call group sex today. I was repelled, but laughed and said, 'However, first I've had a brainwave. I've thought of something very amusing, but I'll need to have my coat on before I tell you.'

'We can't wait!' said our hostess, and brought me my coat. Everyone was looking at me, waiting for the point of the joke. 'I'm leaving now,' I said.

Then her son Wolfgang spoke up. 'I'm going with her,' he announced calmly, and the two of us left the building.

'Where are you going?' I asked him.

'I've no idea.'

So I took him home with me. We stole into the Jacobsohns' apartment. I didn't want anyone to hear me bringing a young man home. There was nothing for it but for the two of us to lie in my narrow bed. We were very proud of ourselves for lying there side by side like brother and sister. Next morning he crept out of the building first thing.

Later I realised that I had let myself in for something else through my acquaintanceship with Toni Kirschstein. Frau Jacobsohn had told me about her brother-in-law. He suffered badly from Parkinson's disease, was confined to a wheelchair and had great difficulty in sleeping. My landlady asked whether I couldn't get hold of a large quantity of really strong sleeping pills. She would pay well for them, she said.

I put the problem to Toni Kirschstein. 'Nothing easier,' she said cheerfully. She had already broken the law by selling prescriptions for morphine to addicts. Now she made out a few prescriptions and told me to buy the pills at different places all over Berlin. If the pharmacists asked questions, I was to say, 'It's not for me, it's for my neighbour.'

I acquired the pills, and shared my earnings half and half with Toni Kirschstein. Soon after that, Frau Jacobsohn's brother-in-law died. Months later I noticed a strange couple at a funfair. The woman was wearing an immaculate tailor-made skirt suit, pre-war quality, the best English cloth; the man, who must have been seventy, was constantly stroking her behind with a large paw, which she seemed to enjoy. When she turned, I recognised Frau Jacobsohn's sister, the widow of the sufferer from Parkinson's disease. A little awkwardly, she introduced me to her new friend, a doorman who lived in her neighbourhood. She told me that his wife had also had Parkinson's disease, and their respective spouses had died at almost the same time. 'We're companions in misfortune,' she added.

I felt very queasy on hearing this story. But I told myself that all I had done was to get hold of sleeping pills to help a man suffering from insomnia, no more. I examined my conscience and told myself that I had suspected nothing wrong in what I'd done. However, Toni Kirschstein had grinned and said, 'These would fell a mammoth.' With all her experience of life, of course she had immediately realised what was going on.

THREE

A rainbow of unimaginable beauty

Attempts at Flight;
Going Underground

1

It was not long after I had moved into Schmidstrasse that Ernst Wolff came to see me. He arrived out of the blue. The son of a very distinguished Berlin Jewish family, he was unmarried and at the time was approaching fifty. His father had been chairman of the Old Synagogue in Heidereuter Gasse for many years.

I had worked for some time unpaid in Ernst Wolff's family research archives before I was forced to go to work for Siemens. At the time I had fallen in love with him. My feelings were stormy but still rather naïvely emotional. I had hoped in vain for some sign that he returned them. It was out of the question for a girl to make the first move.

And now he made this surprise visit. 'Your papa would probably have been very angry with me for making advances to his little girl,' he announced, 'but now there's no one to protect you from the importunate attentions of men.' I was startled by the poor taste of this remark, when my father had been dead for only a few weeks. But all the same, I was in love, so a relationship soon developed between us. For me, it became the first deep love of my life.

Ernst Wolff was profoundly rooted in tradition; it would be difficult to think of anyone Jewish whose attitudes and upbringing were more Jewish. He consequently had a great and significant influence on the development of my personality.

But my intimacy with him did not bring me the fulfilment I longed for. I found our physical relations disappointing, but I didn't know why. I had little experience in such matters, and I knew no clever, adult person to whom I could pour out my heart. Only much later was I to find out what the matter with Ernst Wolff really was.

I was often in the kitchen these days when Frau Jacobsohn was cooking or washing the dishes. We had made friends by now and could talk for hours on end. Once I told her I had heard that Jewish girls could get a Chinese passport by marrying Chinese men. It protected them from persecution and even meant that they could emigrate.

'Try it,' my landlady said. 'You don't have to think about anyone else. Over in Neue Jakobstrasse there's a building where a lot of Chinese live. Quite high up, I think, the second or third floor.'

I went in search of it at once. Most of the apartments had names like Müller and Schulze on their doors, but one of them bore the names of Ping Pang, Ding Dang, Jang Jau and so on. I rang that doorbell. The door opened, and the entrance hall filled up with a whole crowd of Chinese men. The oldest and most dignified-looking seemed to be the spokesman for the group, and I turned to him.

'Excuse me, please – I'm looking for someone who can give lessons in your language. Chinese is so wonderful, and linked to such a high level of culture, that I'd like to learn the language myself.'

'You not wanting Chinese learning,' he replied, 'you wanting sham marriage making.' He spoke broken German with a heavy Chinese accent.

'You're right,' I admitted. 'I'm Jewish, and I want to leave this country. But I didn't like to come straight out with it.'

'Sham marriage cost forty thousand marks,' he explained. Well, I don't remember the precise sum, but it was a crazy one and entirely beyond my means.

'Then forgive me for disturbing you. Goodbye. I don't have that kind of money.'

Once again it all happened very fast. 'Wait, wait!' he said. 'There is other way. We make real marriage. That cost nothing. I come this evening and we celebrate engagement.'

He asked me for my address, and I willingly let him have it. Sure enough, he turned up a couple of hours later in Schmidstrasse bringing a lot of food and a bottle of wine with him. What a feast! Of course I shared it with the Jacobsohns, so for once the children had a proper supper.

From now on I was engaged to Shu Ka Ling – or Ling Shu Ka, in the Chinese manner of arranging names. But to marry we needed permission from the mayor of the city. I had to apply to the relevant authority, and didn't know what I would need to do so. Moritz Jacoby, my guardian, sent me to see a lawyer called Lignitz, who was an Aryan and specialised in foreign law. I introduced myself to this elderly gentleman as the daughter of a late colleague of his, and began by asking him what this consultation would cost me. He patted my hand reassuringly and said, 'It won't cost anything. What's this about, then?'

I told him my story, and he explained how and to whom I should apply. He also dictated a specimen letter into a recording machine and gave it to me to take away with me.

My Chinese fiancé was a nice man, and generous. He gave me presents now and then. But we did not come any closer; after all, we could hardly converse with each other. Privately I thought: if I can get a Chinese passport through him, that would be excellent, but this isn't a relationship that will come to anything. He too probably felt that there was no real attraction on my side, and that at the same time I was conducting a very different relationship, one that mattered a great deal to me.

Once he arrived at my lodgings on Friday evening, just as I was setting out for the synagogue in Heidereuter Gasse. I simply took him with me, and enjoyed showing off to the other Jewish girls arm in arm with him. That gave them all something to gossip about, miserable as these times were. Many of my friends knew that I was really in a relationship with Ernst Wolff, who moved in the best conservative Jewish circles.

A few days after this incident I had an unexpected visitor. Hecht, the cantor, was at my door. I had been seen in the synagogue with a Chinese man, he said. On behalf of the head of the community, he wanted to point out to me, poor orphan child as I was, that this kind of thing would not do. We had a long dispute in which I quoted from the Bible and cited Saul in support of my arguments. When the cantor left, he said, 'After all, you're right. I have three daughters of marriageable age myself. Do you happen to know any Chinese who might suit them?'

The process of applying for permission to marry dragged on and on. We tried to speed it up by going to the authorities together. 'I'm expecting a baby by my fiancé,' I claimed. 'We really can't wait any longer.'

'Then you must produce a certificate,' I was told. 'How long have you been pregnant?' At this point my Chinese fiancé intervened. 'Since last night. My fiancée has a craving for pickled gherkins,' he announced proudly. The whole office roared with laughter, and I could have sunk into the ground with shame. But Shu Ka Ling simply gave the Hitler salute and marched out.

Now Ernst Wolff, who knew about my plan, lent me a helping hand. He took me to Wilmersdorf to see his cousin, a Jewish gynaecologist who of course could describe himself now only as someone who treated Jews. He warned me that this man was a cowardly and unattractive character who would go along with anyone, and I must leave the talking to the two of them.

'I want you to do me a favour,' Ernst Wolff told his cousin. 'Now, in this of all terrible times, something has happened to us; my girl-friend is expecting, and only an abortion will help us.'

'Well, for you I'd do any favour, but an abortion, no!' said the cousin. 'You'll have me on the gallows!' So the argument went on for a while, and in the end Ernst Wolff seemed to give in. He realised he was asking too much, he said. 'But at least give us a certificate of pregnancy so that my parents will agree to our relationship and we can marry!' So the gynaecologist made out a certificate to the effect that I was three months pregnant. It was no use, however; I still didn't get official permission from the authorities to marry.

My relationship with Shu Ka Ling gradually petered out. When the group in his shared apartment went their separate ways, I found him a room in Blumenstrasse with a Frau Ury, who was living with a cousin of my father's. Months later, I heard that my Chinese fiancé had begun a relationship with the daughter of the concierge of that apartment block.

*

At that time you usually had to be twenty-one before you came of age. But I didn't want to wait until 4 April 1943: I wanted to assume responsibility for my own affairs before that. My guardian Moritz Jacoby agreed, and made the application for me. I allowed myself to make a joke before the guardianship tribunal. 'I want to be officially of age because I'm sure that otherwise it will be difficult for me to correspond with my guardian, moving from one concentration camp to another.' The judge thought this remark deeply embarrassing. He went red in the face and wanted to end the scene as quickly as possible. 'Granted with immediate effect,' he said brusquely, and with that he was rid of me.

2

Early in June 1942, I met Frau Nossek in the street. In the old days we always used to see this simple-minded household help, who worked alternately for my parents and for Grete, in the Old Synagogue on religious festivals. She always sat in one of the cheapest places in the second women's gallery. After the service she would come over to us out in the yard to shake hands with everyone and wish us well.

Now Frau Nossek told me that she had already received her deportation order, and had been duly picked up with her rucksack and her bundle of bed linen. At the railway station, however, she had suffered such a bad attack of diarrhoea – which she described in all its embarrassing detail – that she had to go to the toilet. When she finally came out again ('such bad luck'), the train had left.

So then, she told me, she had gone over to a railwayman and described her situation, whereupon he had run after the two Gestapo officers who were just leaving the platform and fetched them back.

'Those two gentlemen from the Gestapo were ever so nice,' she went on. They had been kind enough to take her back to the place where she had been living and unseal the door of her room, she said, and now she was waiting to be deported in line with regulations a week later.

I was on my way to see my friend Irene Scherhey and her mother, and I told them this story, which was weighing on my mind. 'Drunks, small children and the simple-minded have a special guardian angel,' was Selma Scherhey's comment. It set off a strange idea in my mind, an idea that was to come in useful a little later: you only had to pretend to be simple-minded for a guardian angel to come to your aid.

Another incident also influenced me at this time. Frau Koch knew a clairvoyant through a laundry customer of hers. This woman practised her craft in Grünau once a week, although such things were strictly forbidden at the time. Hannchen Koch had a weak spot for mysticism and magic of that kind, and had insisted that we must both go.

I assume that this Frau Klemmstein, who allegedly didn't know who I was, had some idea in advance of my particularly dangerous situation. In any case, she told me, 'No one can pretend to a person like you. I don't need cards or a crystal ball. We'll just sit quietly together and close our eyes. Either I'll make contact with you and have a vision, or I won't. If I don't I'll tell you so honestly, and Frau Koch will get her money back. And if I do I'll tell you what I saw.'

After we had been sitting in silence for a while, she said, 'I see. I see two people, with a *Schein*.'* I thought: she's crazy. I took her to mean a bright halo such as saints are shown wearing. However, I had opted for the wrong word; she meant a paper document, and more specifically an arrest warrant. 'These men, or one of them, will tell you to go with him. If you do, you are going to certain death. But if you don't – even if you get away by jumping off the top of a church tower – you will arrive at the bottom of it safe and sound, and you will live. When that moment comes you will hear my voice.'

A short time later a man with an arrest warrant did indeed turn up. As it happened, I was not on top of a church tower but in my room. It was 22 June 1942, and the doorbell rang at six in the morning. In the Germany of those days that was not the milkman arriving. There was no one who didn't fear a man who came to the door at six a.m.

He was in civilian clothes. Frau Jacobsohn opened the door to him, and he said he must speak to me. I was still asleep, but woke in a terrible fright when I saw him standing beside my bed. In a calm and friendly tone he told me, 'Get dressed and ready to go out. We want to ask you some questions. It won't take long, and you'll be back in a couple of hours.' That was the kind of thing they always

---

* *Translator's note*: The German noun has three distinct meanings: brightness, appearance, and a piece of paper.

said to prevent people from falling into a fit of hysterics, or swallowing a poison capsule, or doing anything else that would have been inconvenient for the Gestapo.

At that moment I really did hear the clairvoyant's voice in my room, loud and clear, and as if automatically I concentrated on the plan I had already hatched: I wouldn't go with him, I would pretend to be half-witted.

Making out that I believed the man, I assumed a silly grin and asked, lapsing into a Berlin accent, 'But questions like that, they could take hours, couldn't they?'

'Yes, they could take some time,' he agreed.

'But I got nothing to eat here – now my neighbour downstairs, she'll always have coffee or suchlike on the stove, and I reckon she'd lend me a bit of bread. Can I get a bite to eat? I mean, like this in my petticoat – no one sees me this time of day, and I can't run away from you dressed just in a petticoat, can I?'

So I went out. The only thing I unobtrusively snatched up was my handbag with my purse in it, and an empty glass bottle. I knew that they always came in pairs to take people away. And if the second man was waiting for me downstairs, either the bottle or his head would be broken. I wasn't going to do as they told me without defending myself.

When I left the apartment I saw Frau Jacobsohn turn white as a sheet, but she invited the first man into her kitchen and said, 'Come in and sit down; it'll take some time for her downstairs to make a sandwich.' She steered him over to a chair and moved the kitchen table in front of it, so that he was more or less penned in.

The second man was waiting down in the front hall of the building. I spontaneously switched the role I was playing. 'Well, guess what?' I said, giving him the glad eye. 'I come out to polish my door knob before I go to work, and my little boy, he's only two and a half, he slams the door on me! So now I got to get the spare key from the mother-in-law, and me in my petticoat, and here's a fellow as I guess wants a bit of the other! At this time of day, too! I never heard the like of it! Men, I ask you!' And so on.

He laughed uproariously, gave me a little slap on the behind, and thought that my conclusion about what he wanted was very funny.

'Well, there's no one going to see me like this,' I said. 'I'll be back in five minutes.'

It cost me a great effort to walk slowly to the next street corner. Then I ran. I spoke to the first person I met, an elderly labourer, briefly explaining my predicament. 'Here, come into the entrance of this building,' he said, 'and I'll lend you my windcheater. You're small, I'm tall, I bet it'll come down over your knees. Then we'll both go to people you know who can lend you clothes.' He seemed positively pleased. 'And if I'm late to work, who cares? It'll be worth it to put one over on those bastards for a change!'

My hair was loose, lying over my shoulders. He tied it up with a piece of string and escorted me to the Wolff family's apartment. At the time Ernst was living in Neue Königstrasse with his parents, his aunt and his younger sister, the art historian Thea Wolff. His father was already over eighty, so Ernst was the real head of the family. His female relations were indignant about his beginning a relationship with a much younger girl when he was in charge of everything and made decisions for the family. They couldn't stand me anyway.

But now they helped me at once. Thea Wolff gave me a summer dress in which I could venture out on the streets again. Apart from that I had almost nothing left: a few pfennigs in my purse, and my Jewish identity card. For now I kept the empty soda water bottle.

Later, by devious routes, I got back in touch with the Jacobsohns and found out that my landlady had kept the Gestapo man engaged in conversation for a whole hour, even getting around to the silly delaying tactic of showing him family photographs. And I truly revere the generosity of Frau Jacobsohn, a modest soul who had moved from the provinces to Berlin. She knew that she, her husband and their children would not be able to escape, but even taking that into account she was ready to accept that they would all be killed a few months earlier, so that she could give me a start on my pursuers.

I also discovered how it had turned out. After more than an hour, the second Gestapo man had come upstairs and asked his colleague, 'Are you two nearly finished?'

When both men realised what had happened there was a frightful row. Each of them was blaming the other, until Frau Jacobsohn told them, 'Gentlemen, I can tell you you've wasted an hour here for nothing. That young woman, my sub-tenant, isn't the respectable sort. She often doesn't come back all night. I'm afraid you've drawn a blank.'

But each of them was so mortally afraid of the other that they couldn't agree on that version of events. Instead, they were stupid enough to tell the truth. Frau Jacobsohn was asked to go to see the Gestapo and found herself confronted with the two men, who were black and blue in the face.

'Do you know these gentlemen?' she was asked.

'They look very different now,' she replied.

One of the pair added, 'If we'd known a young girl like that was such a tough nut to crack we'd have surrounded the whole block with police officers.'

On that occasion, Frau Jacobsohn was allowed to go home unharmed. Later, in March 1943, her whole family was deported and murdered.

3

It was still early in the day, and I didn't know where to turn. The first person I went to see was my best friend Irene Scherhey. I used to share all my thoughts and feelings, plans and opinions with her. Irene was half-Jewish, and lived with her mother Selma in Prenzlauer Allee. Her Jewish father was dead; her mother was Aryan, and lived in constant fear for Irene.

They gave me a warm welcome, but I realised that I couldn't stay long. It was possible that the Gestapo might come looking for me at my friends' homes. Selma Scherhey gave me a handkerchief and a spare blouse to take with me, and then we all three said an emotional goodbye – 'We'll meet again after the liberation!'

By now I had at least decided where to go for the time being: into the lion's den. I would seek refuge in a police station, and with none other than Emil Koch. He worked full-time for the police as a fireman,* and was based in an eastern suburb of the city.

I spent many hours there kicking my heels, as I sat at a long table. Firemen kept coming and going; for them a woman visiting the place was an unusual and welcome novelty. They all cracked jokes with me, and got a pert and amusing reply. I was in rather good humour. I've taken the first step, I thought, the really deciding one; the Gestapo won't come looking for me here. In fact I felt easier in my mind than in the painfully difficult months I had just passed.

Somehow or other Emil managed to let Hannchen know where I was. He whispered to me that I was to go to them in Kaulsdorf late that evening.

I knew I could rely on the Kochs. While my father was alive, Frau

---

* *Translator's note*: The Berlin fire service was subsumed by the police during the hostilities.

*Irene Scherhey, Marie
Jalowicz's best friend, 1945.*

Koch had kept saying, 'This little house is still yours – our home
is your home.' But I also realised that I couldn't stay in Kaulsdorf
for long. There were neighbours who were fanatical Nazis and so
malicious that everyone living nearby trembled at the thought of
them. Whatever happened, those people must not get to know I was
there. I would have to postpone my arrival until it was pitch dark
outside, and as we had almost reached the longest day in the year
that was quite late.

When I was finally about to go to bed that evening I asked
Hannchen Koch, 'Could you very kindly lend me a nightdress?'

'Oh, so my fine young lady wears nightdresses?' she asked sharply.
I realised that I had made a mistake.

In the end Frau Koch found me a lavishly embroidered nightdress with hemstitching round the neck. She had been given it for
her confirmation, and had never worn it. 'It's a very fine piece,' she
emphasised. She herself always slept in her underwear.

I had learned my lesson: I must tread carefully, and adjust with lightning speed to the habits and lifestyle of anyone who took me in. I depended on the help of other people, and I mustn't tread on their toes.

The very next day I set out into the city again. One of my first expeditions took me to 44 Rosenthaler Strasse. I felt scared of entering the house, familiar as it had been to me since childhood. It sounds rather infantile, but I was afraid that the house I knew so well would recognise me too, and put me in danger.

I wanted to see Hilde Hauschild, who had been Uncle Arthur's girlfriend for many years. He had never married her, because she wasn't Jewish and thus not socially acceptable as our family understood the phrase. But he had helped her to extend an attic at the back of the building, and I had often been her guest in that surprisingly attractive and tastefully furnished apartment.

Hilde and my uncle had met in the market, where Arthur had a stall selling jokes. For instance, you could buy a metal imitation of a big inkblot and put it down on a document to fool someone. Or he sold matchboxes that suddenly began purring and jumping about when you touched them.

Arthur used to flirt with Hilde Hauschild, who helped stallholders in the market, by praising her very strong hair. Her red complexion was not her most attractive point, her nose was not exactly regular, and her teeth were not good. But she had that wonderful hair, and broke a comb almost every day because she couldn't get it through the tangled strands. Arthur had introduced himself to her by saying, 'Fräulein, I'll give you a comb that you'll never manage to break.'

It hadn't been easy for Aunt Grete to run a strictly kosher household for her brother on the one hand, and on the other to accept this very unorthodox relationship. She couldn't stand Hilde Hauschild, and there must have been terrible quarrels between the two women. Grete shouted at her brother's girlfriend in tones that could be heard right through the stairwell, and Hilde would shout back, 'Why don't you cook your brother proper food for a change, so that he doesn't starve to death?'

However, my own relationship with Hilde Hauschild had always been untroubled, even after Arthur's death. I had visited her, she had given me food on the sly, and had always acted as if I were a close member of her family. So now I climbed the steps to her attic with my heart thudding in pleasant anticipation. I felt sure that she would help me. Maybe she could send me to her family on the Baltic coast.

When I reached her door I saw a strange name on it. I rang the bell, but there was no one in. Then I tried her neighbours. Finally a woman opened her door and said, 'Looking for Fräulein Hauschild? She got married all of a sudden, to a good class of man at that, an engineer in Rostock.' No, she had not left an address. I went sadly away.

I spent a few nights with Tati Kupke, the sister of my aunt by marriage Mia Lindemann. The two of them had a very nice father; old Grandpa Lindemann was a joiner, and a communist of long standing who lived in Pankow. In 1933 he had told Mia, 'I know you like the comforts of life, and your husband provided them for you. You and he shared the good times together. If you *dare* to leave him and your children by him just because it's awkward now that the Nazis are in charge, I shall put you over my knee and beat the living daylights out of you. People don't do such things in our family.'

Sure enough, Mia did stand by Uncle Herbert, and just before the Second World War broke out she escaped to England with him, Kurt-Leo and Hannele.

Her sister Tati had never had any Nazi sympathies either. Her husband Willi had been an active communist until 1933, and had remained true to his convictions. They had half a room with a couch in their little apartment in Pankow, and the couch was made up for me with clean sheets at once.

On the very first night I found Willi standing beside my bed. A weedy-looking man with a crumpled face, and in a nightshirt far too short for him, he indistinctly muttered a few revolting obscenities. You can guess the rest of it. I could neither kick up a fuss nor send him back, so I just let him have his way. But I felt sure that Tati knew what was going on.

I felt so embarrassed that I couldn't look her in the eye.

The next night Willi appeared again, haunting the place like a nocturnal ghost. There were other reasons why I couldn't stay any longer. Everyone in that apartment block had sharp ears, and there were any number of Nazis in it. On days of political celebration a sea of swastika banners hung there. Sooner or later I would have attracted attention.

I found someone else to help me. Because he was a Jew, Ernst Schindler, an old friend of my father's, had been forced to retire ages ago. He was living in a mixed marriage with an Aryan wife in Gaudystrasse, in the north of Berlin. I had met him and the teacher Dr Max Bäcker a couple of times in the last few months. We had begun to learn Swedish together. It was Bäcker, a passionate advocate of the educational profession, and left in a wheelchair after the First World War, who said, 'Do we really want to waste our time telling each other that the war is a disaster and the Nazis are criminals? Surely we have better things to do.' Unfortunately we got no further than the third lesson.

Schindler, who himself lived in a very small apartment, found me a place to stay with a woman friend called Lotte in Karlstrasse.* In appearance at least this woman corresponded to the idea of an intellectual *par excellence*. She was in about her mid-forties, had her black hair cut like a man's, and wore a pair of heavy horn-rimmed glasses. Lotte was of working-class origin, but had studied at further education classes, and had then been a secretary for the Social Democrat Party until 1933. 'I will never in my life be a Nazi,' she told me right at the start, 'but I want no more to do with the Social Democrats either. Please don't ask me any more about that.' Otherwise she hardly spoke to me. I realised that she wanted to be left alone, and asked her for something to read.

---

*Today Reinhardtstrasse.

She lived alone in two rooms, one leading to the other, in a cultivated apartment with bourgeois furnishings. Unfortunately the toilet was half a flight of steps lower down in the corridor of the building, and that was a terrible problem. I couldn't leave the apartment to go to the toilet in the daytime.

Lotte went out early in the morning, and did not come back until late in the evening. I either had to leave the building with her and spend all day walking round the city – or stay in the apartment and keep perfectly quiet.

So Lotte asked me to get hold of a container in which I could put my stools. I couldn't empty it until she was home. That was disgusting enough, but there was worse to come. I couldn't find any such container. However, every few days I met Frau Koch in Köpenick. She regularly brought me legs of mutton that she got from an abattoir without ration coupons, handed me the cooked dish in a metal container with a lid, and I had to use the same container for toilet purposes.

Soon I couldn't stand the sight of mutton. It nauseated me, but I had to eat the stuff cold, with a horrible sauce. My aversion to eating from the container in which I also transported my shit became so strong that I felt sick at the mere sight of it. However, of course, I had to thank Frau Koch effusively for the food intended for me. Once she brought me kohlrabi too, in the same metal pot. I couldn't bring myself to eat any of it.

One Sunday Lotte took me with her on an excursion. We met a young married couple who were friends of hers at Bernau Station. I enjoyed getting to know them, for the young couple were very well read. We talked excitedly about all manner of things. At some point I mentioned Kant's *Critique of Pure Reason*. My landlady drew me aside and said, 'You still have a lot to learn. The Augustins are neither Nazis nor anti-Nazis. They're nice people, that's all, so you should hold your tongue.' In other words, I mustn't draw attention to myself with remarks about Kant.

After some fourteen days Schindler found me my next place to stay. This time it was with his former cleaning lady. He himself had not been able to afford any household help for a long time, for he and his wife were living on the tiny salary she earned working in an office somewhere.

Ida Kahnke lived close to him, in Schönhauser Allee. Schindler knew that she was an anti-Nazi. The toothless old woman looked like a witch. The entire area round her mouth had caved in, and she had a prominent nose. In addition she was very thin – dried up, but not thin like a piece of string, flat like a bug.

As toilet attendant in a civil service office, she could use every extra pfennig that came her way. She chuckled happily when Schindler, who had no money himself, offered her ten marks to take me in for two weeks. But she made it clear that she would have done that even if no money was forthcoming. 'When I was young I was a communist, but when you're older you get religious,' she often said. She was a Jehovah's Witness, and they were banned at the time.

Ida Kahnke lived in the back part of what had once been a large and grand apartment. She really had only one room, the former kitchen, which was tiled and terribly uncomfortable. She had rented this room to a friendly young man. Unfortunately he stuttered and wet the bed. He dried his wet sheets in the room, and it made the whole apartment stink. Otherwise there was only a small servants' room converted for use as a kitchen. Part of that room, again, was divided off as the toilet. The old woman slept in a kind of alcove in a back corner of the entrance hall, and I had perforce to share her big old wooden bed.

Her entire library was kept in the drawer of the kitchen table, and consisted of a few well-worn pamphlets prophesying the end of the world. I had nothing to do all day but sit in a decrepit wicker chair and leaf through these pamphlets. As the paper on which they were printed was filthy, I turned the pages with knitting needles.

I couldn't move about freely. An invalid lived one floor below, and would have heard me at once. So I sat there idly, waiting for Frau Kahnke and munching the piece of bread that she left for me.

To make matters worse, Ida Kahnke's brother Hugo was released from prison at just this time. He had served quite a long sentence for killing his wife, or perhaps the woman was his lover. Ida Kahnke was terribly afraid of him, telling me how he could burst in hopelessly drunk, demanding money, and so on. And he turned up just as she had described. I wished I were invisible, but he took no notice of me, and half an hour later he had gone again, because as soon as he got out of prison he had found himself a woman of some kind.

One weekend there was a birthday coffee party at Frau Kahnke's. I sat inconspicuously in a corner, but found it fascinating. There were some men there, friends of Hugo's, criminals by profession, and in addition a couple of Ida's friends, devoutly bigoted members of the same sect. The common denominator, I noted inwardly, was that they were outsiders living a borderline life. They played ancient hit songs on an old gramophone with a horn and danced in the style of around 1900, waggling their hips. It was so grotesque that I pinched my arm and wondered if this was reality or a dream.

However, I also began thinking about social questions. After all, I was living in circumstances that I could never have dreamed of. It was clear to me that this horrid apartment was something perfectly normal, and quite a number of people lived like Ida Kahnke.

One day I was sitting in my wicker chair as usual, when the door suddenly opened and masculine footsteps approached. At first I took fright, thinking it was someone breaking in. But it turned out that the man, who was Bulgarian, lived in the same building, and had a key to this apartment because he had promised Frau Kahnke to decorate her kitchen. He had taken a day off work on the excuse of being sick and was here with a bucket of paint to surprise her.

He too was startled to see me. But he said at once, in broken German, 'Housebreakers aren't nice women like you.' He was charming, and one thing soon led to another. By the time Ida Kahnke came home that afternoon, we were ready to tell her we were engaged. Dimitr Petrov Tchakalov – that was his name – was going to take me home to Bulgaria with him. We only had to find a way to get me there.

I was in love, indeed very much in love. He was a delightful man, with his gleaming black, thick hair, his dark eyes and his snow-white teeth. He often sang Bulgarian folksongs, rather sentimental ones, but in a very attractive voice. I really did want to go with him. Of course I didn't tell anyone that I was secretly hatching a plan to go from Bulgaria over the border to Turkey, and then continue to make my way on foot to Palestine.

After two weeks, Frau Kahnke passed me on to another toilet attendant, a Frau Schulz in Lychener Strasse. Once again Schindler paid ten marks for me to go there, even though he was so impoverished himself. And once again I ended up in an almost identical wicker chair.

Frau Schulz worked all day, borrowed a lot of light literature from a lending library once a week, and let me have one of the books to read. She hardly ever spoke to me. A Frau Lauer, her former sister-in-law but now her deadly enemy, lived one flight of stairs down in the same building. On no account must this woman notice that I was staying in the apartment; that was the main problem.

But Frau Schulz had a good deal of experience, and she pointed out to me one day, 'I see what's up with you – you've got a little one on the way.'

She was right, and it couldn't be ignored any longer. I had been suffering from morning sickness for weeks. I simply could not get down disgusting food like the mutton that Frau Koch brought me any more. I also knew who had made me pregnant. I hadn't had anything to do with my Chinese fiancé for a long time, and I had only recently met the Bulgarian. The child's father could only be Ernst Wolff.

The one person who could help me now was Dr Benno Heller. I had already heard a great deal about this Jewish gynaecologist. All the women who had been treated by him praised him highly. I had crossed his path once already, when I visited Toni Kirschstein in the Jewish Hospital after an operation.

Benno Heller had been to see her, and was about to leave the room when I arrived. With the utmost care, he put an expensive velours hat on his head, checking his appearance in the mirror above the washbasin. It was obvious that he was merely introducing himself by putting on that hat. What a vain show-off, I thought.

Heller had an Aryan wife, and for the time being his marriage shielded him from deportation. He practised in Braunauer Strasse* in Neukölln, as what was now called someone who 'treated the sick'.

So that was where I went. Abortions were strictly forbidden. I couldn't possibly ask him for one without gaining his confidence first. I reminded him of our meeting beside Toni Kirschstein's sickbed, but he couldn't remember it at all. He did say, 'You could hardly make up something like that,' but he was still suspicious; I could have been an informer. Rumour said that before 1933 he had already served a prison sentence for carrying out an illegal abortion. He was Jewish, and politically left-wing, so his situation was precarious. However, he wanted to help.

Finally he asked me to recite the Shema, the Jewish confession of faith.

'*Sh'ma Yisroel Adaunoi elauheinu Adaunoi echod*† – hear, O Israel, the Lord our God, the Lord is one,' I recited.

'All right, only a Jew knows that,' decided Heller. He told me he would give me something to induce a miscarriage, but I must go through it on my own. No curettage would be necessary: 'You'll feel labour pains, and the whole thing will be expelled. You must throw it away, and that will be the end of it.' He used the informal *du* pronoun to me, as he did with all his women patients.

So I set off on the long walk back to Lychener Strasse. When the pains began a few hours later, Frau Schulz gave me the key to a summerhouse that belonged to acquaintances of hers in Nordend, and told me just how to get there.

I went to the colony of summerhouses all on my own, unlocked the gate to the small property, found an old bucket somewhere in

---

*Now Sonnenallee.

† The Hebrew translation is written in the way German Jews in Berlin traditionally pronounced it.

the garden and sat on it. After all that I had already experienced, now came this. But it was over quite quickly.

I hadn't noticed that there was someone else in the garden, an old man who had shut himself in there because he was on his own. After the first shock he was very nice to me, said he saw what was happening and asked if he could help. Then he brought me some water to drink, and I asked him for newspaper so that I could wrap up the contents of the bucket and take them away. I went to Heller and asked him what I should do next.

'Are you crazy, bringing that here?' he asked, horrified. 'Get rid of it where no one will find it.' Frau Koch stepped in and helped me. I gave her the packet of newspaper, and she buried it under a plum tree.

I had no moral scruples. I wanted to live, so there was no option. But I was sad. It had clearly been a boy, the only descendant that the Wolff family would ever have had.

I did not even think, incidentally, of offering Benno Heller money, and he did not ask for any. He examined me briefly and said, 'You're all right. Off you go; your uterus has come to no harm.'

Mitko – the diminutive of Dimitr – knew about this unedifying episode and thought nothing of it. He was still planning to take a long holiday and go to his native country with me. I was still enthusiastic about the idea, and even persuaded Frau Koch to buy me a teach-yourself Bulgarian manual to study. I learned the language at top speed.

Soon I took to walking round Berlin again. If I wasn't going to spend all day in the wicker chair, I left the apartment at the same time as my landlady, six or seven in the morning, and walked round all day. I had to do something. I came home, footsore, late in the evening. At that time I often thought to myself: if one could earn a home by walking the length and breadth of it, then I had earned the city of Berlin as my home.

Before leaving for Bulgaria, I had meant to say goodbye to several people whom I would probably never see again. Among them was Leo Davidsohn, a cousin of my mother's. We had often spent Seder evenings at Aunt Grete's with him and his family, but otherwise we did not have much contact with them. I remembered him from my childhood as a short, stout man who was always cracking feeble jokes.

As a young man Leo was said to have been very lively, a young fellow who always wore his boater tipped sideways on his head. But after some time his amusing little adventures came to an end. He was engaged to Gertrud Cohn, the ugly daughter of a very rich private banker. Shortly before the wedding, her father went bankrupt after an incident involving sharp practice, and shot himself through the head. Gertrud was going to give him his ring back, but Leo refused. 'A human being is a human being as far as I'm concerned,' he apparently said, 'and you have suffered misfortune. I am a Jew and I don't push other people into the abyss.' The couple married, and so he had not a rich but a very sharp-witted wife at his side. She did all she could to build up a wholesale business in velvet fabrics, and it made their fortunes.

Leo was now a widower. His daughter was in Paris, and he was living with his two sisters from East Prussia, who kept house for him. This was the first time I had been to the enormous, grand apartment in Lietzenburger Strasse.

A housemaid asked me to wait for him in the wonderful hall. I looked carefully at everything: small rooms were divided off from it to left and right by velvet portières. I began pacing out that wonderfully comfortable room to measure it. If I survive, I decided, I'll build myself a big villa with a hall that looks just like this. Then Uncle Leo appeared.

'Are you going around without a star?' was the first thing he asked, without even greeting me properly. He was visibly indignant.

'Yes, I'm trying to survive. I came to say goodbye. I'm going on to see Recha Frankenstein,' I replied. She was my mother's favourite cousin, and had also been her closest friend.

'You needn't bother. She was taken away last week,' he said bitterly. The pince-nez on his nose quivered. Leo was furious with me for coming to see him without my Jewish star. 'You're in the way,' he said brusquely. 'We don't have time. My sisters are busy making preparations for the transport we expect at any moment.'

'Sorry. I won't keep you long. I only wanted to say goodbye.'

'What on earth are you thinking of, just not going when you're told to?'

'I'd like to survive.'

'But if they catch you – do you know what they'll do to you?'

'What?'

'They'll deport you straight to the East.'

'That's what I want to avoid.'

At that moment he realised that he was going round in intellectual circles. He said, slightly mollified, out of sheer embarrassment, 'I'll be celebrating my seventieth birthday God knows where in Poland.' There was a long pause, as he tried to find words. 'No, celebrating isn't right. I'll be spending my birthday there.' Then he quoted from the *Pirkei Owaus* – the *Sayings of the Fathers*. 'Do not cut yourself off from the community.' A moral sermon was the last thing I needed now.

'Give my love to my aunts, and I hope you will manage as well as possible,' I said. 'Goodbye.' I was glad when I could close the door of the apartment behind me.

And then an idea leaped up at me like a stray mongrel dog. Uncle Leo was very well off; he couldn't take his fortune to the grave with him. Whereas a hundred marks would have been a real help to me. But I was much too proud to ask him for money.

As I was going down the steps, the door of the apartment opened again up above. Leo called in a loud, carrying voice – he had been whispering to me in the hall of the house earlier – 'Hello! I have something else to say to you, come back.' I quickly ran up the few steps again.

'Perhaps you're doing the right thing after all,' he said when I was facing him. 'If you survive, and see my daughter Hilde again, then give her my love. I want her to know that my last thought will be of her. I will die with the Shema on my lips, and think of her.' With that he slammed the door for the last time.

The mood was very different when I went to see Helene Gutherz the doctor. She lived in Augsburger Strasse with her husband David, a lawyer from Austria. When I told them that I had escaped arrest they both rejoiced. 'Marie, make tea, the good tea that we keep for special occasions. This is a very happy one,' Helene Gutherz shouted to the maid in the kitchen. She and her husband hardly knew how to express their delight. Finally they decided to give me a picture that a friend of theirs had painted; green horses in a meadow. I didn't think it was particularly good. 'I don't have a roof over my head – where could I put it?' I objected. Thereupon they tried to give me their dining-room furniture. It was grotesque. 'We spent more than we could afford on it, we didn't have much money,' said Helene Gutherz. Her husband opened the doors of the sideboard and knocked them. 'Hear what good, solid wood that is?' I admired the first-class quality, but had the greatest difficulty in getting them to realise that I could do nothing with the furniture. Where on earth was I supposed to keep it?

After fervent embraces, blessings and wishes for good luck, we finally parted. I felt not a trace of hatred, envy or aggression in either of them, but I was relieved when I was outside. It had been such a pointless battle against being given the contents of a dining room.

Then I still had many hours to kill, and I sat in the shelter of a tram stop to rest. While I was there an idea occurred to me, and it shook me badly: something had just come to an end. These had been my last visits to Jewish friends and relations. They were going one way, I was turning in a very different direction.

My last meeting with Ernst Wolff in August 1942 was terrible. His family, too, had 'the lists' ready. These lists had to be drawn up a few days before your planned deportation, and summed up all your worldly goods. I was sick of the sound of the word: everyone was making 'lists'. I couldn't bear the fear of the crime that threatened them all, and the strange sense of industry that it induced in them.

There was something of the military man in Ernst, and he told me that he had had the huge dining table where the Seder feasts were normally held extended. The rucksacks for his parents, his aunt and his sister Thea were packed on it, and he had his elderly relations doing exercises. 'Pick up rucksack!' 'Put down rucksack!' and so on. He used a terrible word when he told me about it; he spoke of the 'journey' that they would all be taking. A journey, he called it.

At this last meeting, the atmosphere between us was very tense. I walked down Memhardstrasse and Münzstrasse with him, in mortal fear. He was wearing the Jewish star and I, of course, was not. It was torment.

'Which of us is going the better way we must wait and see; who will live and who will not,' he said. I refrained from running through my arguments again. However, raising his forefinger, he gave me some moral precepts to take with me: I was of a good Jewish family and must not forget myself. I had had enough; I didn't want to hear any more.

We were on the way to see his cousin Herbert Koebner. The former director of a dental clinic, Koebner had now specialised in forging documents. Ernst Wolff wanted us to meet.

Ernst and I said goodbye to each other in Koebner's apartment in Kaiser-Wilhelm-Strasse, hoping we might meet again. It was a banal farewell – how could it have been anything else?

4

My aunt Sylvia Asarch had once lived on the estate of Boldera near Riga, and so she had a Soviet passport, which for the time being protected her from deportation. In the summer of 1942, she was the only member of my mother's family with whom I was still in touch. All the rest had fled from Germany, had been deported or were already dead.

We often sat drinking tea together. Of course I told Sylvia about Mitko and my plans to go away with him.

'What?' she asked, horrified. 'A working man without any education? You should marry a rich man so that you can live in the right style for your station in life!'

Of course, this was grotesque. Sylvia herself knew how upset the family had been when she took a non-Jewish lover who was also from the working class. Otto Starke was in fact an extremely nice man. Long after they had separated, well into the war, he was still regularly sending Sylvia parcels.

Sylvia had fled from the Russian revolution in 1917 without her children, arriving in Berlin with a single piece of luggage, a box containing several very expensive Parisian hats. From then on the family had regarded her as an uncaring mother who had sacrificed her children to save her hats. Only now did she tell me the real story. The Bolsheviks had stormed in at the front of the manor house, while she slipped out of the back of it at the last moment, disguised as a peasant woman. If she had shown that she was mistress of this estate, she had reasoned, they would all be killed; they'd be regarded as kulaks and shot. However, she thought that if she left her children behind the Soviets would spare their lives and send them to an orphanage, where they would get enough to eat, be brought up as communists, and would then have to make their own way in the world. Her great secret was that she still had a photograph of her four adolescent children, Tassja, Bruno, Ruth and Fila. She once showed it to me.

Sylvia was rather small and plump, with a large behind. She considered herself beautiful and a person of great consequence. Indeed, every step she took proclaimed: important, important, important. A salient feature of her face was her large nose with its wide pores. She loved to use heavy make-up, painting her lips bright cherry red, and covering her whole face with shimmering powder in a slightly lilac tone.

Her craving to stand out contrasted oddly with the fact that only help from the family enabled her to live in Berlin for so many years. Once, when Aunt Mia bought herself an expensive tailored suit and showed it off, twirling in front of us, we all admired it except for Sylvia, who said, 'Well, not bad, but the best tailor in St Petersburg would have done it better.'

She herself once bought a length of silk that had been used to decorate the display window of a furniture store. She had this badly faded but expensive fabric dyed dark purple and made into a very extravagant set of matching garments: a dress and jacket, a cape and a scarf. People turned to look at her in the street when she wore it, because of her striking appearance.

Once Sylvia stayed with us in Prenzlauer Strasse for a few weeks. She was going to make herself useful by baking something, and my mother suggested a cake in a circular ring mould, telling her the ingredients: half a kilo of flour, about a hundred grams of butter and four eggs.

'What?' cried Sylvia. 'Four eggs? My God, what a mean little recipe!' A cake as she made it, she said, began with a batter consisting of the yolks of thirty-six hard-boiled eggs pounded.

My mother lost her temper when Sylvia put on such airs. 'What a bloodsucker you are!' she said angrily. Thereupon Sylvia left the apartment, slamming the door and without her coat, although it was winter. We worried about her, but she was back an hour later.

In the early Nazi period, Sylvia planned to leave Germany and move in with her brother Max in London. However, apparently his wife Bobby harassed, insulted and exploited her so much that she returned to Berlin a few months later. By a dispensation of Providence she even got back her old furnished room with two ancient old ladies in Wilmersdorf.

Among the absurdities of the war years was the fact that Sylvia finally got a proper paid job. She was employed by a half-Jewish man called Hofer who was a silversmith, and ran a workshop making costume jewellery, which was very popular at the time. You could bring him an old silver spoon or something similar, and he would make it into a pendant or a bracelet. There was nothing of the kind to be bought in the shops.

Sylvia did all the office work in this business. Her boss was living with a lady whom he couldn't marry because she was fully Aryan. Once, when I visited Sylvia in the silversmith's workshop, she introduced me to this lady – or rather, introduced us the other way round. 'I'm so glad that I can introduce our Fräulein Richold to you,' she told me. Elisabeth Richold was old enough to be my mother, so I should have been introduced to her. She was a full-bosomed, very attractive woman. The expression on her face slipped briefly, but she tried not to let it show.

When we were alone I asked Sylvia, 'How could you do a thing like that? Introducing a much older woman to me as if she were a servant.'

'Well, and is she anyone in particular?' replied Sylvia. This was one of her favourite phrases, indicating that the person addressed was not in fact anyone in particular.

That summer of 1942, Sylvia concentrated all the love she had no longer been able to give her four children on me. She became central to my life, making visits on which I could no longer venture. For instance, she went to see Toni Kirschstein to tell her that I had disappeared. And somewhere in a winding street she found a dusty little stationery shop which still sold something very important to me: ink-erasing fluid, which had been taken off the market long ago and was strictly forbidden because it could be used in forging

Sylvia Asarch with her husband
Boris Asarch, pre-1914.

documents. But the saleswoman didn't know that, and was glad to get rid of her old stock at last.

When we were drinking tea together one day, Sylvia got to her feet and announced, 'I am going to tell you something that will astonish you, and you mustn't forget it. I've lost everything, I have that terrible flight behind me, and I have never seen my children again. But I know one thing very well, and it's the sum of my experience of life: the Bolsheviks were right.' That has influenced me for the rest of my life.

My plan to go to Bulgaria set Sylvia thinking along her own characteristic lines. 'You need a first-class trousseau,' she said. 'You can't go without an evening dress. Pea-green silk would be nice.'

She planned to embark on a major business deal to provide this trousseau. She had a friend who was also Bulgarian, one Herr Todorov who lived in the same building and worked in a tobacconist's. At a guess, the man was seventy, and I couldn't help noticing that she was in love with him. She herself was around sixty, but still had an erotic and very passionate nature.

She gave all she had to the charming Herr Todorov. Doing small deals – getting hold of ten cigarettes somewhere and selling them on at a few pfennigs more – was not in Sylvia's style. She wanted to bring off a really big coup, and it led to her being handed over to the authorities by the man concerned.

I heard about it because Sylvia had arranged for me to talk to Herr Todorov. We were to meet at a certain bench in the Tiergarten. She was sure that it would be extremely useful to me to discuss life in Bulgaria with an educated and well-to-do Bulgarian.

He was to be carrying a sign by which I could recognise him, but that wasn't necessary. I knew who he was before he reached me. He looked exactly as I had imagined him from Sylvia's description: a very good-looking, white-haired gentleman entirely clad in pale grey. He was obviously a shady character. Poor Sylvia, I thought, she's fallen for a Lothario.

And even from a distance I saw how the corners of his mouth turned down in disappointment. I was not his sort of woman. My poverty was obvious, and I was shabbily dressed.

We exchanged a few civilities, and then he said, in a strong Slav accent, 'Asarch is locked up.'

Locked up? I gaped stupidly at him and asked, 'What did you say?'

'Is locked up,' he repeated.

He must have denounced her, thereby ridding himself of her, one or two days after she had given him all her money. I was to go to his house with him, he said, and he would give me a piece of bread. Feeling dazed, I followed him to Schaperstrasse. He kept me waiting in the doorway of his room. Opposite the door stood his desk with its drawer open, and I saw Sylvia's ring inside it. I liked that ring very much, and had often admired it: it was so large that it spread above the lowest joint of her middle finger, and was very beautifully made, with a setting of tiny birds pecking at jewelled splinters. If only because of its filigree craftsmanship, the ring was very valuable.

My last doubts were gone. He had even cleared out her apartment. With an idiotic grin, he turned to me and closed the desk drawer with his behind. Then he gave me a piece of bread. It was so hard that Ida Kahnke and I worked away at it with hammer and chisel, and still we couldn't cut it up small. Although it was all so terrible, we laughed until we cried.

In addition Herr Todorov gave me two pairs of knitted stockings. The thick material would never fit smoothly, but 'absorbed water', as people said, meaning that they got wrinkles in them. Poor as I was, I couldn't wear such things. I gave them to Ida Kahnke. 'To think there are still knitted stockings!' Delighted, she burst into fits of bleating, old-lady laughter.

Next day I went first to the silversmith's workshop where Sylvia had worked. I told Elisabeth Richold what had happened.

'How could she do such a thing?' she sighed. 'A Soviet Jewish lady dealing with a profiteer like that?' After Sylvia's arrest the jewellery workshop had also been searched.

'She didn't do it for herself,' I said. 'She did it for me.'

Frau Richold burst into tears. 'I'm glad you told me that. Sylvia Asarch is rather eccentric, but this shows her in a very different light. I didn't know she was such a good person.'

I never saw Aunt Sylvia again. Many years after the war I happened to be in company where people were discussing Hofer the silversmith's workshop. One of the women present said, 'And would you believe it, there was a Soviet Jewish woman called Sylvia, she'd been enviably well protected, but she was so greedy and stupid that she tried dealing with crooks, and that was the end of her.'

I didn't mention the relationship, but asked, 'Did the lady survive?'

'No. I don't know exactly what happened, but it's said that she was shot.'

5

There was a strange atmosphere on the railway platform in Zagreb. I walked uneasily up and down, waiting for the storm to break. A curiously ominous wall of purple cloud hung over the station, but when I turned round I looked up at a bright blue summer sky.

Then torrents of rain fell. A few moments later a double rainbow stretched in front of the dark clouds, shining in glorious colours such as I had never seen before. I felt a deep sense of gratitude, and put up a silent prayer. 'Thank you for this sign, dear God. The rainbow is a sign of your covenant in the Bible, so you are keeping the covenant with me – which means that I shall live.'

Would I reach my journey's end? Could I succeed in crossing Bulgaria and Turkey and reaching freedom? It was a question that I had asked myself again and again recently. I was in a state of great nervous tension. The train had kept stopping on the way along the line, we kept having to get out, and when we did reach the next station we had often missed our connection. We were now in Croatia, and I felt very queasy in a country subjugated by the Nazis. I had heard that the fascist Ustaše there were even worse than the SS. I would rather not have got out of the train at all in the Croatian capital, but it felt good to stretch my legs. A little girl of about six danced round us, reaching out her thin arms and begging. We got back into the train, and a few minutes later it moved away towards Sofia.

It was now the middle of September 1942. In my last weeks in Berlin I had been busy getting together the papers I needed for this journey. I began by approaching Herbert Koebner, who created or got hold of the documents needed for escaping from Germany. I knew his son Heinz slightly; he conducted the choir in the Old

Synagogue, so I had often seen his face in the pattern, so to speak, cast by the grille behind which the choir sang. He was engaged to a very pretty graphic artist, who lived with the Koebners. Her blonde curls didn't quite go with her complexion and her brown eyes. She had already gone underground (her name was allegedly Fräulein Henze), and she worked on the practical and technical side of the forgery business, paying great attention to detail.

Ernst Wolff had told me that his cousin needed a highly intelligent and reliable person to act as a test case for his forgeries, and in return would not take any money from me. I felt greatly flattered, and believed him. I discovered the truth about this bargain only much later.

First, however, I had to have documents on which Koebner could work. Hannchen Koch immediately offered to get hold of what was needed. She worked in the office of a co-operative laundry which had a great many customers coming and going, and she stole an identity card from the pocket of a coat hanging up in the corridor there.

By chance the name of the woman it belonged to was Abraham, née Hirsch. Presumably she could prove that she was of pure Aryan descent, but both her surnames sounded decidedly Jewish. Frau Koch immediately realised that I couldn't use an identity card that would arouse suspicion. 'It's a judgement from God,' she announced. 'You mustn't go under the name of Hirsch or Abraham or Schulze, you'd better have my papers. If I'm ever in a situation where I have to show my identity card, I'll only just have discovered that I've lost it.' For herself, she got what was known as a postal identity card, a substitute which meant that only the postman had to vouch for her identity.*

---

*In a talk that Marie Simon gave in 1993 she described the way to get a postal identity card: 'Many Jewish women who had gone underground could account for themselves legitimately at any time, and without arousing suspicion, by showing a postal identity card – a genuine identity card made out in a false, non-Jewish name. This is how it worked: Mirjam Cohn regularly wrote herself letters to the same address, sent to Marta Müller care of Schmidt ... She looked out for the postman, asking him to take

She had suffered pangs of conscience in abstracting a stranger's identity card. It was even harder for her to play the part of the honest finder now, and restore the document to its overjoyed owner. She claimed to have found it on a heap of coal in the yard of the laundry, and made a great fuss over accepting a generous sum of money as the reward.

However, I had another problem with Frau Koch's papers: she had been born in 1905, and so she was seventeen years older than me. I, on the other hand, barely looked my real age of twenty. Indeed, I was often taken for seventeen and asked whether I was still at school. All that Koebner could do to tone down this discrepancy a little was to make the figure 0 in the date 1905 into a figure 1. That would make me twenty-seven years old, which still was not very likely.

Thanks to the ink-erasing fluid I had bought, the original ink on the identity card could simply be removed. Koebner exchanged the photo of Hannchen Koch for one of me. Fräulein Henze copied the part of the official stamp that came above the photo, along with the eagle and the swastika, using a very fine brush. Everything else remained as it was: from now on I was Johanna Elisabeth Koch, née Guthmann. I was not entirely happy with this maiden name. More Guthmanns were Jewish than Aryan – but I had no real choice in the matter.

So now I had an identity card, but no passport and visa allowing me to travel, and no rail ticket. All these things were hard to procure in the middle of the war. Herbert Koebner therefore thought up a special ruse: he gave me a life as a freelance canteen manageress travelling at her own expense. I would not need a ticket issued by the Wehrmacht for that, and indeed I would not have got one, but I would seem to be vaguely connected with the Wehrmacht, and

---

her letter, chatted him up a little, offering him a cigarette, and after a certain time she would ask the postman to tell them at the post office, for the purpose of making out an identity card, that yes, he knew Marta Müller personally. At this point a packet of cigarettes changed hands. I don't know of any case where a postman refused to do a nice woman this small service.'

Johanna Koch's identity card with a photo of Marie Jalowicz. The stamp over the photograph was drawn in by hand and the date of birth forged.

it was to be hoped that my documents would not be checked so closely.

The document he thought up for me was a travel order allegedly made out at a Luftwaffe air district command post in Warsaw. Fortunately that was a long way off. Such a document apparently issued in Berlin would have been far more easily checked to see if it was genuine. The son of a woman who was a neighbour of the Koebners, a young man of about my age, had been stationed at the Warsaw air district command post and stole the blank form there. His mother was a convinced supporter of the Resistance movement, and was later to save my life yet again.

It would have been simpler to travel by way of Poland, for that route led entirely through Nazi-occupied territory. I would not have needed a visa. But I couldn't do it; I was panic-stricken at the thought. Passing a concentration camp in broad daylight, a place where my own people were being killed? It was a nightmarish idea.

So Koebner let me persuade him to devise another route by way of Vienna and Zagreb. With my heart in my mouth, I went to the Croatian embassy, situated in a villa with polished parquet floors in the elegant surroundings of Grunewald, to apply for a visa to pass through the country.

I did not have to wait long to show a member of the embassy staff my travel order as manufactured by Koebner, although it was obvious to the man at once that there was something wrong with it. First he looked sceptical, then he thought for a moment, and after that he began to roar with laughter. 'Well, of course we'll do it!' he told me, with the air of someone anxious to please. I tried to keep my anxiety under control, and then I realised that he was more frightened of me than I was of him.

I don't know what he really thought about me, but anyway, during this official transaction we both chuckled unconvincingly, as if we were acting in a silly farce. 'Given that our countries are such close friends,' he said emphatically more than once, 'we'll put a stamp on it.' The Croatian coat of arms was a kind of chessboard, and the stamp looked very impressive.

The whole plan almost came to grief when I went to buy my ticket. The ticket clerk, a disobliging character, was suspicious. 'You have a travel order? Then why hasn't the Wehrmacht given you a ticket?' he snapped. 'There's something fishy about this. I'll have to get you arrested.'

'I'm in a great hurry,' I replied as calmly as possible, 'but if you can't give me a ticket now, then I'll just have to wait until next week and get the passport and visa first. Heil Hitler!' And I made off. Luckily he couldn't leave his desk unattended and run after me.

I went to another station, where they made me out a ticket to Sofia with no more fuss than if I were buying a tram ticket from Schönhauser Allee to Pankow. The ticket clerk there couldn't have cared less what my plans were. The money for the ticket was a present from Frau Koch's boss, a former client of my father's. He even gave me an extra hundred marks for the journey. I hid the banknote in the sole of my shoe for emergencies, and didn't even tell Mitko about it.

*

The journey to Sofia took three days and three nights in all. Of course we went in the cheapest class, sitting on wooden benches, and it was a great strain. But I was not on my own. Mitko was with me, and we were newly in love. I was convinced that we were made for one another, not least because of the symmetry of our birth dates: I was born on 4/4/1922, and he was born on 5/5/1911.

We stopped off briefly in Vienna. My first impressions of the city disappointed me. I had expected something wonderful, imagining Vienna's famous coffee houses and cake shops. But walking in the surroundings of the station, I found them as grey and dismal as any Berlin suburb. We had a cup of ersatz coffee in a cheap café, and then the journey went on.

When we finally arrived in Sofia the first thing that Mitko did was find us a hotel room. It was a cheap, shabby place, and he had to pay a lot for my papers not to be checked. He still had money; he had been working in Germany for two years – not as forced labour but voluntarily, as he reluctantly admitted. He really meant to use his savings from that time to buy a plot of land in Bulgaria, build a little house on it and get married. But now he was spending all his money on me, and it was rapidly dwindling.

On one of our first nights in this hotel there was a police raid, and all the guests had to show their papers. I had a fine for vagrancy imposed on me, and Mitko paid it at once. When he offered to pay a little extra to keep the case out of the records, the police officers agreed at once.

Sofia struck me as rather colourless. The city did not particularly impress me. One of our first visits was to a cousin of Mitko's who ran a hairdressing salon with her husband. They lived in a large apartment building in the Mediterranean style, with long corridors and many tenants. Without understanding much of what they were saying, I heard Mitko talking to the couple excitedly, describing my situation and asking how my presence in Bulgaria could be legalised. He wanted to marry me, that much was certain.

His cousin and her husband were obviously upset to find that he was in a fix yet again, but they wanted to help, and told us that a writer who lived nearby was head of the communist Resistance. Presumably that last bit was something of an exaggeration.

This elderly gentleman, to whom we turned for advice, was called Christo Christov. He looked rather impoverished and down at heel, with gaps in his teeth and shabby clothes. There was much agitated conversation with him, too. After a while he asked to see my papers and have them translated. 'It's a miracle and a mercy that you got here with this rubbish,' he commented. 'These papers are useless. There are no Wehrmacht canteens here. You'd better bury the documents at the bottom of your bag, and don't show them to anyone.'

But Christov did give us some good advice: Sofia, he said, was much too dangerous for us. We had better go to Tarnovo, where another cousin of Mitko's lived.

Our journey through Bulgaria was a wonderful adventure for me. It was my first encounter with the strange, southern world of the Balkans. We took our time, seeing all the sights and staying in hotels here and there. I was fascinated by the climate, the flora and fauna, the food, and the way people sat together over meals. Every Bulgarian word and expression that I picked up made me happy. I didn't worry much about anything, I just relied on Mitko, whose country this was. My plan of making my way towards Turkey retreated into the distance.

It was the vintage season, and we lived almost entirely on grapes. I ate them by the kilo, and that built up my strength again. After my experiences, after horrors like the mutton eaten from the container also used for my shit and other such unpleasant things, I was making an excellent recovery and getting my strength back.

In Tarnovo, the old imperial city of Bulgaria that clings picturesquely to a high rock, we saw the introduction of the Jewish star under pressure from the Germans. Or rather, I should say we saw the attempted introduction of the Jewish star. It was a curious and unique spectacle, resisted by the entire nation. I witnessed several street scenes that deeply impressed me.

Once I saw three or four Jewish girls wearing the yellow star on their school uniforms as they walked through the streets. Their non-Jewish friends had formed a protective cordon round them. With heads held high, those girls looked aggressively into the face of every passer by, including me, as if to say, 'If you dare to touch our friends we'll strike you dead.'

On another occasion I observed a Jewish girl of ten or eleven walking by herself when a policeman abruptly beckoned her over. He grabbed the child, who went white as a sheet, tore the Jewish star off her, flung it to the road and trampled on it with both feet. As he did so, he was saying – and even I could understand him – 'We don't do that here! Bulgarians are not criminals.'

Within a few days that saying was in general circulation: 'We Bulgarians are not criminals.' An ancient man with a shepherd's crook and a shaggy sheepskin asked us, 'Where do I go to demonstrate against our fellows citizens being deported?' All the former political parties protested, so did the lawyers' association, the dentists' association and the Church. It was magnificent. Only I, sadly, was barred from demonstrating against the Jewish star, which distressed me. But I was not in the country legally and must not attract attention, however much I wanted to protest.

Mitko's cousin in Tarnovo was a realistic woman, and she asked us after a few days what our further plans were; we couldn't be her guests for ever. She asked around to find out what could be done to make my stay legal, and chanced upon a lawyer who would do all kinds of crooked things for money. Mitko went to see him at once.

The man had seen us in the street. 'You are here with this enchanting lady from Germany?' he asked my lover. 'I could use her as a governess for my little boy! The papers wouldn't cost anything, if you take my meaning?' He winked in a vulgar manner. Mitko, a naïve but decent character, was indignant at this improper suggestion. 'We can do without your services,' he said brusquely, and he stood up and left. 'As you like,' the lawyer called after him. 'We'll see what comes of this.'

It was he who denounced me. He must have told the police that

I was illegally there in Bulgaria and suspected of spying for Russia. Next morning we found two Bulgarian police officers standing by our bed. I was abruptly torn away from an intense and delightful dream of flowery meadows – it was a rude awakening.

The uniformed officers spoke to us calmly and reasonably. 'We're sure you wouldn't find it difficult to run away from us,' they said, 'but then we'd know that you're guilty. We're family men, so do us the favour of going to Sofia and reporting voluntarily to the authorities, or it'll be we who pay for it.' We looked at each other. It was obvious at once that we didn't want to get other people into trouble.

My first experience of prison was a shabby hotel in Sofia. I was not allowed to leave the room, and was under police supervision. Down below, my lover Mitko, in floods of tears, stood under my window waving. We communicated through notes passed on for us by a cleaning lady, in return for a small tip.

Once in Sofia, Mitko had immediately gone to see Christo Christov. The old gentleman must have cursed to find himself involved in a case like mine. But he remembered that there was a man in Sofia responsible for the employment of Bulgarian workers in Germany. Hans Goll was regarded as a decent man and a firm opponent of the Gestapo. Through intermediaries, an arrangement for me to meet him was made.

I was collected from the hotel in a car, and Mitko, who was standing in the street, was allowed to come too. It was all very strange, like something out of a fairy tale. We were led into a large waiting room, and were soon called in to see Goll.

From the first, he addressed me in a pleasant tone of voice. He was prepared for my visit, but I couldn't tell how much he knew about me. For a while he stared in silence at the documents I put in front of him. I asked him, openly, 'Can you imagine someone who has never done any harm to another human being, who has never broken the law, let alone committed a bad crime, being in great danger?'

Marie Jalowicz with Dimitr Petrov Tchakalov in September 1942, in Sofia, Bulgaria.

'I take your point,' he replied. 'I'll try to help you.'

Mitko was in the room with us. He had done some interpreting on a transport of foreign workers, and at this wholly inappropriate moment began to ask for money for his services. He could communicate only in broken German, so it was clear that he had no real skill as an interpreter to offer. To make matters worse, he turned up his trouser leg, pushed down his sock and began scratching his shinbone very thoroughly. I could have sunk into the floor.

Hans Goll, a sandy-haired man with a redhead's tendency to go crimson in the face easily, did so when he saw that and shouted, 'Get out!' When Mitko had left the room he said to me, rather more calmly, 'I don't think you should be in a relationship like that, it's beneath you. But you are worth helping.' He spoke to me as if I were a close relation.

Then he telephoned someone while I was still in the room. 'Well, she doesn't have proper papers, it's a silly love affair – remember

Hans Goll, aged thirty-four in Sofia in 1942. Goll was responsible for Bulgarian workers coming to Germany.

Viktor Koch and his little daughter?' I heard him saying. I had no idea who this Koch was.* 'Young people today do the silliest things when they're in love,' he went on. Then he put his hand over the receiver and breathed a word to me, probably 'Gauleiter'.

After he had hung up, I said anxiously, 'It's my married name that's Koch, at least in my papers – so my father can't be called Koch, can he?'

'Oh, my God, how naïve you are,' he said. 'It's not a question of checking your papers. The whole point is to act from the first in such a way that no one asks about them.'

Then he sent me out. I sat down beside my unfortunate lover Mitko. It was odd, but at that moment I felt, for the first time, that Goll was right. There was no future in my relationship with Mitko.

---

* Probably Heinz Koch (1894–1959), visiting professor at Sofia University in 1940 and director of the entire educational system of the city.

It had been a really enchanting, spring-like love affair, but a flash in the pan. Now it was burning out, and soon there would be nothing left of it but a little heap of ashes.

After some time Goll called me into his room again. 'Go back to the hotel,' he said, 'but you can go as a free woman. Walk about all you like. Tomorrow or the day after I'll pick you up in a car. You will get a genuine German passport on trust. It will stand up to any amount of checking, but it will be marked *Valid for Return to Germany Only.*'

He also explained the course that this return journey was to take: I would go by ship from Lom on the Danube to Vienna, by way of Budapest. He would discover in good time whether there was a warrant out for my arrest in Germany. If there was, he would send me a telegram to the ship containing some innocuous message. 'If you get a telegram, never mind what it says, leave the ship in Budapest. Pick up a shopping basket, wait around by the shipboard galley, and leave the ship with the crew.' He gave me a sealed envelope. 'Open this only if you have to disembark in Budapest, and go to the address you will find inside. They will help you there. If you don't receive a telegram, stay on board and burn this envelope. Give me your word of honour that you will.'

I promised, solemnly assuring him that I was absolutely reliable. One or two days later he drove me to the German embassy in Sofia. Once again I had to wait while he disappeared into the back rooms. When he came out, he said in a loud voice, 'Having known your family for so many years, I've been able to guarantee your identity as Johanna Koch. Get your marriage certificate in order, and then you can legally come back to Bulgaria. But for now my office will pay your passage back to Germany. Good luck, and I hope we meet again.' I didn't even have a chance to thank him properly.

I was given my passport by a very nice young woman who volubly wished me luck and all good fortune. She herself was married to a Bulgarian, she told me, and he was a wonderful man. She hoped I would succeed in marrying my own Bulgarian fiancé. As she talked, she caressed both my arms.

*

Mitko went as far as Lom with me. Once again we stayed in a hotel there and ate the excellent Bulgarian grapes. Once again Mitko was my lover, a delicately built man with fairy-tale colouring, white as snow, red as blood and black as ebony, and with an enchantingly mellifluous voice. But now I clearly felt how different we were. He often sang a German hit song that was all the rage on the radio in Berlin, a terribly sentimental piece – and when it turned out that he had misquoted the line *Schenk mir dein Löchlein, Maria*, substituting *Löchlein* [little hole] for *Lächeln* [smile], I finally realised that yes, it had been a nice love affair, but it was just as well that it was over now.

After one or two days in Lom, Mitko asked me to understand that he couldn't stay any longer. He had been in Bulgaria for weeks, he said, and hadn't yet even been in touch with his parents. He was going back to his village, but he left me all the money he still had. It was a tearful farewell. We embraced, wept together, and encouraged each other to hope that we would meet again some day. But we never did.

Lom was a miserable place. If there were any sights worth seeing there, I didn't discover them. And once Mitko had left, there was no one to show them to me.

All the same, I tried to delay my journey. Every day that I didn't spend in Berlin, I thought, was another day in safety, a day closer to the end of the war. I thought up all kinds of reasons why I had to stay in Bulgaria. The man organising shipments from Lom was German. He sat at a little table in the street, drawing up passenger lists. I offered to certify that I hadn't yet finished a course of medical treatment. I said I had to wait for a date to appear in a law court. None of it was any good. 'You're being thrown out,' he said abruptly. 'That's what it says in your passport.'

Before giving up I made one last try. 'Then I'll have to leave without my winter coat, what a nuisance! I left it in Tarnovo,' I said miserably. 'They were going to send it on here in a parcel.' That did work. The man began shaking dramatically, a facetious imitation of someone shuddering with cold. It was mid-October, and he obviously regarded Prussia as something like East Siberia. 'Prussia without a winter coat?' he said. 'Dear me, that won't do. You can stay here another ten days.' He crossed my name off one list and put it on another.

So I had gained a little time, but I didn't know what to do with it. Since I had no occupation, I just wandered round the place. As I did so I noticed a large group of Greek men who looked lost and impoverished, and were probably foreign workers bound for Germany.

Once an elderly Hungarian officer spoke to me. 'You speak German? May I invite you to take a glass of wine with me?' I accepted the invitation, and soon regretted it, because he was dreadfully arrogant. We drank wine together for five or six evenings running. He was always making remarks such as, 'Asia begins beyond Budapest.' He was also a traditional anti-Semite, well informed about the military situation. He told me, 'We shall win, you know. But I'm aware how hard it will really be; I expect a catastrophe.'

I could no longer restrain myself. I answered in such a loud voice that people at the nearby tables turned to look at us. 'I don't expect any catastrophe. I'm firmly convinced that the just cause will win.'

He looked at me foolishly. 'What do you mean?'

'Are you in any doubt of what the just cause is? Do you need such things explained to you?' I retorted defiantly.

To that, he said, 'Something about you strikes me as odd. The extent of your education compared to your financial means, your putting up here in the cheapest accommodation and your generally poor appearance – none of it really fits together.'

I told him some story about a large suitcase that had gone astray. Once again I had been taught a lesson: I must be more careful. This man could have been dangerous to me. Fortunately he was leaving next day.

At the end of October I left Lom on the ship. Because it had got around that I spoke some Bulgarian, I was asked to interpret. There were many Bulgarians on board who didn't speak a word of German. It was only a case of giving them simple instructions such as where to go on the ship. But I was proud that I could make myself useful.

A woman who was one of the organisers told the man in charge of this transport about me, and he wanted us to meet. He sat beside me on a bench on deck. It was fine weather, and we saw the landscape passing by. He was bored, hoped to get some amusement from our conversation, and kept laughing cheerfully. Then he asked why, as a citizen of the German Reich, I was being sent back from Bulgaria. I told him the usual story – I had been planning to marry a Bulgarian, but had left Germany in too much of a hurry and without the necessary papers.

'Would you be kind enough to show me your papers?' he asked. 'I've never seen a passport in which a German citizen is obliged to leave the country, although there is a guarantee of her identity.' Naturally I was alarmed. I opened my bag, meaning to show him my identity card first, but I found that I had my passport in my hand. I noticed my mistake too late. Put the passport back in the bag and take out the identity card? That would have looked suspicious.

Temporary passport for 'Johanna Koch' to enter Germany, made out on 9 October 1942 at the German embassy in Sofia. Comment in the passport: 'The holder of this passport has not proved her citizenship of the Reich. It is valid only for her

The man produced a magnifying glass and inspected my passport closely. Then he gave it back to me. 'There, now we can be comfortable together. Your passport is fine. So far as I'm concerned it could say anything, for instance *If my aunt had wheels she'd be an omnibus*, or –' he was looking for something equally silly, and I supplied it: 'Or *There's a funfair on in Heaven*.'

'Yes, just so long as the stamp on the passport photo is genuine,' he went on. 'You see, I've recently been on a course showing us how to recognise forged papers. After that we were able to unmask several Yugoslavian partisans with apparently faultless German papers. They spoke good German, and only one little thing in their papers was wrong: the edges of the official stamp were forged.' He pointed to the bank of the river. 'Look over there: we strung up those partisans on meat hooks a little farther on inside that forest.'

I was shocked and upset, and had the greatest difficulty in hiding it. If I had handed him my identity card he would have

return to Germany by the Danube route.' On the right-hand side, the stamps document her journey out of Bulgaria from Lom on 31 October 1942, and her arrival in Vienna on 4 November 1942.

121

seen at once that it was forged, and that would have meant my certain death.

He went on to tell me about other Slavs who had forged papers and spoke excellent German, but could not pronounce the letter H. I immediately thought of my Russian grandmother, who was said to have called her son 'Gerbert' and her son-in-law 'Germann'. And then I fell victim to a strange phenomenon: for a few hours I myself couldn't pronounce an H. I had to steer a course around any word with H in it, like 'heaven', or think of an alternative. Such was the absurd result of the mortal fear that, once more, I had survived.

I was very glad when we had left Budapest behind us. The outline of the city rooftops, considered so beautiful, did not appeal to me at all. I associated Budapest with the appalling Hungarian officer who had drunk wine with me in Lom. Until we reached the Hungarian capital, moreover, I was waiting in great suspense for a telegram from Goll. He had assured me that he would be told exactly when I was travelling, and had asked me not on any account to get in touch with him on my own initiative.

I spent the last part of the river voyage on deck in fine weather, talking to the workers who, like me, were going on to Vienna. One of them had a copper ashtray with him. I borrowed it for a moment on some excuse, took it into the toilet and burned Goll's unopened letter, with a certain sense of personal pride: I was not such a moral wreck as to break my word out of mere curiosity. I threw the ashes away and gave the man his ashtray back.

We reached Vienna that evening. The ship emptied, and a long line formed on the quayside. After we had gone through the first passport control, I asked the man in charge of the transport, who was standing next to me in the queue, 'Can I go now?'

'No,' he told me. 'Everyone has to be checked by the Gestapo men in Morinplatz. You too because of that unusual passport. So stand in line here with the rest of us.'

It was a long way, and the column of weary figures weighed down by their packs moved slowly. As we passed a railway station,

I suddenly had an idea. I went into the ticket office, handed in my case at Left Luggage, and rejoined the queue a little later. I felt more mobile and could move more freely now.

On reaching Morinplatz, we were accommodated in a huge concourse full of camp beds and straw mattresses. It was a terrible night. I couldn't get a wink of sleep, terrified as I was of what might happen next. That meant, of course, that I was exhausted in the morning, when we would all be called up for the Gestapo to check our papers. We had to wait for hours.

When my turn came, I forced myself to go into the Gestapo office in total control of myself. 'Wait here,' someone told me in a heavy Viennese accent, offering me a chair. He said he had to telephone and find out whether my personal details and my address were right. After he had gone out, I heard him talking behind the closed door. He was obviously calling the police station responsible for Nitzwalder Strasse in Berlin.

A few minutes later he came back, beaming. 'Yes, all in order: identity card number, address, maiden name and date of birth.' I felt enormously relieved. No one had noticed the forged date of birth, 1915. That obvious discrepancy could have been the death of me.

'Can I go now?' I asked, casually. 'I have to do a few things in Vienna before I go on to Berlin.'

'Not yet, I have to ask you to wait. We still have to speak to police HQ in Berlin.'

'I see. Will it take long?'

'Well, right now I don't have the time to make the phone call, so it could be quite a while.'

I asked him where the toilet was. My body was reacting violently to all this upheaval, and I suddenly felt unable to stay in the building a moment longer. In the toilet I took my hundred-mark note out of my shoe. Then I looked out of the window. Two German soldiers were on guard only a few metres away. Within seconds I had an idea.

'Hey, you fine gents, run after them! Those bloody Balkan guys stole my case! Look, there they go!' I shouted at the soldiers.

'Can't be done, we're on guard, we have to stay put.'

'Whoever heard of such a thing?'

'On guard means on guard!'

'Then help me out of this window! I'll have to go after them myself,' I snapped furiously. The two young soldiers helped me out of the window like the good boys they were, and I chased after the supposed thieves.

After that everything happened very fast. At the next street corner I asked someone the way to the railway station. Soon after that a tram came along, I got on it, and was at the station within a few minutes. I quickly went over to the Left Luggage counter, where I got my case back without any difficulty. Then to the ticket office, where I bought my ticket. No problem with passport checks either; Vienna was in the Ostmark area. I asked when the next train for Berlin left.

'Don't worry,' I was told. 'Up those steps, you can take your time. You have five minutes.' It was pure chance that a connection to Berlin ran from Franz Joseph Station in Vienna, and at that very moment too.

I found myself in a compartment with a nice bunch of young Austrian soldiers as my travelling companions. When I asked them to lift my case up to the luggage net, they laughed themselves silly at my Berlin accent. Then they brought out a wonderful rustic loaf, sliced it, spread the slices with butter, topped them with cheese and sausage and invited me to share their meal. I certainly didn't go hungry on that journey.

And so, on the morning of 6 November 1942, I was back in the city of Berlin that I had left seven weeks earlier.

FOUR

The enemy is doing all this to us
The First Winter in Hiding

1

Early in the evening we all met at the Koebners' apartment in Kaiser-Wilhelm-Strasse. Once again I noticed the vanity of Benno Heller, the gynaecologist, not to mention the great care that he devoted to his wardrobe. When he took off his scarf and gloves, he put them down so that everyone could see they came from an expensive sports shop on the Kurfürstendamm.

We sat down at the large, handsome dining table, and Frau Koebner made herbal tea. I had asked for this meeting soon after my return in November 1942, and it was at my suggestion that Heller was also there. For he, too, had turned to Koebner's forgery workshop; he wanted to get out of Germany, and that could be done only with forged papers. I wanted to warn the men against making any more use of the blank forms from the Warsaw air district command post. Judging by my recent experience, it seemed that they would do no one any good now.

Hannchen Koch spoke first; I had spent the first night after my return with her. While her husband was on shift duty at the police station, I had slept soundly in the Kochs' marital bed for almost twenty-four hours. Hannchen had decided to keep Emil out of my affairs in future. 'I will see to it that you're safe on my own. I'll make all the necessary sacrifices,' she had told me, as usual rather too emotionally.

Now, shyly and quietly, Frau Koch made some remarks mingling, in wild confusion, all she knew about magic, mysticism, the occult and the interpretation of dreams. She told us that she was trying to influence the political situation by damaging Hitler's astral body. I felt that this was incredibly embarrassing, but everyone kept a straight face. After a few minutes I reached over the table to take her arm and said, I'm afraid in far too loud a voice, 'Hannchen, that's wonderful.'

At the same moment the shrill sound of the doorbell was heard. We were all terribly alarmed. Who could be at the door?

Then we all set to work very fast. While Frau Koebner went to answer the door, her husband and son cleared the living room. The table and chairs were pushed aside, the rug rolled up. Someone wound the gramophone, put on a record, and immediately music began to play. We were staging a dancing party. With an elegant bow, Heller invited Frau Koch to dance, while the gramophone belted out an old hit song with a catchy rhythm. *I'd like to be the lodger in Miss Liesbeth's downstairs room, For I'm a merry dodger, we'd have such fun – zing boom!*

The music carried me away: Fritz Koebner, one of the sons of the family, had led me out on the improvised dance floor. His elder brother Heinz and Heinz's fiancée were not there. I saw Frau Koch closing her eyes. In spite of all the anxiety and alarms, she looked ecstatic dancing with her dream-doctor, who looked exactly the part of a film star playing a gynaecologist in a sentimental romance. Her face expressed wistful delight – she might have been on the point of coming to orgasm. While Heller skilfully guided her round the floor in his well-disciplined style, Hannchen Koch arched her back and moved her behind half a metre to left or right with every step of the dance.

Fritz Koebner led me into a corner of the room, tapped me lightly on the shoulder and breathed into my ear, almost inaudibly, 'I'd better warn you.' I looked inquiringly at him, but he fell silent, for just then Frau Koch, waggling her behind, sashayed past us. 'Warn you against my father,' he whispered. My conscious mind refused to take in this information; it was too full, so to speak, to admit anything else.

All this happened within a few bars of the music. Then the door was flung open, and we heard Frau Koebner's voice. 'All clear! It was only Frau Hansl from downstairs kindly bringing us a bag of sugar.' The gramophone was switched off at once, and normal conditions were restored. I was slightly sorry when the music stopped. I'd have liked to go on watching Frau Koch doing her grotesque dance.

But now it was time for me to tell the story of my journey, and then we would decide what to do next.

When I had finished, someone asked me where I would really like to go. 'France. I'd love to see France,' I heard myself saying, to my own surprise. But reality, as I knew, was very different: I needed a place to hide in Berlin, and I depended entirely on the people here at the Koebners' to help me. I didn't want to get in touch with my Jewish friends and acquaintances, not with Irene Scherhey, or Ernst Schindler or Max Bäcker. They mustn't even know that I was back in Berlin.

Frau Koebner had been very friendly to me from the first. I had liked her at once: she was a pleasant, clever woman. Her husband, on the other hand, behaved with courteous civility to me but showed no personal warmth. I thought I even detected a certain dislike in his attitude. Now, rather reluctantly, he said he would have to think up a new strategy. Heller suddenly seemed to be upset; he had spent a good deal of money on his blank forms from Warsaw, and now he didn't know whether they would be any more use to him.

Finally, Fritz had an idea. Before 1933 the Koebners had often spent the summer holidays as sub-tenants of an old man who lived beside the Wannsee. Until his retirement he had commanded huge ocean-going steamships, and then had captained a barge on the River Spree. This captain, Fritz thought, was a sad and lonely bachelor, and would surely be glad of a little female company in his basement apartment. In addition, said Fritz, he had never concealed his poor opinion of the Nazis. After they came to power, he had written letters to all the Jews he knew personally, telling them how indignant he felt about the treatment they were suffering.

Fritz Koebner said he would go to see this Herr Klaar in Kladow the next day. Our little party broke up. I went a few steps further with Hannchen Koch to Alexanderplatz. This was the part of the city where I had grown up, and where I had always had many friends and relations. But now I didn't know where to spend the night. Emil Koch's night shifts had come to an end, so I couldn't go back to Kaulsdorf. In any case, it was close to miraculous that the Gestapo hadn't long ago turned up at Hannchen Koch's home. After all, I had travelled under her name to Bulgaria, where I had attracted the attention of the police several times.

When we said goodbye, Hannchen pressed a milk can into my hand. She thought that would protect me from suspicion; if I happened to come up against a checkpoint I should just say I was off to get milk for my child. Only when we had parted did it occur to me how pointless this idea was. No one went to get milk for her child in the middle of the night. And as I clutched the metal handle of the can my fingers were slowly turning numb. It was a cold November evening.

I got on the Ringbahn, the circular line of the S-Bahn railway, and rode round it a couple of times. After a while I had had enough of it. I knew that all I could do was stay awake until next morning by walking through the city.

I also had a very pressing problem. I needed the toilet, for the full works.

I was in an area that I didn't know, somewhere in the south-west of the city. The front doors of all buildings had to be left unlocked at night because of the air raids, so that the emergency services could storm in to the rescue if there was a fire. I went into one of these unpretentious apartment buildings and crept quietly up the stairs. When I saw a name that I didn't like on a door, because it had a Nazi ring to it, I squatted down and did my business. I left some newspaper there too. What would the people in that apartment think next morning when they found what I had left on their doormat?

Then, next day, I did think of someone I could visit in Berlin. On board the Danube ship I had met a Bulgarian called Todor Nedeltchev, a fair-haired giant about my own age with a primitive, rather childlike face. He had often hung around me on the ship, telling me over and over again, 'I German speak very good, very nice.' Those assurances, however, exhausted his entire German vocabulary.

I knew that Todor was going to Berlin himself. He had given me the address of his lodgings, in Teltow next to the factory where he worked. I set off for it.

Sure enough, I found Todor at once. He was glad to see me again, and showed me the hut where he and the other foreign labourers lived. I was worn out and very short of sleep. I could think of nothing but where to stay for the next few days. Todor was my last hope, so I came straight to the point.

'Where can we find somewhere private here?' I asked in my broken Bulgarian. I was going to offer him a tender interlude and then suggest that we get engaged. If we did he would be able to find a place for us both – not as a long-term solution, of course, since I had no papers that I could show the police. But perhaps I could get through one or two weeks in that way.

Rather clumsily, Todor led me to the communal shower, which was entirely empty at that hour in the morning. I drew him into it, bolted the door on the inside and said, 'I know what you men like! Let's not bother about long preliminaries – we'll do it now and then we can get engaged.' A fuse had somehow blown inside me.

The man looked rather foolish. It reminded me a little of the idiotic expression that Charlie Chaplin sometimes wore – a mixture of bafflement and awkwardness. He stood there perfectly still when I tried to take him in my arms. Then, hesitantly, he admitted that he had never had anything to do with a girl before. He felt very embarrassed about it.

I tried to make it clear that I was offering him an engagement. When he had grasped that, and overcome his shock, he was enthusiastic. We set off at once in search of accommodation.

We spent all day together, without much more to say to one another than 'very good' and 'very nice', and we asked various acquaintances of his, but no one had a room for us. So we parted that evening with many good wishes, and that was the end of my relationship with Todor Nedeltchev.

Fritz Koebner had been more successful. He had found Captain

Klaar at home, and the captain had immediately agreed to take me in.

Fritz took me to see him next day. We travelled separately to the Wannsee S-Bahn station. Fritz was dark-haired, looked distinctly Jewish, and of course had to wear the yellow star. But he had a second jacket with him in a travelling bag, and he put it on in the toilet of the S-Bahn station at Wannsee. Then we walked the rest of the way to Kladow together, while he told me about his father.

Herbert Koebner, he said, had always been the best and kindest of fathers, a man who loved and respected his wife, and led an exemplary if not strictly orthodox Jewish life. But, said Fritz, he had obviously lost his wits. 'He's involved in some kind of business with Gestapo and SS men, making them forged papers just in case the war doesn't turn out as expected,' he told me. 'And he has the crazy notion that this will make him a dollar multi-millionaire. In his mind he's planning a world cruise for the whole family, looking at atlases and thinking up routes.' His mother, he added, was in despair. 'Have you noticed the nasty grin he sometimes has on his face?' Fritz asked me. I nodded. Something about the man had always seemed odd to me. 'It must be a symptom of his madness,' said his son. 'He never used to grin like that.'

Captain Klaar welcomed us warmly. He was a friendly old gentleman, but he did indeed seem very melancholy. He lived in the basement of a two-storey house, and reassured me by saying that his neighbours were far too cultivated to feel curious or denounce anyone. He had told them, he added, that he had given a woman he knew a key to his apartment, so I wouldn't need to hide, and must make myself at home. He showed me the kitchen and the larder, the heating arrangements, and his bedroom. He was just about to set off on a river trip lasting several days.

In spite of all he said, I hardly dared to move in his apartment. I kept my hands off his stocks of food, for I was so starved that otherwise I would simply have fallen on them. It was damp and cold in that basement, but I dared not put the heating on. I slept in the unmade bed, and lived solely on a piece of bread and a jar of beans that Frau Koch had given me. After all that I had been through, I felt exhausted and depressed.

I could get away from Kladow only by taking the ferry across the Wannsee. The captain had warned me against the ferryman, saying he was very inquisitive, a shockingly bad character and a fanatical Nazi. Sure enough, the man asked persistent questions when I set off for the city after a couple of days to go and see Frau Koch. He wanted to know where I lived, and questioned me about my family circumstances.

'Can't you guess why I'm here?' I hinted. 'I mean, you're not past it yet yourself.'

'I wonder who the lucky man is,' he replied. 'There aren't many young men around here.' I was glad when I could get off the ferry.

Then I marched towards the city centre along one of the large, western arterial roads. I wanted to go as much of the way to Köpenick as possible on foot, but I was very hungry. As I came to a café that must once have been very elegant, I decided to stop for a rest. Every restaurant offered what was called a standard dish of the day, for people who didn't have any coupons on them, usually very poor quality food consisting of swedes and pieces of potato without fat of any kind. It was well known that deserters and other dubious characters who had no food ration cards took up this offer.

What devil got into me, making me go into that café? And what even sillier devil told me not to sit at a small table, but instead go over to a huge slab of oak clearly frequented by the regular customers?

No sooner had I ordered than several well-dressed gentlemen, probably from some official authority, sat down with me. Their glances showed what they thought of the uninvited guest at their table: a harmless madwoman who had lost her way. I ate my dish of the day as calmly as possible, while listening to their conversation. They were talking about Ribbentrop. Then I paid and fled into the open air. That way, I left the gentlemen unsure whether I even knew any German. It had been rash enough to sit at a table with them.

*

When Captain Klaar came back to his apartment after a week away, he was obviously very disappointed. He had expected to return to a comfortable, warm home, with the beds freshly made up and a hot meal on the stove. I explained that I simply hadn't ventured to touch anything in his apartment. However, it was clear that I couldn't stay with him any longer. We said a friendly goodbye, wishing one another good luck.

I went back to the centre of Berlin. My route took me straight to Kaiser-Wilhelm-Strasse, where Koebner lived. Hoping that the forger might have thought of a new scheme for me, I climbed the stairs.

But I did not get far. The door of one apartment on the first floor was open just a crack. A white-haired old lady put her head out and whispered, 'Are you looking for the Koebners?' It was their helpful neighbour Frau Hansl. She quickly led me into her apartment and closed the door. 'Gestapo upstairs,' she breathed into my ear. She had been standing in her front hall in the pitch dark for hours, watching the bottom of the stairs and heading off any visitors to the Koebners.

Looking through the peephole in her door early in the morning, she had seen several people, bound together, being taken downstairs. Now the Gestapo were back again to search the apartment. She had seen little bottles of ink and erasing fluid, paper and other items of equipment from the forger's workshop being taken away on trays. The Gestapo men could still be heard rummaging around upstairs as we stood in her hall in the dark.

'Are you the girl my son brought those blank papers back from Warsaw for?' she asked me quietly. I nodded. Koebner had been furious, she told me, when he heard about my return to Berlin. 'Silly cow, almost gets to the Turkish border and then comes all the way back again! She should be ashamed of herself!' However, his wife had raised her own voice and said it was a stroke of sheer genius on my part to get out of Bulgaria alive and without being arrested. 'If anyone should be ashamed it's you. Instead of getting properly informed, you make her out a stupid travel order like that, and then spend your time planning those crazy round-the-world trips!'

Now we heard footsteps rapidly going downstairs again. From the window of her front room, Frau Hansl saw the Gestapo men getting into their car and driving away. 'You can venture out into the street again now,' she told me.

'Many, many thanks,' I said as I turned to leave. Frau Hansl had saved my life. We don't say thank you often enough for the truly great gifts we are given.

When I emerged from the darkness of that front hall, first into the stairwell and then out into the street, I was dazzled by the daylight. It was as if the sky had fallen, covering the road with a concrete roof from side to side. I felt as if I were caught in a tunnel. I wanted to get away from there, fast. I was afraid of being recognised. But I had to wait until I could see better again. Feeling weak at the knees, I leaned against the wall of a building.

A little later I was running down the steps to the U-Bahn. I was going to Neukölln to see Heller and warn him. He could be in danger now himself. I interrupted him in the middle of his consulting hours, but I managed to speak to him in private for a few minutes.

'Koebner and his whole family have been arrested,' I told him breathlessly.

Heller turned pale. 'It's very good of you to come and let me know at once,' he said.

'As for me, it means there's no one who can help me to get away now,' I said. 'I'll never find anyone else to forge papers for me – and if I did I couldn't afford them.'

'We don't know whether Koebner would have forged new papers for you anyway,' replied Heller. 'After all, your travel order was bought with the Wolff family's last savings, and at a high price, too.'

This revelation shocked me. I tried not to show my emotions as it dawned on me that, solely out of civility, Ernst Wolff had played on my vanity. Meanwhile his family had paid for me, and had spared me having to thank them – even though they were not particularly fond of me.

Heller went on, without noticing how moved I was. 'What's more, Koebner said it was a funny relationship his cousin had with that young girl, meaning you. You'd have been the ideal boy for Ernst Wolff.'

Once again light dawned on me. I had never seen it, but Ernst Wolff was homosexual, and that was why he was a bachelor. It was also why the ladies in his family had been so indignant about our relationship.

Now, of course, I also realised why a group of boys gathered round him in the yard of the Old Synagogue after every service. I had often seen one of the choirboys with Ernst Wolff, a lad called Georg Blumberg. Georg and I were friends after a fashion. He was a little younger than me, and had hinted a couple of times that we had something in common. I had never understood what he really meant.

Georg Blumberg had been one of Ernst Wolff's boys, then, and so had I. I was in great emotional turmoil, but there was no one in whom I could confide about it.

2

In his youth, Benno Heller had been on the extreme right of politics. He had belonged to a Christian and Jewish student fraternity, and wore the duelling scar on his face with pride. Later he had changed sides, becoming an enthusiastic communist and intermittently a Party member. After a journey through the Soviet Union with his wife, however, he returned in sober mood, horrified by the conditions that he saw there.

Heller must have left the KPD, the Communist Party of Germany, before 1933. At least, he was never persecuted as a communist. All the same, he was still firmly on the left politically, and in practice as well as verbally he opposed Paragraph 218 of the law, proscribing abortion.

It was therefore not only Jewish women who turned to him when they needed help. The Aryan patients whom he was no longer allowed to treat after 1933 remembered their Jewish gynaecologist when they were in trouble. One of them was Karola Schenk, who lived in the street in Neukölln where Heller's practice lay, on the corner of Pannierstrasse. He had helped her when she became surprisingly and very inconveniently pregnant, and did not ask for a fee. From then on, however, she was in his debt.

He now reminded her of that. While I waited in his consulting room, Heller went to his former patient and told her that for two weeks he wanted her to take in a Jewish girl who had gone underground. It was only with reluctance that the former circus artiste agreed to shelter me in her apartment. She was no fanatical supporter of the Nazis, but she was a conformist who felt that resistance was unseemly, and took no interest at all in politics. Accordingly, this slightly built and very cultivated lady received me into her home courteously, if coldly.

After I had spent two or three days sitting in a wicker chair, she suddenly thawed, and told me how she had been testing me: she had put tiny pieces of matchsticks in the hinges of all the cupboards to see if I had been opening them when she wasn't in. She couldn't bear the idea of someone rummaging through her things, she said. But she herself could hardly have borne to sit idly all day in someone else's apartment without looking at other people's property. My exercise of such restraint seemed to her the pinnacle of distinction.

'Let's say *du* to each other,' she offered, 'and as a reward you can try on all my hats. Any woman would enjoy that!' She showed me her wonderful hats, made of the finest velours. They were all made-to-measure, none of them were standard goods. I was even allowed to slip into her jackets and skirt suits. I told her how a man had once spoken to me in the street saying he would like to engage me as a model. Apparently I had just the sort of face for modelling hats. He promised me good pay, and I wanted to say yes at once, but my father wouldn't let me, saying that such work was unseemly and beneath my dignity.

Karola and I soon became close friends. Her family were prosperous Bavarian entrepreneurs, and as a girl she had run away from home several times to join the circus, where she had turned her baptismal name of Karoline into 'Rola' and met her husband, stage name Dannas. But finally she had been reconciled to her family, and took a proper training for her work as an artiste. She and her husband had built up a troupe of performers, and while practising their profession lived an ordinary settled married life, just as other couples might run a shop selling soap or a dental practice.

To their great grief, they had no children. So they took on an apprentice, whom they called 'Boy'. 'Rola-Dannas-Boy' sounded as if he came from a circus family, and had an emotional appeal to the public even if the supposed child was in no way related to them.

When Dannas, whose real name was Alfred Schenk, fell severely ill the troupe had to give up performing. Karola took an office job, and nursed her husband with great devotion. Their former apprentice stayed with them, living in half a room in their apartment. It was with him, of all people, a youth who could have been her son, that Karola had begun a brief relationship after her husband's death, and immediately become pregnant.

After my first few days in her apartment, Karola asked me, 'How can you bear to sit around on a chair all day doing nothing?'

'With difficulty,' I replied, 'but there's nothing else I can do.'

'We'll find a better solution,' she said, and she introduced me to her neighbour Ella Steinbock, a seamstress who worked for a firm in the clothing industry and could do with an assistant to sew on buttons and turn up hems. Karola told her I was a circus artiste, but I couldn't perform because of a knee injury, and would be glad of something to keep me busy.

So now I sat for a few hours a day in a warm, well-lit room, and I even got paid for my work. I didn't have to hide, I could go to the toilet when I liked, and I could even listen to music on the radio.

Frau Steinbock was very silent. Only when the conversation happened to turn to politics, and the Führer's name was mentioned, did this lonely and introverted old maid smile in a curiously enraptured way, half-closing her eyes. It was in her that I first encountered the phenomenon of a passionate enthusiasm for Hitler bordering on religious mania.

Karola too worked for a fanatical Nazi. This man, one Herr Lehmann, did official (and also unofficial) business. Since Karola, as his secretary, was a great help to him in it, he allowed her a certain amount of freedom. She didn't have to observe her timekeeping slavishly, and through her boss she could get black-market goods of which other customers could only dream. Who had a tomato for supper these days, or smoked fish?

Her boss was much younger than Karola; he was married and, in line with the Führer's wishes, he and his wife had several small children. But he made unwelcome advances to his secretary, and was always pestering her. She was repelled: 'Lehmann is a bastard.'

She spoiled me for those two weeks by employing all her charm to seduce me. At the weekend she cooked us a festive meal, and decorated the table with coloured ribbons. We had roast mutton, and the best kale I had ever tasted. Once I mentioned in passing that I hadn't eaten poultry for years. Oh, she said, how she wished she had thought of getting a boiling fowl to make soup for me.

Every evening she came to my bed, which was beautifully made up with white sheets, to give me a goodnight kiss. Once she heated the bathroom stove specially for us. When I was sitting in the water she came to wash me; she had found a cake of the finest, sweet-smelling pre-war soap specially for the occasion. This very cool, reserved woman with her delicate complexion and deep-set eyes suddenly said, 'I've been waiting for you for decades. You're my friend, my little sister, you're what I've always longed for, you're my daughter.' Then she kissed me all over, praising the separate parts of my body and speaking as I had only ever heard men speak before. It was a remarkable outburst, but not unpleasant. I gave myself up to it, without showing any reaction, but thinking all the time: Oh God, this is a sin, this is a perversion.

She ended the scene after a few minutes by rubbing me dry. I went to bed, repeating the confession of sins as a way of somehow coping with the incident.

One day Karola told me that in the afternoon she was going to Zeuthen, a little place outside Berlin, to see her sister-in-law. When she came back late that evening, she put her arms round me and said, 'I've done it. My hopes are fulfilled, Camilla will take you.'

My time with her was over. Karola had suffered from knowing that she was doing something forbidden, even though we had larked around together a great deal, often laughing until we cried. She didn't invite me to come and stay with her again.

Before I could move to Camilla Fiochi's, however, Heller had found somewhere else for me to go. Frau Janicke lived a little further to the south of Neukölln. The poorest streets of this part of the city were becoming familiar to me. There had never been many Jews living in these lower-class areas; they had not been considered good addresses. The advantage of that was that no one here knew me. I didn't have to live with the constant fear of running into an informer.

I was to go and stay with Frau Janicke, allegedly as a nurse for her grandmother. This old lady, who came from a small town in Thuringia, had pneumonia. She wouldn't have been comfortable in hospital, but could not stay at home alone; there was a shortage of doctors, for most of them were at the front. No doctor paid home visits these days to ordinary patients on a health plan – except for Benno Heller. Of course it was against the law for him to look after this old Aryan woman, but he was happy to do it in order to help me find a new refuge.

Gerda Janicke had a small son about two and a half years old. Her husband was at the front. She lived in her apartment – one and a half rooms at 18 Schierker Strasse – with her grandmother, her adored little boy, and now me. I found myself in an environment that was the quintessence of the lower middle class. Many Nazis who prided themselves on supporting the cause lived in this apartment block, which was still a new building at the time. On festive days the place was thick with swastika banners.

I hated having to play the part of a nurse. Frau Janicke gave me a white overall and I tied a white scarf round my head, but I had no idea what I ought to be doing. The old lady was always calling out, 'Nurse!' in her Thuringian dialect, and I scurried around the apartment looking busy. Heller had persuaded Frau Janicke that nursing her grandmother would be a great strain on her, and it would be useful to everyone if she took me in to help with the work of the household. But there wasn't really much to be done.

There had been no agreement on my board, so I was terribly hungry. Once a week I met Frau Koch in a cheap café in Köpenick, and ate the standard dish of the day there. She also gave me a little pocket money, a bread roll and perhaps a hundred grams of margarine. But that was nowhere near enough to satisfy me. Meanwhile I watched chubby-cheeked little Jörg, Frau Janicke's son, thriving and eating any amount of food. In my mind I called this voracious child the 'Little Teuton'.

And her grandmother, that silly old woman who thought the world of the Führer, distrusted me from the first. Once, when Frau

Gerda Janicke, who gave me shelter in the winter of 1942–1943, with her son Jörg, the 'Little Teuton'.

Janicke was taking the child for a walk, she called, 'Nurse, I'd like some bread and butter.' There was a beautiful loaf of rye bread in the kitchen. Its aroma rose to my nostrils so strongly that I was afraid I might go mad with hunger. I had to spread slice after slice of bread for the old woman, at least four of them. Then she told her granddaughter that she had eaten only two slices, so I was under suspicion of stealing food. Frau Janicke cut notches in her loaf from underneath so that she would notice at once if I secretly took a slice.

All the same, I found ways and means. When the mistress of the house was out, I would turn the butter dish upside down on a hot, damp cloth to make its contents fall on the cloth. That was because the pat of butter was stamped on top with a pattern that I could not have reproduced, but I could shave a very thin slice off the bottom of the pat and eat it. Frau Janicke wondered why the butter was disappearing so quickly, but did not see through my trick.

To soothe my guilty conscience, I mentally drafted a set of rules for my situation in legal jargon. I called it the 'Reich Law on the Theft of

Victuals as Applied to Those Who Have Gone Underground'. I couldn't write it down complete with all its clauses, since I had no paper, but mocking the authorities in that way made me feel a little better.

Once a week at midday I went to see the Hellers, who lived next to Benno Heller's practice. Sometimes I just looked in for a moment to say that everything was all right, and I had no news. On one such visit I saw the couple's dining room, which was furnished in very good taste with a large mahogany dining table and other items in the style of the Neue Sachlichkeit [New Objectivity] of the Weimar Republic period. There were no fancifully ornamented old sideboards or dressers here.

The chairs were covered with royal blue velvet. When Heller asked me to sit down, his wife instantly interrupted him. 'Wait a minute! Newspaper first!' He then put a sheet of newspaper on the seat of the chair to protect it – as if I had been wallowing in the dirt. That was just one of the dreadful humiliations that I suffered at the couple's hands. Later, I found out that everyone who entered that dining room was made to sit on a newspaper in the same way.

This room was the apple of Frau Heller's eye. She looked after it with the most meticulous care. Once, when she had visitors, she thought the cleaning lady hadn't polished the wooden parquet flooring well enough. She picked up the heavy broom used for that purpose and worked away on the floor until, since she had chronic heart trouble, she suffered a bad attack.

That was what the Hellers were like: on the one hand heroically ready to risk their lives for others, on the other thinking as much of their polished floor as of resistance to the Nazis.

I was under observation in Frau Janicke's apartment. A doorman's wife by the name of Krause lived one floor down, a woman who thought herself every inch the member of a superior class. Her son was an engineer, and she was a great supporter of the Nazi regime. She was always asking Frau Janicke, 'Why don't you get that woman who's living with you and looking after your grandmother properly registered?' Frau Janicke had to think up excuses. She claimed that I only occasionally slept in the apartment, but all the same she often sent me out to fetch milk early in the morning, when anyone could see me.

'Frau Janicke, do I have to?' I asked.

'Please, couldn't you make yourself a bit useful? I'm doing enough for you. And anyway I'm still in my dressing-gown.'

So I would slip out early in the morning to the dairy, which was a great place for gossip. I got milk on the ration card for small children, and the first thing I did was to disappear into the front entrance of a building and drink a good gulp of it. But now I had to fill the milk can up again. As it happened, there was a pump very close, but I didn't know how to pump just the right amount of water into the can, working it on my own.

Then an SA man came along. 'Can I help you?' he asked in friendly tones. 'I see you have your hands full.' And he pumped water for me. I let some of it run into the hollow of my hand, which meant I could fill the can up to the right level again. I thanked him heartily, and the SA man said goodbye as if it were the most natural thing in the world for him to help me dilute the milk. Frau Janicke was alone in noticing that the milk in the can had a blue tinge to it. 'How can I help that?' I asked. 'How am I to know what quality of milk gets delivered to the dairy?' When she next went to get milk herself, it wasn't as blue as before.

There was also increasing tension between me and Dr Heller. He learned that Frau Janicke was dissatisfied with my nursing skills.

Once I told him, 'That sick old lady is so thin, I get the impression she has a tapeworm. I've seen something like that when I sat her on the toilet.'

'That would explain a lot,' he said. 'Another day you must keep whatever comes away there.' Next time he paid a home visit he looked at the results, and said, 'You silly girl, that's not a tapeworm, you've seen but scraps of the intestines that can come away at any time. Really, you have no idea what you're doing!'

'How am I supposed to know that?'

The gynaecologist Benno Heller and his wife Irmgard, around 1930.

'A student nurse is expected to have mastered the basic elements of nursing the sick after two months.'

'But I'm not a student nurse!'

'No, you're the distinguished holder of a school-leaving certificate, you know Latin and French and you're highly educated, but when it comes to anything practical you're hopeless.'

Quarrels like that were quite common between us, and they did much to damage my self-confidence. We fought like cat and dog, and then made up the quarrel and felt close to each other again.

His wife, however, clearly couldn't stand me.

Irmgard Heller was a tall, very slender lady, and she always wore her hair in the traditional German style. In the war, that was known as the 'all-clear hairdo', referring to the All Clear when an air raid was over, and everyone could come out of the shelters. When she put her head back a little way, I felt I ought to address her in medieval language as 'Most noble lady'.

She came from the upper middle-class society of Leipzig, and should really have married someone from the same circles. But then the First World War broke out, she had gone to work at a field hospital, and there had fallen in love with Benno Heller, a medical student assisting the doctors. She married that son of a Jewish merchant family in Bad Dürkheim, and adored him for ever after.

Heller's wife had good reasons not to like me. It was my fault that a tender relationship of the past between her husband and Frau Janicke had been revived. He sometimes visited Frau Janicke's apartment with his Jewish star concealed, and not only to treat her sick grandmother. Heller himself once asked me angrily, 'Do you suppose I'm doing it for fun? When I have so much on my mind, and we're all of us malnourished? I have to pay Frau Janicke for sheltering you with my prowess in bed.' That was dreadfully embarrassing to me, but what could I do about it?

Frau Janicke herself, on the other hand, tried to keep the relationship secret from me. She claimed to have a new lover who was a dentist. When he was with her, I had to stay away from the apartment. Afterwards, she would put the doormat outside the door lengthwise as a signal to me that it was all clear.

So although Irmgard Heller had good reasons for her jealousy, she and her husband stayed together when it really mattered. Benno Heller's marriage to an Aryan protected him from deportation. However, when he had the chance to emigrate and join his brother in the United States, he chose not to go because his wife's heart trouble meant that he could not have taken her with him.

3

I had first come into contact with the fascinating world of the circus through Karola Schenk, and now I learned more about it from her sister-in-law when I went to stay with her in December 1942.

Camilla Fiochi was one of ten children in the Schenk family. They had all been born in a caravan, and their parents had given them exotic-sounding names, since they were destined for careers in the circus.

Camilla Fiochi had seldom attended school, but she had been very ambitious and successful as a circus artiste. She did so well that she could turn her back on the life of the travelling circus and get engagements at permanent venues, like the Friedrichstadt Palace theatre. After many years on the stage, she had fallen in love with Paolo Fiochi, an Italian who was also a performer and a little younger than she was. They became a couple, married, and Camilla used her savings to build a pretty villa in Zeuthen.* She was planning to live happily there with Paolo and hoped, although it would be late in the day for her, to get pregnant. That wish was not to come true. One day Paolo travelled to his native Italy, where he met a very youthful dancer, fell head over heels in love with her, and soon the two of them had a baby.

Meanwhile Camilla was still living in her villa in Zeuthen, southeast of Berlin in the Brandenburg Mark, and she welcomed me to it. 'My colleagues have always been properly put up here,' she told me by way of a greeting. She took me into a charming room, suitable for a young girl, with white-painted furniture, where I was to stay. I was enchanted.

Then she asked me to guess her age. Her hair was bleached

---

* Miersdorf at that time, now Zeuthen-Miersdorf.

platinum blonde, and she had very well cared-for skin; her figure was delicate, and she had made herself up like a girl. Of course I wanted to compliment her. 'I could say that I thought you were twenty-five,' I said, 'but that wouldn't really be honest. Looking at you I'd put your age in the thirties, maybe even in the second half of your thirties.' She crowed with laughter, chuckled happily, and was delighted with me. As I had seen the yellowish spots on the backs of her hands, and the fine white line in the iris of her eyes, I knew that she must really be somewhere between her early fifties and mid-fifties.

Karola Schenk had warned me in advance. 'Camilla is crazy. You'll have a tough time with her,' she had said as we went by rail to Zeuthen. 'She throws fits of rage if there are no cigarettes in the house, no cognac and no real coffee.' All those things were available only at unaffordable black-market prices, and by this time Camilla was impoverished. Sometimes the gas was cut off because she couldn't pay her bill, sometimes it was the electricity or the telephone. 'It's touching, really, that in spite of it she's ready to give you shelter. For all her faults, she's a warm-hearted person,' Karola had added.

Since Paolo's departure, the Trio Fiochi had been wound up, but Camilla had plans for a new troupe. However, she had only one trainee available, a girl of fifteen called Inge Hubbe. Secretly, both of them knew that Inge would never make a circus performer. She had certainly earned good marks for gymnastics at school, but that wasn't enough. Frau Fiochi was very strict with her and sometimes even beat her. I was often present when she did ballet exercises with Inge Hubbe or tried to teach her the 'bridge' position: going from a handstand to arching over backwards like a bridge, and then slowly moving forward into a handstand again.

I was supposed to lead her through the moves, but it was no good. Inge couldn't manage them, and let herself collapse on a chair, bathed in sweat, as soon as her teacher left the rehearsal room. Frau Fiochi generally remained within earshot.

As Inge sat there, I kept calling, 'Come on, Inge, do the bridge! Do a better bridge!' And finally, 'Yes, now you're coming on! That

Postcard advertising 'The Fiochi Sisters and Paolo', around 1927. One of the artistes is demonstrating the bridge position at the top of the picture.

was a good arch!' Hereupon Camilla Fiochi came back in, and surprisingly enough Inge really could do a successful bridge position at that point.

Inge was going through all the problems of adolescence, and was bored to tears for most of the day. My own relationship with the girl was friendly, but on the cool and indifferent side. I had no idea at the time that her family would come to play an important part in my life.

All the Schenks had specialised in what were known as 'Icarian' performances: spectacles in which people were thrown through the air as if they could fly, emulating the attempts of the classical Icarus. For instance, three acrobats formed a tower: one stood on the shoulders of another, while the music first died away and then played a flourish. Each movement had to be worked out exactly to the millimetre so that the three people could keep their balance. The real show began when two such human towers faced one another and the two men at the top threw another performer, usually a delicately built young girl, back and forth between them.

The Trio Fiochi had simplified this turn long ago to one forming a tower three men high, but Camilla and Inge didn't have a third person so that they could put it into rehearsal again.

I was well off with Camilla Fiochi, who was a passionate opponent of the Nazis. She had grown up among circus artistes, had a soft spot for travelling people, and couldn't stand the police and the authorities; she felt deep sympathy for all nomadic peoples, who of course included gypsies and Jews. 'You won't find me denying anyone food,' she said emphatically. 'We artistes are special people who believe in sharing what we have.' I contributed the food that Frau Koch gave me to the common housekeeping, and ate breakfast, lunch and supper with Camilla Fiochi and Inge Hubbe.

In the evening we played games: board games like draughts, or games I hadn't known before like backgammon or the Chinese game of mah-jong. Camilla was so childish that she always wanted to win, but she didn't play with any particular acumen. I had to make mistakes on purpose so that she could beat me. Then she would clap her hands with delight.

On the other hand, she worked me terribly hard. She took the opportunity of having me clean the whole house thoroughly. Crawling round on my knees, I had to leave every corner spotless. The trouble was that Camilla was unable to articulate clearly just what she wanted me to do. She spoke in a curiously affected way, and unfortunately her grammar wasn't always correct. In addition, she kept mixing up the meaning of single words that sounded similar. When she was agitated her voice rose to a hysterical screech, and all I could understand was that I mustn't do something 'like this' but 'like this'. At the same time she went red in the face with fury, called me an idiot and pulled my hair. Half an hour later she would be apologising profusely, caressing me and saying, 'I'm an idiot myself, I'm mentally sick, I'm crazy! I don't have any money to buy bread, and here I go bringing another mouth to be fed into the house.'

An appearance at the Friedrichstadt Palace: Paolo Fiochi, Camilla Fiochi and Lieschen Sabbarth with her luxuriant hair.

Sometimes Lieschen Sabbarth came visiting. She had been trained by Camilla, very successfully too. Privately I thought of her as the three-wigs girl; Lieschen had such strong, springy tresses that she looked as if she had three heads of hair, one above the other. At the top was a kind of nest made of as much hair as would cover another woman's entire head. Then there were very abundant locks of medium length, and under that ringlets peeping out. It was a wonderful colour, as well, a glossy chestnut brown. Lieschen Sabbarth often said, 'I must be the only circus artiste in Germany who doesn't have a perm or dyed hair.' She had grown up in a housing development with gardens in the Nordend district, the daughter of an anarcho-syndicalist of long standing. He had succeeded in bringing up all his many children to be anti-fascists. So Lieschen was particularly nice to me; she would offer me cigarettes and give me sweets.

Karola Schenk came to see us at the weekend. We were all happy to be reunited. The performers practised the three-man tower together. 'Oh, this is nice,' Camilla told Karola as the latter climbed up on her shoulders. 'You're as light as a feather!' Inge watched, but was as stolid as a block of wood, and did not react at all to the performance being rehearsed in front of her.

Not all the Schenks were with the circus. Camilla's sister Amanda, for instance, had married a master tailor who was a fanatical Nazi. It was against him of all men that my father had once been involved in a trial. He was representing an impoverished Jew from the East, who did preliminary work for the tailor's establishment and was never paid for it. By chance I had been present in my father's chambers when both parties met: the tall, stout master tailor had threatened the thin, red-haired and destitute Jew in a way I had never before seen.

All that came back to me when Amanda visited Zeuthen, and told me her husband's name. Fortunately she hadn't brought him with her in person. I was introduced as Camilla's Russian household help. I served coffee in silence, and later cleared away the china with an enigmatic smile.

Camilla had also told some kind of story about me to the couple living above us on the attic floor of the villa. Unfortunately she had immediately forgotten what it was. Was I a Russian to them too? Or was I a Polish worker?

I once had to take something up to that floor, and delivered it in silence. The young woman was busy at the time, with a dressmaker kneeling in front of her pinning up a hem. She was having a dress for a special occasion made, and looked enchanting in it.

Another time I had to clean out the coal cellar. In the process I found a tattered Reclam paperback copy of Kant's *Critique of Pure Reason*, sat down on the heap of coal and began reading it. Suddenly I saw the young lady from the attic apartment standing in front of me. Like me, she got a terrible shock, and went bright red in the face.

'Do you speak German?' she whispered. It would have been pointless to deny it in view of my reading matter.

'Wait a moment,' she said, and went upstairs. Then she came back with several biscuits wrapped in silver paper, and gave them to me.

'Thank you,' I said simply. I never saw that neighbour again.

In part of the cellar that had been converted into a garage, I discovered a large, expensive car. It belonged to Herr Lehmann, Karola's boss, who lived in Zeuthen with his family. Camilla and Karola knew that he was urgently looking for a household help; his wife was overworked, what with looking after their small children and organising the many large evening parties that he had to give as a prominent Nazi.

So the sisters-in-law had thought of suggesting me for the job. They thought that Lehmann could even get me the P sign worn by foreign Polish workers. No one would have suspected that a Jewish woman was hiding in his house. However, I was greatly relieved when I heard that Lehmann couldn't make up his mind to go along with their idea. I wouldn't have wanted to act the part of maid-servant to a Nazi bigwig.

A stay of two weeks in Zeuthen had been agreed for me. When that time was up, Camilla Fiochi said goodbye to me in a distinctly cool tone. She wished me luck, and thanked me for my work. But something was wrong. I just didn't know what it was.

I was back on uncertain ground. Another stay with Frau Janicke had been agreed for me, but not until the New Year. Benno Heller was the only person to whom I could turn now.

He gave me two addresses of women in Neukölln who were said to rent rooms, but they both turned me away. He did not mention the very last emergency solution to me until both these attempts had failed; then he sent me to see Felicitas in that gloomy bar in Wasser-torstrasse. And she sold me to Karl Galecki, the 'rubber director', who lived in a hut in the back yard of the place where he worked.

4

When I woke in the morning after my first night in the hut, the rubber director had already left for work. He had let me sleep in, but the evening before he had asked me to leave the place before his cleaning lady arrived. For the time being, he didn't want her to know that a woman was staying there. But he did want to introduce me to his employees, so he asked me to go to the workshop in the course of the morning.

Many years later, when I was watching the *Threepenny Opera* performed by the Berliner Ensemble and the beggars made their entrance, I thought: my God, they're the very image of the people who worked for the rubber director!

The men whom Galecki summoned, barely a dozen of them, were a most unlikely assortment: pensioners, invalids and veterans, all of whom he had hired, and he paid them well.

His speech impediment meant that he had to make several attempts to tell them, if indistinctly, that they were to listen to him, and he went on until he was sure they understood him. Then he continued, 'This is my wife. I'm not on my own any longer, and you must obey her as you would obey me.' I said a few friendly words and smiled at them. 'I know we'll get on well,' I told them, and then I left.

That evening Galecki said to me, 'I watched you walking across the yard. Did you notice how Felicitas shuffles? There's a world of difference, and that matters to me. She shuffles, you stride out proudly and freely.' I was very pleased with the compliment, which I took not personally but as something that could be said of all Jews. 'You stride out proudly and freely.'

However, that comment also implied an unspoken but suspicious question: so you're not the lower-class semi-prostitute I was expecting? Then who are you, and where do you come from? That same evening he told me how he hated Jews so much that he could smell them from some distance away. I turned to look at the fish in their aquarium again so that he wouldn't see me blushing. I ventured to ask what Jews smelled like, but he couldn't describe it.

One evening we were invited to supper with his mother, who lived quite close. Her first husband, Galecki's father, had died prematurely. She had married again, but now she was a widow once more. This elderly woman received me with great curiosity.

I ate the worst meal of my life there. In honour of the day she had made a meat loaf. It had long ago cooled off on the side of the stove, and was now only lukewarm. Its main ingredient was rotten onions, and the poor quality fat in the sauce had solidified so that it was almost uneatable. Galecki, who loved and honoured his mother, watched me anxiously in case I said anything disparaging. But I remained courteous and friendly and ate a little of it. Once again, the extent of my tolerance amazed him.

After supper Galecki lay down on the sofa as usual. His mother went into the kitchen, and I said I would help her with the dishes. The old woman was a real sight, with her hair, which was dyed raven black, accentuating every wrinkle in her face. But what followed was genuinely touching. She told me she had been watching me all the time. 'There's nothing false in your face,' she said. 'You don't mean any harm. I know my way around life, but these days I can't understand what's going on. What do you want with my Karl? He's a cripple, and you are a nice young woman. I warn you, I'm sorry to see you setting up house with him and making yourself unhappy.' I managed to turn the conversation in another direction with a few civil remarks.

But a few days later Felicitas told her customers at the bar in detail that she had been to hospital on a gynaecological matter, and that was a near-disaster for me. She named several doctors, and also said that she had been treated earlier by Heller. Thinking of this, Galecki said to me, 'She's been to a Jewish hospital, she mentions all those Jewish names – and that makes me suspicious of you, too.' 'What?'

I asked him. 'Jewish names?' Suddenly I was in full control of the situation. I tried persuading myself that the fish in his aquarium were my friends and would protect me. 'Jews don't have names like that,' I objected, and put together any number of idiotic nonsense syllables at random, saying something like 'Pitshipatshiklatshput-shpitshpappakakak'. He laughed until he cried, thought it very amusing, and then I added more imaginary names, along the lines of 'Pingpangpong' and 'Dingdangdong'. He was splitting his sides, and exclaimed, 'Oh, you're priceless! What it is to be young!'

Around now the rubber director was wondering whether it was time to introduce me to his drinking companions in the bar. I felt terrible misgivings. But before it came to that he turned suspicious once more, and this time I really was in danger. He had been secretly rummaging in my handbag while I was in the kitchen or the bathroom, and had also asked me embarrassingly pointed questions about the situation that, supposedly, I had been obliged to leave. I had learned that to sound credible you must describe familiar circumstances – rather than lies that must then be committed to memory – in realistic detail, even if you are transferring them to another context. So I simply told him how shockingly cramped it had been in Frau Janicke's apartment, and turned her horrible parents into what I said were my own in-laws. I really had met those two sour-faced pensioners at Gerda Janicke's. They looked as if they had just bitten into a rotten lemon, and always thought that everyone was out to do them down. They were unpleasant to their sensitive daughter and showed no consideration for her. Of course I didn't tell Galecki that they were also passionate Nazis.

But then Felicitas said things in the bar that, yet again, made the rubber director very suspicious about my background. 'I don't believe your story any more,' he said. 'This has to be cleared up, and fast. If there's something the matter with your racial origins then this is all over. It would be catastrophic.'

I knew I was in mortal danger. Galecki was no match for me in physical strength, but he could go into his workshop at any time and phone the Gestapo from there. I couldn't simply run away, because that would have put Hannchen Koch in dreadful danger. He knew her name and address.

Calmly and apparently indifferently, I said, 'You can clear it up in the morning. Now let's get some sleep.'

'All right,' he said. 'And you can do some shopping for me tomorrow.'

He wrote a shopping list, and left a banknote in a large denomination for me. He wanted a few small things bought from the baker, the butcher, and so on.

Then a miracle happened. As soon as I was out in the street next morning, Felicitas came shuffling towards me. The hem of her petticoat showed under her winter coat, and she was still very sleepy. 'Oh, I'm so tired,' she said, yawning ostentatiously. 'And I quite forgot to tell you something. I was to tell the rubber director as well, but I forgot about telling him too.'

'What was it?' I asked.

She yawned again. 'Dr Heller came to see me specially yesterday evening, just as I was going to the bar. That young lady, he said, you found her a place somewhere, well, there's something you must tell her.' He had drummed the wording into her head, and got her to repeat it several times. Now she came out with it, like a child reciting a poem. The lady at the villa in the Brandenburg Mark apologised for her behaviour to me, and was inviting me to come back at once as her welcome guest.

I didn't show what a relief this news was to me. 'If only you could have told me that a couple of days ago!' I said calmly. 'But there's still time.' Then I added, 'Goodbye – I must do some shopping for the rubber director.'

At that time people had to queue in the shops for ages. But now there was a second miracle; I went into the baker's to find it entirely empty, bought what Galecki had put on his list, and was out again within a minute. The same thing happened at the butcher's and the greengrocer's.

With a certain pride, I folded the net shopping bag like a flower in bud, put it on the kitchen table, and arranged my purchases and the change from the banknote round it. As I did so, I thought: people in your circles might go off with the change, but in ours we wouldn't do a thing like that. We're different.

Then I went into the workshop and asked the first man I saw, 'Is the boss here?'

'No, he's gone to buy some stuff.'

'Well then,' I said, 'I've locked his living quarters and put his shopping on the table. Here are the keys, and goodbye. It's possible that I won't be back. I'm going to make things up with my family.' And then I walked away.

Incidentally, there was something strange about that workshop. It contained the kind of Boley lathes that I knew from working for Siemens. The material for the small parts made on them had been abstracted from the armaments industry, by very elaborate means, and the rubber director paid a high price for the method. Then, with much emotion, he delivered those parts back to the armaments industry and thus to his beloved Führer. Galecki was a curious case of split personality: he was passionately devoted to an ideal that at the same time was the means to an end, and he fraudulently exploited it.

5

I went to Görlitzer Station at my leisure. Once there I made my way to the platform from which the train for Zeuthen left. It wasn't five minutes before the steam engine moved elegantly into the station hall. I got into the train, feeling so free and happy on this journey that I could almost have called out loud, 'Oh, how pretty this is!'

The extreme cold had gone, and slushy, dirty snow lay in the streets of Berlin. But now I was passing through a glittering white landscape in bright sunlight, admiring the snow-capped fences and telegraph poles. I remembered my childhood. On Sundays my father often took me for a little outing in the Tiergarten, the Grunewald or to Wuhlheide. Once, when I was ready to go out, he asked me to wait. 'Just a moment, I have to finish going through this file. I won't be long.' Looking over his shoulder, I saw him write 'erl' followed by a full stop on the last page of a set of files – *erl.* – and I said '*Erlpoint!*'

He laughed and explained that it was an abbreviation of the word *erledigt*, meaning 'dealt with' or 'finished'. Then we both had the same idea at the same time. While my mother was packing a picnic for us in the kitchen, we began to sing. Doing the goose-step, we marched round the big dining table, lustily bawling, 'Dealt with, dealt with, dealt with, dealt with,' to the tune of the German national anthem. Since that day, when I had dealt with some tiresome task, I had often said, 'I'll sing this thing out of existence.' And I did just that now. I sat in the steam train singing our 'dealt with, dealt with' ditty, to the tune of the second movement of Joseph Haydn's Emperor Quartet, as a way of dumping my memories of the rubber director episode once and for all.

Oddly enough, Camilla Fiochi was already expecting me. From a distance I saw her standing outside her garden gate in the sun.

She was wearing an elegant lounging outfit dating from peacetime; the heavy silk was beautifully designed with the dull surface on the outside, and the shiny surface only trimmed with piping. With it, she wore an old-rose blouse.

Her arms were outspread. It took me only a moment to realise what she expected of me, and then I ran to her, fell into her arms, and let her rock me back and forth like a child. I wondered whether this was reality or a dream. The woman who had shouted insults at me and pulled my hair, now holding me blissfully in her arms?

First of all I complimented her on her outfit. 'Black and old rose are a classic combination,' she said. 'I'm sure it will suit you later.' Arms entwined, we walked through the garden gate.

'Karola was terribly annoyed,' she began telling me. 'She said you don't get goblins except in fairy tales.' It was some time before I could work out the gist of her disjointed remarks: Camilla Fiochi had assumed that her divorced husband's new wife, who was totally crazy, was invading her house on the sly and getting up to all kinds of mischief.

I was at a loss, but I realised that she wanted to keep me in suspense for a while. She made funny faces, I responded in kind, and we fooled about a bit. In the process I discovered that she had been sure I would arrive in Zeuthen by the three o'clock train, as in fact I had. This was the third day she had been waiting for me in her pretty lounging suit, with the coffee table laid for two. If I hadn't arrived today, she said, she would have given up.

We sat by the big window. Cold, snowy light flooded in from outside. Frau Fiochi had the ersatz coffee already standing on the side of the stove. She brought us a cinnamon pastry each from the cellar. She had made a great sacrifice in buying these sweet pastries with her white-flour ration coupons. I was happy, I felt safe in an atmosphere where I had been affectionately welcomed and entertained. My joy over all this was much greater than my curiosity about what had actually happened.

But now she wanted to hear my own story first. I began by telling her about the rubber director and his aquariums, but then

I interrupted my own account. 'I don't really want to go on. I'm afraid all this sounds incredible.' Camilla didn't agree. 'Some things are so absurd that no one could make them up, not even the most imaginative film director.'

Finally, she told me what had happened: while she was at her expensive hairdresser's in the Kurfürstendamm, someone had been rummaging around in her desk, and had spilled some ink in the process. The perpetrator of this dreadful deed had taken a pair of expensive and delicate lacy French panties from the bedroom and used it to mop up the ink, then throwing the incriminating garment out of the window, for fear of being caught in the act. Next day a neighbour had rung Frau Fiochi's doorbell, returning that unusual item, which he held in his fingertips.

The intruder had also broken into all her cosmetics and tried them. And someone had opened the preserving jars in the cellar to sample the contents. She had been absolutely sure I was the culprit, she said, and she hadn't even been cross with me, because she thought such conduct was a normal reaction to the situation in which I found myself.

Then she had discussed all this with her sister-in-law Karola Schenk. Karola, however, had thought her suspicions far-fetched. 'Hanni?' she asked – it was by that name that the two of them knew me – 'Never!' But Frau Fiochi insisted on her point. 'It would be perfectly understandable, considering the way she was exploited and overworked here. In her place I'd have set fire to the whole villa!'

However, some time after saying such a cool goodbye to me, there had been other incidents in her house. So now her suspicion was turned on the new Frau Fiochi, who lived far away in Italy.

One evening she had come home from Berlin and called for Inge. She had finally found her trainee in the cellar. The girl shrieked when she saw her mistress and upturned a jar of strawberry compote over her own head. Camilla described the scene to me about twenty times, and I had to keep asking about it and expressing astonishment. 'Strawberry compote, really? Strawberry compote!'

Preserved strawberries were the height of luxury at this time. Camilla Fiochi had only one or two strawberry beds in her garden, and you could hardly ever buy strawberries in the shops. Presumably Inge had opened a jar out of sheer boredom, and was just drinking some of the juice from the strawberries when Frau Fiochi entered the cellar. The real identity of the kobold haunting the villa was now obvious; hoping not to be caught *in flagrante*, the girl must have tried to hide the jar behind her in a hurry, but succeeded only in tipping the compote over her head.

While Camilla told her tale, darkness had fallen outside, and it was time to make supper. Inge was summoned. She came in with her head bowed, and when told to apologise to me muttered, 'Sorry.' She couldn't get anything more out.

'That's all right,' I replied. I wasn't for a moment angry with her; the whole story was a matter of complete indifference to me.

My second stay in Zeuthen was not so very different from the first, but now I knew that all those unedifying scenes between Camilla and me would soon come to an end, and we would be friends again. If there were times when she called me an idiot, that soon turned to laughter, and she shook her head at herself. Once we needed to cut another slice of bread during supper, and I said, 'Do let me do it. The kitchen's in spotless order, and I wouldn't want crumbs falling on the floor.' At that she giggled like a child, came round the table, hugged me and said, 'You're every bit as crazy as I am.'

As a performer, she always wore trousers because they worked well as a training costume. In all kinds of situations, she would suddenly jump up, legs straddled wide apart, and do the splits. She thought poorly of her trainee Inge for not practising ballet positions or arching her back, hands on the floor, in the bridge pose.

Gymnastic training often took place in the rehearsal room of the Kaufholds' place. This roller-skating troupe, who were friends of the Fiochis, lived nearby. My job was to hold the suspension harness, a block-and-tackle device securing a trapeze artist who had been hoisted up into the dome above the room.

Inge, fastened to the suspension harness, would climb a ladder to the trapeze where she rehearsed her act. Or rather, tried to rehearse her act: while I held the thick, unbreakable rope, she dangled from the domed ceiling like a dead weight.

On one occasion Frau Fiochi shouted and raged, finally said she would rehearse the act herself, and went over to the suspension harness. Just before, she had been bullying me yet again, sending me over to a corner of the room with a cotton-wool ball and checking while I made sure that there wasn't a speck of dust left there.

I was furious myself, and now I took my revenge: when I was to let my host down from the dome again I did it very slowly, on purpose. 'Are you going to leave me hovering in the air for the rest of my days?' she screeched angrily. Thereupon I let her drop like a stone, pulling the rope taut again only just before she reached the floor. She cried out in alarm.

Camilla Fiochi regularly went to see her lawyer, Dr Hildegard Stahlberg, who had her legal practice close to the Kurfürstendamm. One day Dr Stahlberg told her that she could no longer afford to spend several hours on every consultation with her client. She simply could not make head or tail of Frau Fiochi's chaotic tales, and asked her to write down exactly what demands she was making of her ex-husband. It was up to me to do the job; I spent hour after hour sitting with Camilla, reducing her flow of words to four or five clear points, which I noted down clearly and objectively on a sheet of A4 paper. I then made a fair copy of the whole thing under the heading 'Information', as I remembered they used to do in my father's office.

When Dr Stahlberg saw this document, she apparently said, 'You've got another lawyer!' Camilla Fiochi told her that she had a young Jewish girl whose father had been a lawyer hiding with her. Dr Stahlberg was a confirmed anti-Nazi, and on hearing my story gave Camilla the handsome present of some ration coupons. Later, Frau Fiochi told me that Hildegard Stahlberg had also given her twenty marks and a packet of cigarettes for me. Camilla spent the money on food, and smoked the cigarettes herself. After the war, she promised, she would pay it all back to me. She also kept the money that Lehmann had given her for me when I cleaned his filthy car that was hidden in the cellar.

To my great delight Lieschen Sabbarth soon came to visit us again. She brought me a bag of sweets, and her kind heart and friendly nature did me good as well. At the weekend Karola Schenk also visited the villa.

I told Lieschen and Karola all about my stay with the rubber director. I was very worried about the way it had ended; I feared that after my sudden departure Galecki might have made inquiries about me. He knew Johanna Koch's name, and I had also given him her address in Kaulsdorf. She could have been in great danger.

But Karola and Lieschen reassured me. 'That rubber director of yours would never pursue the matter,' they said. The man had certainly been glad to find a nice woman, they thought, and then it had gradually dawned on him that there was something odd about my background. When the relationship came to an end without getting him into any trouble, he would simply have let his vague suspicion drop.

Late that evening, Camilla asked me to go to the station with her sister-in-law. I was happy to do so, for I still felt rather fond of Karola. She looked wonderful in her pale mink coat and an expensive velours hat. On the way she linked arms with me, and we nestled close to each other as we walked along. Then she told me about her visit to Heller.

Karola had gone to see the Jewish gynaecologist to put in a good word for me. She had heard from Camilla about the false suspicions cast on me in Zeuthen. It was a difficult step for her to take as a law-abiding citizen who was not known as either an anti-Fascist or an opponent of the Nazis. She was terrified of falling into the hands of the Gestapo when she went to see Heller, unlikely as that might be.

The doctor had just shown a patient out of his consulting room when he saw Karola. He was about to ask her to go into the dining room for a moment, but when he had opened the door and looked inside the room he closed it again. 'Oh, my God, we can't talk in there. That's my second set of patients for the day come to see me.' At a fleeting glance, Karola had seen only that there was someone sitting on every dining chair, each of the occupants of the chairs, naturally, on a sheet of newspaper.

Here my companion stopped in the street and turned to me. 'Promise me one thing,' she said with great urgency. 'Never go to see Heller as one of his second set of patients for the day. Never!'

'I can't promise that. I don't know what may yet happen to me. But what would be so bad about it?' I asked.

Then she said a surprising thing. 'The people sitting on those elegant dining-room chairs, without saying a word to each other, were all of them Jews in hiding.'

'How could you tell?'

'I just know. I wouldn't have taken any of them separately for a Jew, but all together, yes.' She couldn't express her meaning any more precisely, but now I knew what she meant.

'Yes, let's take the typical caricature of a Jew as it appears in *Der Stürmer*,' I said thoughtfully. I was referring to the infamous anti-Semitic weekly newspaper of that name. 'The *Stürmer* Jew has an assortment of about ten different characteristics: curly hair, a paunch, flat feet, a huge nose and so on. If someone has all those features, people immediately think: ah, a Jew. But a Jew with only one such characteristic doesn't stand out in a group of nine Germanic types. Only if you get ten Jews together, each with one such feature, are they unmistakably a Jewish group.'

'Exactly!' she said. 'I couldn't have put it so precisely myself.' Then she hugged me and held me close. And once again she whispered in my ear, 'Please remember, never try to get in touch with Jewish groups.'

Inge's mother also visited Zeuthen one Sunday. Trude Neuke's first marriage had been to Rudolf Hubbe, a communist functionary in Magdeburg. He had been killed by SA men in April 1933. A little later, so as not to be alone in the world with her two small children, she had married another communist, Julius Neuke.

Trude was a small, plump woman with sturdy legs. Her most striking feature was her fiery red hair. She wore it neatly parted and pinned up into a heavy bun at the nape of her neck.

She greeted me warmly, and we were on familiar terms at once. 'I've already heard about you – you're Hannchen. Of course that first name is false, and I don't even want to know your surname. I'm usually called Red Trude, and not just because of my hair. My opinions are redder still,' she told me. Even at this first meeting I noticed that the corners of her mouth sometimes turned down for several seconds, while she went on talking in a loud and apparently cheerful voice. Then she suddenly looked very melancholy.

The four of us sat drinking ersatz coffee. Inge's misdemeanours were the main subject of conversation. Trude shouted and raged, and fired off tirades of abuse at her daughter; it wasn't the first time she'd had trouble with her. 'You dreadful girl, you dreadful girl!' she kept saying. 'Here's a human being who, sad to say, has to live in hiding, she falls under suspicion on account of your idiocy and the disinformation you spread, and you haven't cleared that up yet!' Inge sat there perfectly still and didn't react at all. Then Trude told her daughter to apologise to me.

The girl got to her feet, came round the table in her blue gymnastics outfit, offered me her hand and yet again, in a tone devoid of any emotion, said, 'Sorry.'

After that Trude, without exaggeration or excessive emotion, calmly said something that meant a lot to me. 'From now on, until the victory of the Red Army, I will take responsibility for saving your life from our common enemies.' She offered me her hand, a small, delicate, ladylike hand that reminded me very much of my mother's. I took it and held it firmly. I was to feel, later, that this was one of the best moments of my life.

Camilla too sensed that something out of the ordinary had happened. 'We must drink to that,' she solemnly declared. She went down to the cellar and brought up the remains of some cherry brandy that she had saved for very special occasions. She divided it out between four tiny liqueur glasses that she took from a glass-fronted cupboard, which also contained various kitschy items and *objets d'art*.

We stood up and pushed our chairs under the table. Then Camilla Fiochi made a short speech, phrased with surprising clarity. 'All of us gathered here are Germans, and we all love our Fatherland. But a country that is committing the greatest crimes in human history can't be called a Fatherland. Let us raise our glasses to the downfall of the Wehrmacht, so that humanity and ultimately Germany can live. We will drink to the victory of the Allies.'

'Victory and freedom!' Trude agreed, drinking to us. At the word 'freedom', something like a bright spark of life was to be seen in the unfortunate Inge's face. She too raised her glass to me, and I nodded at her. That was our real reconciliation.

I took Trude Neuke to the station that evening. With a crook of her finger and a nod of her head she directed me, as we parted, to a dark corner of the building, where she bent over to me and whispered in my ear, so quietly that no one else could hear it, 'Red Front!'

A few days later I told Frau Koch about this first meeting with Trude. That was stupid of me, naturally, for she immediately conceived mortal hatred of the second woman to have said that she would protect me, thus proclaiming herself Frau Koch's rival.

On 3 February 1943, sitting with Inge Hubbe and Lieschen Sabbarth in Camilla Fiochi's house, I heard the dramatic radio broadcast announcing the surrender of the Sixth Army in Stalingrad. The news had me in a state of excitement greater than any I had known before. It was clear to me that the course of the war was decided, the Allies were going to win, and the history of the world would not be pointless. Humanity, and with it Germany, would be saved from final disaster.

In the middle of this transmission, with the Nazi newsreaders describing the catastrophe, Camilla suddenly said, 'Oh, my God.

My nephew Gunther!' This nephew of hers, she had suddenly realised, had probably fallen in the 'kettle' surrounding Stalingrad.

I reacted to this remark with a totally inappropriate urge to laugh. It may have been the result of my own powerful feelings. I had to run out of the room and shut myself into the bathroom, feeling ashamed of myself for such foolishness. It was some time before I could calm down.

That afternoon Lieschen Sabbarth told me that her father, the anarcho-syndicalist, had been trying hard to find me somewhere to stay. That asthmatic old man, who found walking difficult, had dragged himself laboriously round his old acquaintances. Many of them were no longer alive, he found that many more had gone to live at another address. Often the door was opened to him by careworn women who told him that their husbands had been imprisoned years ago, or taken to a penitentiary or a concentration camp. But unfortunately, she said, his search for shelter for me had not been successful. I was much moved by this story. 'You can't imagine,' I told Lieschen to console her, 'how much it does for me to know that an old man, a total stranger to me, has spent days on end looking for a place where I could go. And yet he doesn't even know me.'

Soon after this I left Zeuthen, with many heartfelt thanks. For the second time my stay with Camilla Fiochi was over, and another with Gerda Janicke was agreed. 'Remember today's date,' Frau Fiochi told me. 'If the war is still on in a year's time, and if I haven't hanged myself yet and if you're still living in hiding, you must come here again and stay for four weeks.'

'Stay alive,' I replied, with the casual phrase that so many people used when saying goodbye in wartime.

6

Basically, the Janickes' apartment in Schierker Strasse consisted of a single room, which was also difficult to heat. Like all other such rooms in this apartment block, it was used as a bedroom; bedroom furniture with a handsome bed frame was the pride and joy of the lower middle classes of our society. A cupboard for crockery, books and bed linen all combined stood in another, half-sized room. This ice-cold little room also contained a sofa, and that was where I slept.

Instead of the grandmother in need of nursing, who had gone home to Thuringia, there was now another young woman who had gone underground in this tiny apartment. Eva Deutschkron was a few years older than me, and had also been sent to Gerda Janicke by Benno Heller. The two women were in total agreement about everything, including young Jörg, whom I now saw again.

Eva Deutschkron was a trained dressmaker, and sat at the sewing machine all day. She made rompers for the little boy, altered his clothes, and also worked on renovating Frau Janicke's wardrobe. Eva saw no reason why this needlework should ever come to an end. Her hostess enjoyed having her own personal dressmaker, as Heller put it, to the amusement of both women. 'You know, your sewing is like the *Tales of the Thousand and One Nights*,' I once told Eva.

Our real life was spent in the kitchen. Even this room was never really warm, despite the presence of a coal stove. The two ladies ate their meals there with cute little Jörg, while I watched – or rather, turned away. My mouth was watering, but they didn't give me anything to eat.

Otherwise, Gerda Janicke sat about on the coal-box unoccupied for most of the time. She was a pretty, rather plump woman, but she let both the corners of her mouth and her shoulders droop. 'Even her clothes are weeping,' my grandmother would have said.

My hostess had grown up in very poor circumstances. She had been treated as a child all her life, bossed around first by her horrible parents, whom I had met, then by her husband. She had never been the kind of woman who could give other people instructions. That had changed when I came to stay with her. There was no doubt that she was risking her life for me, but she also enjoyed being in charge for once. 'You must be available to do housework at any time,' she told me, for instance, although there wasn't really much housework to be done. 'I can't have you going off to Köpenick all the time to see that friend of yours.' That meant I didn't even get the meagre diet that Hannchen Koch saved for me out of her own rations. For days on end I had absolutely nothing to eat, and I was hungrier than I had ever been before.

In these days I began hating Eva Deutschkron like poison. At the same time I was ashamed of myself for it, considering my feelings inappropriate, unseemly and ungrateful. She did me no harm. But I could hardly think clearly because I was crazed by hunger.

I kept repeating the words of the confession of sins, and in a kind of childish superstition I wanted to prove myself guilty of as many sins as possible. I hoped that my suffering, my fear and my need were a punishment for my misdeeds – because then there was a prospect of their coming to an end when I had atoned for everything.

Unlike me, Eva Deutschkron had ration cards of her own. She told me how she had come by them when we were washing the dishes, and had been passing the time by finding out whether we had any acquaintances in common. In that way we came to Mirjam Grunwald, who had been in the same class as me at school.

She was an intelligent, talented, highly educated girl, and came from a distinguished and cultured Jewish family. Like me again, Mirjam was one of the best students in the class. We had been very polite, but had not really taken to each other.

Mirjam's parents had been given an opportunity to go abroad, but when it came to Mirjam herself the trap closed on her. She was called up to do forced labour. Of course it was terrible for her parents to leave Germany without their daughter. To find some way out of this conflict, they left all their fortune behind for her as a 'black-market' fund. I imagined this, picturesquely, as a large sack of money consisting of coins painted black. The money was to make it easier for Mirjam to survive, and they hoped she would be able to follow them to the United States as soon as possible.

The two girls got to know each other in the firm where Eva Deutschkron and her husband were also doing forced labour. Eva talked about her early marriage there, and passed round a photo of her husband. One weekend, to their surprise, the young couple were invited to coffee by Mirjam Grunwald, who entertained them very hospitably.

Then Mirjam told the couple that she had means of going underground; she had money, an address to which she could disappear, and a source of ration cards. But she could bear her mortal terror only in the arms of a man. So she suggested a very unusual bargain: Eva was to lend Mirjam her husband for an indefinite period of time, getting money and ration cards in return. Part of the deal was that Eva would see her husband just once a month: no love-making, no emotional outbursts, their meeting would be only so that they could know they were both still alive.

This proposition left Eva utterly baffled. She went to the Hellers to ask what they thought. Their advice was: 'In absurd times, everything is absurd. You can save yourselves only by absurd means, since the Nazis are out to murder you all.' So in the end the young couple agreed to the bargain. Eva Deutschkron told me all this amidst fits of terrible weeping. Frau Janicke knew about it, but Eva asked me not to let her know that now I knew as well.

Myself, I had reached the lowest point of my life. I was freezing all day, my teeth chattered with cold and hunger. And suddenly I had another very unpleasant affliction; I felt stabbing pains in my bladder and couldn't contain my urine. When it happened I was in the dairy, fetching milk for Frau Janicke. A pool formed beneath me. I don't know whether the other people there noticed anything, but I couldn't help it. I thought, desperately: *the enemy is doing all this to us.* Perhaps such repellent things are actually easier for others to understand than piles of corpses, than the really great crimes of human history.

It was particularly uncomfortable that I had no way of washing and drying my clothes. My underclothes stuck to my body, dried slowly – and stank. Now Eva Deutschkron and Gerda Janicke really could consider themselves a class above me.

I wasn't allowed to go to the toilet at night. Early in the morning I had to fetch milk. So I simply took the milk can to my ice-cold bed with me and used it as often as necessary. In the morning I emptied the can in the bathroom and rinsed it out – sneakily, I have to admit – with cold water. This disgusting business too, I told myself, can be chalked up to the enemy's account.

One afternoon the two other women set out for a long walk with Jörg, the Little Teuton, leaving me with the task of polishing the kitchen furniture to a shine with a piece of leather. I soon realised that no shine could be achieved by that method, and I didn't have the strength for it either. So I simply lay down on the sofa and read. At some point, Herr Janicke had acquired a wonderful leather-bound edition of the works of Dostoevsky. This diversion saved me for a little while. I was reading *The Brothers Karamazov* for the first time, and was fascinated even as my teeth chattered.

Suddenly I was aware that the three would soon be back. I quickly climbed on a chair and wiped the furniture at the very top, expecting Frau Janicke to check up on it there. Then I lay down on the sofa again, but was ready to jump up as soon as I heard footsteps on the stairs.

I didn't notice that the dust on top of the cupboard was now running black and slimy down the sides like ink.

Of course this incident was reported to the Hellers, hot off the press. Both Eva and Gerda were enthusiastic about Benno Heller, with his resemblance to a dream doctor in a Hollywood film. They, like me, regularly visited him to tell him how things were going. They particularly liked to describe my disastrous influence on the housekeeping.

'Ah, so here's our distinguished holder of the school-leaving certificate,' said Heller the next time I went to see him. 'Fabulous. You should be proud of that certificate, Marie, since you can't do anything of the least practical use.' He sat down at the piano and played a few bars. The doors to his consulting rooms were open, and all his patients could and were intended to hear him. Then, with his wife joining in, he adapted the refrain of a walking song from *fal-lal-lee, fal-lal-la* to '*Grubby girl, dirty girl*', which they sang in two parts.

'I can explain what happened,' I said desperately. 'I'm not well, I have an inflammation of the bladder. Please give me something to cure it.'

'Out of the question,' he replied angrily.

'But there must be something to make it better, isn't there?' I asked.

'No,' he replied again, and he added a strange remark. 'Jews who go underground don't get sick.'

I couldn't sleep the following night. My thoughts were in confusion. I was afraid of simply falling down in the street unconscious in my hungry, wretched condition. And then, if I was taken to the police, my whole struggle so far would have been for nothing.

As I lay in bed, shivering all over, I suddenly heard the nursery rhyme about 'Hänschen klein' [Little Hans]. It wasn't me singing it but a boy, the son of a cleaner who had been very helpful to us in the year of my mother's death. Even as a child, Fred Heinzel had been against the Nazis.

I thought: why am I suddenly hearing this song? There must be some connection between Heller's refusal to help me and little Fred Heinzel. And then, in my strange mental state between dream and reality, I made up my mind about something: if I could solve that puzzle I would take it as a good omen. But if I couldn't solve it I would not take it as a bad omen, because that would be superstition, which is not allowed in Jewish tradition.

Meanwhile, I kept hearing Fred Heinzel's voice singing 'Hänschen klein'. And suddenly I had a picture in front of my eyes. We were sitting by the open hearth in the dining room of the Prenzlauer

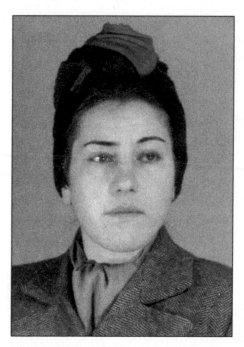

Marie Jalowicz in the winter of 1943.

Strasse apartment of my childhood. The boy was telling my father about school, where he had trouble with the very demanding gymnastic exercises in the military style that he was expected to do. They had made him cry in the sports lesson. He had told his gymnastics teacher, a staunch Nazi and a sadist, that he couldn't do the exercises any more because he was in pain. Thereupon the martinet had shouted at him, 'German boys don't get sick!' That was the connection. Heller had said, 'Jews who go underground don't get sick.' Although he was a good doctor, intelligent when it came to making a diagnosis and psychologically skilled in treating his patients, he couldn't bear the visitors in his two waiting rooms to mingle with each other. To him, I might be a Jew who had gone underground, but I mustn't be a sick Jew.

I woke up next morning feeling relieved. I had solved the puzzle and I would get better. And sure enough, after exactly a week I had thrown off the infection.

*

By this time Eva Deutschkron had run out of new fashion ideas to keep Frau Janicke happy. She had once dreamed of being a fashion designer, and she had already designed a beach outfit, a walking costume and evening dresses for her friend. It was February, so I suggested, 'Why not design a Carnival costume?'

'Oh, what a good idea. I can spend a whole afternoon with that,' replied Eva. She was genuinely grateful to me.

When she showed us her costume designs, we went on to talk about New Year's Eve, and Gerda Janicke mentioned the custom of telling fortunes from the shapes taken by molten lead dropped into water. That reminded me of my encounter with the clairvoyant, and the idea came up of asking for her services again. 'I'd really like to know whether my apartment is going to be bombed,' said Frau Janicke.

I knew where Frau Klemmstein lived, but to get permission for an extra outing I claimed that I would have to ask Frau Koch. Trying to telephone her could take a long time, because she was often out and about in the extensive laundry building where she worked. 'Stay out as long as you need,' said Frau Janicke generously.

I used this opportunity to celebrate my recovery. I ordered and ate the cheap standard dish of the day in two different cafés, a cabbage one-pot dish and a swede one-pot dish – that was luxury, even thought there wasn't a gram of meat or fat in either, but at least they were hot. Then I went to a shabby coffee-house for a cup of ersatz coffee. I could be as extravagant as this only because I had prospects of money – I had decided that my visit to Frau Klemmstein would be purely fictional. I was going to keep the money for her clairvoyance and for the telephone and travelling, and I would spend it on myself.

I went happily back to Schierker Strasse, told them that Frau Koch had given me the name of the village where the clairvoyant lived, and that when I got there I would have to ask the way, because fortune-telling was illegal. It cost five marks per fortune. Then Frau Janicke cast the lead herself, and a woman she knew joined her. On the day when I had arranged to visit Trude Neuke for the first time since leaving Zeuthen, I told them that I was going to see the clairvoyant.

Trude had told me her address only once. You didn't write things down at that time, but I would never have forgotten it: Number 13 Schönleinstrasse in the Kreuzberg district. I happily climbed the stairs. I saw an oval porcelain plaque on the first floor, with the name Neuke on it. When I had rung the bell I heard dragging footsteps coming to the door. A tall, thin man in his forties opened it. A mild smile crossed his stern features, forming dimples in his cheeks. I liked that mixture of severity and human kindness in his face at first sight.

The master of the house, Julius Neuke, was known as Jule. I knew a little more from Inge Hubbe about her stepfather. He was a lathe operator, which meant that he had to do heavy work while standing, but he suffered from leg ulcers that made the job a torment. As a result he often had to be off work sick. His family had a hard time making ends meet financially.

Jule Neuke knew all about me. He steered me into the kitchen. On stepping into it I thought at once: Hello, you nice kitchen! Yet the room was very conventional, neither particularly handsome nor lavishly furnished. But it had an atmosphere in which I immediately felt at ease.

'Do sit down,' said my host, offering me a chair. He spoke with such formality that I wondered if he was addressing someone else in the room, but there was no one. Apart from his old-fashioned way of speaking to me, Jule Neuke welcomed me with great warmth. His wife, he said, was in Magdeburg, where she sometimes went to visit her old mother Anna Aernecke and her three sisters, who were still living in their home town. But today the special purpose of her trip, as I guessed, was to look for someone in her extended family who would take me in.

Jule Neuke offered me a cup of ersatz coffee and set off in search of some biscuits hidden in the next room for special occasions. It took him some time to get back. As I waited, my glance fell on a postcard stuck into the frame of the glazed front of the kitchen cupboard. It was obviously from Trude, and I could read only the side showing, but I didn't want or need to read any more: she had arrived all right, she said, and her mother was well. Then came the news that I read at least ten times; I soon knew what it said by heart. With wonky punctuation, and her own unique mixture of capital and small letters, she had written: 'Elle, Could but says no. Erna happy To for six weeks.' I knew at once who and what the meaning of that was.

My relationship with Julius Neuke stayed just as it had been on our first meeting; he was one of the few men who simply liked me without the slightest trace of sexual innuendo. He would never have been pushy. We arranged a time when I could come back, and soon after that I said goodbye.

It was a very cold day, and as I didn't know how to kill time I soon went back to Gerda Janicke's apartment. She and Eva were surprised to see me home so early. I told them an untruthful story: it had all gone well, I had asked after Frau Klemmstein and been told the way to her as soon as I reached the village. I had asked Gerda Janicke in advance what problems interested her and her friends in particular. One of her acquaintances, a young widow, wanted to know if there would be a new love in her life. I thought up remarks that might refer to the subjects they suggested in some way, and told them, with much stammering and stuttering and pauses for thought, what the fortune teller had allegedly said. It went down very well indeed. They were all happy, I had had a day off, had eaten something, and made twenty marks for myself.

I was beginning to get my self-confidence back, and my relationship to the other two women in the apartment also improved. One day they said they would like to go to the cinema. A film with Marika Rökk was showing, and at this time everyone wanted to see it. People longed for something to take their minds off reality, and long lines formed outside the cinemas. Even in great cold or driving rain, they were ready to queue for several hours with the prospect of such enjoyment ahead.

I loved to see these kitschy films myself. I identified with the women stars, imagining myself in their wonderful dresses, dancing gracefully through ballrooms. Meanwhile a second part of my mind was closely analysing the political ideology of the films, which were designed to encourage the populace to see things through while also looking for such diversions, and I despised the sentimentality served up by the Nazis.

So I went to stand in line and get tickets for the two ladies. After I had waited in the cold for hours, someone came out of the cinema and called, 'Please don't wait any longer. The tickets will be sold out in five minutes' time.' I was so furious that I just stood there defiantly, even when the ticket office had closed and everyone else had gone away. I would so much have liked to make myself popular by going back to Schierker Strasse with those tickets.

Suddenly a distinguished-looking old gentleman came over to me, and said, 'I have two tickets available.' I stared at him as if he had fallen from heaven.

'In this cold,' he explained, 'I didn't set out just to get back the small sum these tickets cost. I knew how many people would like to see the film.' His wife, he said, wasn't feeling well, and so she had given up the idea of going to the cinema. I showed my delight so obviously that he asked, 'Does your eternal bliss depend upon it?'

'Yes!' I replied, in all seriousness.

'Then in those circumstances, allow me to make you a present of our two tickets,' he said. 'And you ought to have a hot drink at once to revive your spirits.' We shook hands as we parted.

I decided, then and there, that if I survived and was still a decent human being, I would try all my life to listen to people and see whether they needed me. For it sometimes takes only a few words, a small gesture at the right moment, to help someone in need to recover.

I got home late, but in triumph, with the cinema tickets, and of course I didn't refuse to take the money for them. Eva Deutschkron looked at me and said, 'My God, Hanni is frozen blue! Gerda, may I?' Frau Janicke understood her at once and nodded. Then Eva went into the kitchen, cut me a thick slice of bread, spread it with plenty of butter, and poured me some hot ersatz coffee. And my spirits gradually did revive. It was a wonderful moment of solidarity and companionship between us three women.

7

To the last, the Hellers were a deeply contradictory pair. When Irmgard Heller threw her head slightly back, so that you saw her beautiful profile beneath the old German hairstyle, I had the feeling that she regarded those Jewish women in the waiting room who wore the star with traditional anti-Semitic prejudice. It was all the more to her credit that she devoted the last of her strength to saving Jews from the greatest criminals in human history.

I sometimes talked politics with her husband, the ardent left-winger. Once I said the war would have to be lost to liberate Germany and mankind from Hitler's regime. 'But you can't envisage the defeat of our Wehrm—' he began to protest impulsively, and then clapped his hand to his mouth to keep the rest of the word Wehrmacht in. I was horrified. I had never met an opponent of the Nazis – from Ida Kahnke the toilet cleaner to Emil Koch the fireman – who hadn't been convinced that the Allies must win the war. I didn't start arguing with Heller, because he himself had noticed what he'd said. But the attitude he had betrayed went with the duelling scars on his face.

We quarrelled again and again. Once, Frau Heller, who had heart trouble, was lying on the sofa in their dining room. A box of sweets stood on the table. My mouth was watering. It was a long time since such good things had been available on the open market.

Benno Heller noticed my glance. 'We share the sweets,' he said, smiling. 'First she eats half of them, then we divide what's left between us, then we divide what's left next time between us and so on – until she's eaten them all by herself.'

'I hope to lead a perfectly normal life some time in the future,' I replied, 'and then I'll invite you both to coffee. And we'll nibble some sweets too.' That last sentence had just slipped out of me.

Such a remark was of course idiotic, and tactless to Frau Heller, ill as she was.

That did not escape Heller. He raised his hand at once and slapped my face. It was not a hard slap, and it did more damage to my mind than to my face. I took it as a deep humiliation.

I went out without another word. The doctor ran after me. 'Mariechen, I didn't mean it like that!' he cried. I was halfway down the stairs, and turned back. He was overwrought and didn't mean to hurt my feelings, he said. I accepted his apology. We didn't have much time to make up the quarrel.

A little later we had our last and worst argument. We talked angrily. I felt that he was obsessed by the idea of saving as many Jews as possible. There were half a dozen of them sheltering illegally in his apartment during the day, trying to look as if they had some good reason to be there: wiping down the window frames or cleaning vegetables. And Heller was always urging his Aryan former patients to take someone in. I feared that sooner or later it would end in disaster.

'What's going to happen when someone who's gone underground is staying with people who've changed their minds and give him up to the Gestapo?' I asked. Such cases had been known. Many of the Jewish women whom he helped to escape had not been prepared for a life underground. 'You're simply pushing those women in at the deep end. But many of them can't swim, and certainly not under water,' I warned the gynaecologist reproachfully. He had no idea what I was talking about, and got angrier and angrier. Then he exploded. 'I've seen through you, and I don't think much of your character! You don't want me to help anyone but you! If I find a dozen refuges, you want them all for yourself, a week here, a week there. That's how you aim to survive until the end of the war. But it's not all about you. We have to save as many people as possible!'

To me, that was the end. 'You're insulting my honour,' I said, 'and this is the end of our relationship.' I walked out without saying goodbye. Once again he followed me to the stairwell and called, mockingly, 'You'll be back on the day we next agreed to meet, won't you? You'll come, oh yes, you'll come!' I turned, and cried with all the pride of which I was capable, 'No, I won't! Never again!' And then I was gone.

I didn't have the courage to go back to Frau Janicke and describe this terrible scene to her. I wandered aimlessly further and further out of the city. It was very cold; my feet were frozen stiff. To warm them up I stamped hard on the ground at every step I took. In my sense of desolation and misery, I wished heartily that I could meet the only friend and ally of many long years still left to me: Hanni Koch. 'Want to meet Koch, want to meet Koch,' I muttered to myself, stamping my feet, but I knew that she couldn't possibly be in this part of the city. She was probably sitting on her stool in the office of the Köpenick laundry.

And then, suddenly, a familiar figure did come towards me. She was a delicately built woman, and I knew very well that she wasn't Frau Koch, however much I wished for that. She was wrapped in a wonderful green stole of the finest wool, an expensive garment such as Hannchen Koch had never possessed. This person came closer, stopped right in front of me and said, 'My word, you do look cross!' It was Lieschen Sabbarth.

The three-wigs girl, whom I had met by chance that day in a street in Neukölln, was also in a temper. Lieschen had just been to see a colleague who claimed to have sprained her ankle badly. Because of that injury, the whole troupe of acrobats were obliged to cancel a show for a Wehrmacht audience, which would have been very well paid. With typical solidarity, however, Lieschen had gone all the way from the extreme north of Berlin to the south to visit her colleague. But she had found only the supposed invalid's mother at home. 'What, sprained her ankle?' asked the mother. 'I don't know about that. She's met this officer, he's in Berlin for three days and treating her to all sorts of good things.'

At this news, Lieschen Sabbarth had turned round in a fury to go home again. On the way, we had met. We went a few steps together, and then she invited me into a café, ordered ersatz coffee for both of us and bought me a piece of yeast cake. We sat there for a long time, enjoying our conversation.

'I'm going to tell you something that no one else knows,' she said at one point. 'Give me your word of honour not to breathe a word about it.' The secret was that she, who had been trained by Camilla Fiochi and was friends with her to this day, had an illegitimate child by Paolo Fiochi. It had happened five or six years ago, when they were all living under the same roof in Zeuthen. At the time Paolo Fiochi was already in a relationship with his great love the Italian dancer. But he and Lieschen were young and bored, and so they had started an affair. I was shocked. At that time I couldn't understand how such a thing was possible.

When we parted, Lieschen Sabbarth gave me two packages that had really been meant for her colleague. 'Here, I don't want to keep these. You have them,' she said. One was a prettily wrapped fifty-gram chocolate bar, the other a packet of twenty cigarettes tied up with a coloured ribbon bow. Fortified by these presents, I went back to Schierker Strasse.

It was evening by now. Gerda Janicke and Eva Deutschkron were waiting for me, and they were overwrought. Not primarily for my sake, of course, but if anything had happened to me they would be in danger too. To mollify them, I took the two packages out of my bag, and said, 'I had a very special experience today. And I brought this back for little Jörg.' I meant the chocolate. Two minutes later I was calling myself an idiot, as Frau Fiochi herself so often had. I had given away expensive luxuries that I would have enjoyed myself, and there hadn't really been any point in it. Frau Janicke hardly even said thank you, but carelessly threw the packages into a drawer.

And then an idea jumped at me, like a dog barking in my ear and telling me what to say to the two women: I delivered a long lecture extempore. I took my aunt Grete as my subject, and it was brilliant. I told them her entire life story, described her appearance and her character – and I didn't say she was my aunt, I claimed she was a former Aryan neighbour of mine whom I had met in the street. She had insisted on giving me a couple of presents for my hostess and her dear little boy, I said, but she had to go and buy them first, and I was kept waiting for a long time.

I saw Gerda Janicke making a face. I had obviously laid it on too thick. She sensed that I was not being honest, because she knew that I did not particularly like Jörg, the Little Teuton.

I was already in bed when I heard steps making their way along the corridor, and then a quiet tap on my door. 'Are you still awake?' asked Gerda Janicke.

'Yes.' I sat up, expecting an explosion.

'Stay where you are,' she said, standing in the doorway. 'I just want to ask you something. You see, I was fascinated by your story. I didn't believe a word of it, but at the same time I was thinking: how can anyone can lie like that? Every detail sounds right, but as a whole it doesn't. Will you tell me the real truth now?'

'All right,' I said. 'I took a photograph that hadn't been retouched, every detail of it true to life. But I removed it from its frame and put it in another one. I told you all about the life and character of my aunt Grete, but transferred to someone else.'

'And what really happened?' she asked.

'I'd rather not talk about it. Something happened today that's weighing terribly on my mind.'

She accepted that. She came even closer and sat down on the side of the sofa. 'Hanni, I must say you're a genius.'

'Goodness no, Frau Janicke! There are far cleverer people than me about,' I said, dismissing the idea.

'But you are! The doctor said so himself the other day, and his wife nodded, so she agreed. He told me how fond of you he is. He may make fun of your school-leaving certificate, but only because he wants you to learn practical things.'

That nocturnal conversation was a comfort, and it reconciled me with the Hellers. I didn't yet know that I would never see them again.

A few days later, Gerda Janicke went back to the gynaecologist's practice. Eva looked after the toddler while she was out. She thought he was sweet, and the Little Teuton loved her like a second mother. He felt just as clearly that I didn't like him, and he was afraid of me. It's true that I sometimes felt like pinching him or calling him names. I felt unspeakably sad to think how many Jewish children had been murdered, and then I could hardly bear the sight of that crowing lump of flesh who loved his food so passionately, but was late learning to talk.

'I'm worried,' said Eva that afternoon. 'Gerda's been out for so long. Something must have happened.' When Frau Janicke finally came home she was white as a sheet, in floods of tears and hardly able to speak. At last she told us, sobbing, that Heller had been arrested. Two officers had taken him away from his apartment. As usual, there had been several people there illegally, but the police hadn't taken any further notice of them.

We were shattered, all three of us, and we sat together for a long time, shedding tears. Then Gerda Janicke stood up, went to a calendar hanging on the wall and marked the date, 23 February, with a small line. 'From now on we fight against all injustice.' This was no time now for romantic effusions. 'If you agree, Eva,' she went on, 'Hanni will eat with us now. I know that you're paying a high price and a difficult one for your ration cards, but after this we'll share everything.'

'I've wanted it to be like that for a long time,' Eva agreed at once. I thanked her with real feeling, and apologised for not always behaving well to her. And to mark this as a special day, we all had a cup of real coffee.

But once we were sitting at the supper table, there was an air-raid warning. Gerda Janicke had asked Eva to light the bathroom stove because she and Eva wanted to have a bath, but now they had to go down to the air-raid shelter in the cellar. I didn't go with them, because officially I wasn't here at all. Eva was explained away as a friend who sometimes stayed the night.

'Hanni, you have a bath,' said Gerda Janicke. 'Otherwise the bathroom stove will overheat.' I jumped at the chance, got into the bath and made waves with both hands, playing around in the water. 'I'm tipsy on coffee, tipsy on coffee,' I chanted, and indeed the unaccustomed caffeine had left me slightly intoxicated.

When the all clear had been given the other two came upstairs again. 'You're sitting pretty,' said Frau Janicke reproachfully. 'There were we, freezing down in the air-raid shelter, while you were wallowing in a nice warm tub.'

That reminds me of a Soviet joke that I heard years later: crowds are standing outside a butcher's shop, but no delivery of meat arrives. First the Jews in the crowd are sent away, then people who don't live in the area, and after several hours more those who are not Party members. Finally the butcher comes out and says, 'I'm sorry, I've just had a phone call and I'm afraid I must send you all home. There won't be any meat delivered today.' The crowd disperses, grumbling, 'As usual, the Jews get first preference.'

Gerda Janicke kept her word. She cared devotedly for Frau Heller, who had suffered a severe heart attack when her husband was arrested. Gerda went with her to her lawyer's and to remand prison. Irmgard Heller also told her where all of us who had gone underground were staying – Cohn with Müller, Levy with Meyer, and so on. Frau Janicke went to see them all, told them what had happened, and found out what they knew. That was how we discovered why Heller had been arrested.

A Jewish woman about thirty-five years old, and entirely non-political, had been persuaded to go to ground by the gynaecologist. He had sent her to stay with a grateful patient of his in Neukölln for two weeks. But once those two weeks were over, she didn't want to leave. Her hostess told her she couldn't possibly stay any longer. There were Nazis living all round her place. She had been telling people that her cousin from the country was visiting, but neighbours had already been telling her she ought to register her guest with the police.

So the Jewish 'non-swimmer' had nowhere to go. She wandered around for several days and nights, hungry and freezing, with nowhere to wash or go to the toilet. She went back to the woman she had been staying with and asked, 'Can you take me in again?'

But her hostess refused. 'I'm afraid it simply can't be done,' she said.

'Then I'll tell you something: what I've been through in these last few days was so terrible that it can't be worse in a concentration camp. I'm sure there are no creature comforts and the food isn't restaurant standard, but at least I'd get thin soup and a straw mattress under the shelter of a roof. That doctor is a criminal, driving people into misfortune.' And the woman did indeed go to the Gestapo, gave herself up of her own accord and denounced Heller. However, she never told them the name of the woman who had taken her in for those first two weeks.

A little later Irmgard Heller went to live with her sister in Leipzig. She died there a few months later, in September 1943. She was suffering severely from heart trouble, and she had to assume that her husband was dead; the police had told her that on the way from the remand prison to Sachsenhausen, Benno Heller had been shot for resistance to the authority of the state. In fact, he was still alive early in 1945.*

After Heller's arrest, Jews who had gone to ground went on living in his apartment. Irmgard Heller had paid the rent for months in advance before leaving Berlin. They were supplied with food that Gerda Janicke begged from former patients of Heller's, taking them to Braunauer Strasse in a small suitcase. This resistance struggle of hers became a full-time job, while Eva Deutschkron looked after her little boy.

---

* After his arrest on 23 February 1943, Benno Heller was first held in police custody in Berlin, and then deported to Auschwitz, where he was probably forced to work as a doctor. In the autumn of 1944 he was sent to Sachsenhausen concentration camp, and then to the satellite camp of Lieberose-Jamlitz. He was last seen there in the middle of January 1945. The circumstances and precise date of Benno Heller's death are not known.

8

Little girl
All alone
To the Hellers' house has gone.
What a fuss, who's to blame?
I must bear it all the same.

As so often, I was singing to myself in my mind as I carried my suitcase from Schierker Strasse to Schönleinstrasse. It was a day late in February 1943. I wondered whether it was wicked to sing when Heller was possibly being tortured to death at this very minute. Then I adapted a little more of the 'Hänschen klein' nursery rhyme to suit my own situation.

Never fear
Be of good cheer
Things may yet be better here.

Anyway, I thought, what harm does it do anyone if I feel cheerful and optimistic? After all, something wonderful and extraordinary lay ahead: my meeting with the woman who had said she would be responsible for keeping me safe until the day of liberation came.

Trude was at home and gave me a warm welcome. 'Every day that passes is a day gained, and a day closer to our liberation,' she declared. I felt at ease with that family at once. The living room where I slept on the sofa contained oddly assorted old pieces of furniture, but it looked very tasteful, because Trude had a brilliant sense of colour and avoided anything kitschy. The room also contained a small library of belles lettres and a desk.

For the time being I was to spend about a week there. At first Trude wouldn't let me help with the housework, but my fingers simply itched when I saw dishes waiting to be dried, so in the end she let me have my way. As she saw it, Camilla Fiochi was a mean-minded, despicable capitalist exploiter. When we talked about the villa in Zeuthen, she would swing her clenched fist belligerently through the air. 'After the war, when it's all over and there are trade unions again, you must go to them and complain that you weren't paid a proper wage!' she announced. I thought that was absolutely absurd. 'So what do you think of Camilla risking her neck for me, taking me in at such short notice, and feeding me even though I had no ration cards?' I asked. Trude was magnanimous enough to listen to such arguments, and then to say, 'Now that I think about it, I can see that you're quite right.'

The name of her neighbour on the same floor was Steinbeck. 'That woman is stupidity incarnate, and a passionate Nazi,' Trude told me. 'And to make matters worse, she's bosom friends with the most unpleasant female Nazi in the whole district.' All the same, she wanted to introduce me to her neighbour as soon as possible; she didn't want the woman to think she had something to hide. She openly took me shopping with her, and we made a lot of noise climbing the steps on the way back. The door to the neighbouring apartment promptly opened, and Frau Steinbeck looked out. 'Someone else from Magdeburg,' said Trude cheerfully, indicating me, 'my cousin who's come to spend a few days in Berlin.'

'You have a never-ending number of relations,' said Frau Steinbeck in amazement.

'Yes, hundreds,' joked Trude, and after a friendly handshake we went into the Neukes' apartment. No sooner had Trude closed the door of the corridor than she put a finger to her lips. She knew that Frau Steinbeck was standing next door, listening. Only when we had closed the door into the hall and the door into the kitchen could we talk.

I called the neighbour 'that receding lady', and Trude laughed herself silly. Frau Steinbeck had a receding forehead and a receding chin in front, and her hair and her bottom stuck out behind. She plucked at her hair to make it fly out behind even more, and she hollowed her back, emphasising her behind. She really was a comical figure.

One of Trude's sisters who lived at the back of a building on the Planufer in the Kreuzberg district took me in for a weekend. I had to cross several courtyards before I came to that part of the building in the shabby apartment block where Trude's sister, Anne Adam, had what was called a kitchen room. The water pipes for these apartments lay down a long corridor, and there was a cupboard for each apartment.

The room itself wasn't as bad as I had feared. Everything in it was polished to a high gloss and spotlessly clean. A large cooking stove that also served to heat the room stood against one wall. The opposite wall was equipped as a kind of living room, with a bed and some seating in a corner. The picture of a child stood beside a lamp. It was Anne Adam's great grief that she had lost her only child, a little girl, to diphtheria. After that her marriage had broken up.

In the Aernecke family, to which both she and Trude belonged, political conviction was like a religion. Accordingly, Anne Adam was a communist too. She shared her food supply for that weekend with me, and was very friendly in other ways as well. During the day she worked in a canteen. She had coarse features and a skin with large pores; she amused herself as best she could and was a rather vulgar woman, or at least nothing like as intellectual as her big sister.

I very soon developed a warmer relationship with Trude Neuke, but it was never really close. Well as we understood each other, we met not as individuals but as symbolic figures. To me, Trude personified the resistance of a communist woman, and to her I was the typical figure of a persecuted Jewish girl whom she must help as a matter of principle.

My hostess was also constantly tormented by her inner uneasiness. She often unloaded her anger on her husband Jule. Then she would scold him soundly, and he usually took it without protest. She often wanted her husband and her son Wolfgang to rearrange the furniture of the apartment. 'This is ridiculous!' she would shout. 'The kitchen table is standing lengthwise, and it would be much better across the room!' The two of them had to move the table and other pieces of furniture back and forth, until in the end everything was in its original place again.

Jule Neuke was a thoroughly decent human being. Trude was always running him down for apparently doing something wrong. There was constant trouble with Trude's children Inge and Wolfgang, and it was a disadvantage for him that he was only their stepfather.

Once, when he and I were talking on our own, he told me that he had met Trude's first husband through their work for the Party and greatly respected him. He himself had been out of work at the time, and in a wretched situation. He had married Rudolf Hubbe's widow soon after Hubbe's violent death to help everyone concerned. He was tactful enough not to let a word slip suggesting that he was unhappy, but it was obvious.

Trude and Jule had had a child of their own, thus fulfilling an ardent wish of his. 'I've never usually had my way,' he said, 'but I did in this case.' They had called the child by a name that I thought particularly beautiful: Rosemarie. But after a short while the little girl died.

However, there were less depressing aspects of Neuke's life. As a native of Magdeburg, Trude was a confirmed local patriot where that city was concerned, and she had an old friend who had been at school with her and had made a career as a singer under the name of Lisa Letko. When she appeared on stage in premières at the Metropol Theatre in Berlin, Trude regularly received complimentary tickets, and these visits to the theatre were the elixir of life to her. At such times she generously overlooked the fact that her friend's parents were members of the hated plutocratic class, and Nazis into the bargain.

Jule was extremely musical, and had a beautiful singing voice. He had belonged to a male voice choir for many years. Trude herself sometimes sang a song aloud in her clear voice.

*

Just before I left for Magdeburg, Trude had a special request to make. 'You'll have realised that I belong to a communist resistance group,' she said. 'Would you be prepared to help us by taking some leaflets to Magdeburg?'

I enthusiastically said yes. I dreamed of being able to do something at last, and would have liked it to be a great, heroic deed. But then I realised that Trude wasn't entirely happy about my enthusiasm. Calmly, in a very matter-of-fact tone and with a touch of irony she asked, 'Are you really sure that would be sensible?'

After that she went away and gave me time to think about it. I imagined myself sitting in the station with a case full of leaflets, perhaps being asked to open the case to have it checked in case I had been hoarding something. If that happened, all my earlier struggles to survive – and all that other people had risked for me – would have served no purpose. It wasn't worth it, that much was obvious.

Then I wondered how I could get rid of the leaflets, unnoticed, before my train journey. I would have to ask Hannchen Koch to come to the station and give her the package in the toilet. She would have to take a day off specially, and try to destroy the leaflets without attracting attention.

When Trude came back, I asked, 'Can I see one of the leaflets?' I was rather disappointed by the contents. 'End the war!' they proclaimed, and Trude asked me, in a sharply ironic tone, 'Any idea how to do that? A prescription for ending the war?'

'No,' I admitted. I admired the way that on the one hand Trude was a real heroine of the Resistance, but on the other thought critically about everything she did.

'Then why do you do something so dangerous if you're not really entirely convinced of it?' I asked Trude.

'You don't have to do anything like that,' she replied. 'You don't have to take leaflets to Magdeburg. There are murderers after you. But I can only go on living with myself if I try to frustrate those murderers. Otherwise I have no right to life.'

She told me that she was going to give me potatoes to take for her sister Erna's household, not leaflets, and the potatoes had been donated by Red Aid 'for this Soviet girl parachutist'. The last words just slipped out of her.

Trude, it seemed, had told the group that she was helping a Jewish girl. And the group were not happy with that idea – not out of anti-Semitism, but for reasons of Party discipline and on account of 'the great tasks' that they all had to perform. This had made her so furious and left her talking so chaotically about it that I could hardly follow her. 'They can lick my arse, crossways and spirally at that!' she shouted. 'What good does it do anyone for us to meet in secret, whisper passwords to each other and clench our fists in our pockets? Saving human life is all that matters!'

Trude had solved the problem in her own way. At their next meeting she had told her comrades that she had seen the light, and was now rendering aid to a Soviet girl parachutist.

9

The journey in the slow train to Magdeburg took several hours. I sat in the cheapest class and observed my fellow-travellers. A young woman holding a small child on her lap whispered audibly to the man sitting next to her that it would be nice if he asked the little girl her age. He obliged. The child flung her arms in the air and announced, 'I'm three and I'm not married yet.' Everyone roared with laughter.

When it was a little quieter in our compartment, I leaned back and conjured up my memories. I had decided that on this journey I would concentrate on the domestic staff who used to work for us.

For instance, I remembered Erna Neigenfind. We had met her when my mother went to stay at a spa resort in the Riesengebirge for the good of her health. I was seven years old at the time, and my father and I visited her there for a couple of days. We slept in a boarding house in Krummhübel,* where Erna was a waitress. I thought she was lovely, with her thick braids of fair hair pinned up so that they covered her ears and a large part of the back of her head. I kept looking at her the whole time. In my eyes Erna was beautiful, although she was very short-sighted and wore metal-framed glasses that cut deeply into the bridge of her nose.

The boarding-house proprietors, whose daughter she was, didn't treat her well and were always snapping at her. I begged my parents to bring her to Berlin. And indeed, Erna Neigenfind came to us, proved to be pleasant and a good worker, and stayed for quite a long time. She taught me a Silesian folksong about picking blueberries, with a refrain that ran, 'And when our cans are full of fruit, we'll go back home again.'

---

* Now Karpacz.

After her came Vera Sobanyak, a farmer's daughter from the Brandenburg Mark. We were once invited to eat at her parents' home, and they were bent on serving us a good dish of meat. Huge platters of roast chicken legs and escalopes were brought in, and naturally we all helped ourselves, for it was my family's principle to adjust to the customs of their hosts. When I was out I sometimes even ate Viennese sausages. We lived in the city of Berlin, not in some Polish ghetto.

At home, however, as I remembered now, we ourselves, also naturally, ran a kosher household. I was horrified to learn that my parents had not followed a kosher diet for some time before I was born, because they found the Jewish dietary rules inconvenient, and an unimportant outward sign of our religion. However, when I was born they had decided to go back to kosher food. 'If one stone comes loose, the whole building may fall,' as a Talmudic saying goes. My parents wanted to pass the Jewish tradition on to me, even if it wasn't always easy. Kosher meat was very expensive.

When I was nine, we had another household help, a young woman called Gretel Stiewert. After she had been with us for a while, she told me, 'Here's six months gone, and I haven't had sex for all that time. It's more than a person can bear!' I had no idea what she was talking about.

Gretel Stiewert was a pretty, delicately built creature, blonde and hard-working. She had been orphaned young and was then engaged to a young man who died after a motorbike accident. For a while she went on visiting his parents every other weekend. These people, whose name was Tschoepe, rang one day to tell us something about Gretel that was not, in fact, news to my mother: the young woman had forgotten all about her late fiancé and walked the streets in the evenings. She earned well, and was often very elegantly dressed; she had a white pleated skirt made of the finest wool, which she wore with a royal blue jacket, and a cap that looked like whipped cream piped on top of her head. I thought the outfit beautiful, and wished I could dress as well as that some day. I don't find her profession so bad. To be honest, it can feel much more degrading to do dull, stupid work for other people. Unfortunately, she soon stopped working for us and took up street-walking full time.

Soon after the Nazis came to power, we visited Herr and Frau Tschoepe in their apartment in Taborstrasse to discuss what they called the Gretel tragedy. Two old people, broader than they were tall, led us in felt slippers through a front room full of any number of kitschy knick-knacks. Then we sat in a large and beautiful conservatory. Herr Tschoepe, who like his wife was a member of some kind of sect, spoke poorly of the Nazis, although with restraint. Where deeply religious subjects are concerned, one does not speak in Berlin dialect, which often replaces the letter G with J, but Herr Tschoepe overdid it a bit, using G even where it should have been J – 'in the name of the Lord Gesus' – and then, on becoming excited, he lapsed into full-blown dialect again. I could hardly keep from laughing at the contrast.

On the way home we saw small pieces of paper, obviously produced with the aid of a child's printing set, hanging from a tram stop. 'Goebbels says Guns Before Butter' they read. My parents immediately linked arms with me to right and left, and strode on at an unaccustomed tempo, positively dragging me on with them. Similar notes were hanging from the next tram stop. We did not linger, but turned the next couple of corners at a smart pace and then took the U-Bahn home. My parents were terribly afraid someone might suspect we had put up those notes. As soon as we were out of the danger zone, however, they calmed down and were cheerful again. In fact they were glad to see that free speech like that was still possible.

By now Martha Sill was working for us, a slow-moving, apathetic girl who lethargically pushed the vacuum cleaner over our carpets. One day she turned up unannounced in our dining room with her fiancé, a man in an SA uniform. He said 'Heil Hitler' politely, put out his hand and said he had come to collect the wages that had been withheld from her. 'Do by all means come into my study and look at my accounts,' said my father obligingly. 'I'll show you everything.' My father then, at his leisure, proved to the SA man that no wages had ever been withheld. All the man said was, 'That's all in order, then.'

After this incident my parents were very cool to our household help. 'Martha,' they said, 'we are giving you notice as from the first of the month, but you can leave at once. We will pay you your full wages at the end of the month. Do you know where you can go? Do you have family here?' Martha slouched away without saying goodbye, while the SA man shook hands warmly, said goodbye to us, and even added his thanks.

Afterwards, my father explained to me, 'That was a rather stupid but good-natured young man. One of his SA friends had told him that the fiancé of a maidservant who works for Jews must blackmail them. But his instructions obviously went no further, and when I showed him that everything was in order he did as he has been brought up to do and gave us a civil bow.'

Martha Sill was our last non-Jewish maid. After the Nuremberg Laws came into force in 1935, no Aryan woman under the age of forty-five was allowed to live in the same household as a Jewish man.

The square outside Magdeburg Station looked exactly as Trude had described it to me. I turned to a very old woman to ask which tram I should take. Instead of telling me, she stared at me suspiciously. 'Where are you from, then?' she remarked. 'You don't come from these parts!' I felt that her face was uncomfortably close to mine, quickly shook her off, and asked a middle-aged man, who immediately gave me the information I wanted.

This little encounter was helpful: I had never attracted attention in Berlin. My voice, my appearance and my behaviour all made it obvious that I was a local woman. I could mingle proudly and freely with all the other inhabitants of the city. As soon as I arrived in Magdeburg, however, I stood out as a stranger. I drew an important conclusion for future reference: if I wanted to live underground without hiding all the time, I could do so only in Berlin.

From one stop to the next, the tram steadily emptied. As agreed, a youngish woman was waiting for me at the terminus. Trude's sister

Erna let go of the little boy whose hand she was holding, to welcome me with outspread arms and a warm smile.

She had a round face, rather bad teeth and small, blue button eyes. Her hair was dyed blonde, as many women wore it in those days. In her case, however, there had been a minor accident: small patches of green mingled with the fair hair. As a result her face looked rather doughy.

When she took my suitcase from me to put it on the handcart she had brought, she was surprised. Contrary to her expectations, it did not weigh very much. All my possessions in it amounted to a single spare set of underwear. The few kilos of potatoes that I was bringing had fallen out of their paper bag and were rolling about loose in the suitcase. However, she had been told that I was bringing leaflets with me. Now, in her rather hoarse voice, she said, 'I suppose that's the leaflets rumbling in there.'

She lived in a light, clean ground-floor apartment in a new building near the South-East Magdeburg Sugar Factory. She was putting me up in a room just off the kitchen. Her husband was not at home, but at the front.

On the first morning I heard a light tap on my door, and then Erna's hoarse voice whispering, 'Shall I help to lace you up?'

'What?' I asked, intrigued. The misunderstanding was soon cleared up. Cautiously, and without making her feel silly, I had to let her know that I didn't come from the last century. Erna had worked for a time as a maid for a Jewish family in Magdeburg, and in the morning she had helped to lace up the corset worn by the old mistress of the house. Ever since, she had thought wearing a corset was a Jewish custom.

Trude had told me how hard the whole family had worked to instil the basic elements of education into Erna. Trude herself, incidentally, was the undoubted head of the Aernecke family. To her little sisters, what she said was law, and she had ordained that I was to be treated like a patient in a sanatorium while I was in Magdeburg. I fought in vain to be allowed to dry the dishes, and instead sat in a wicker chair as if nailed to it. It had been brought into the kitchen especially for me. Because I had mentioned in passing to Trude that I liked knitting, I had been provided with material for that handicraft: a knitted top of very thin machine-knitted yarn to be unravelled. The threads kept breaking, and had to be knotted together again. I made up my mind to use this yarn to knit a scarf. Knot upon knot adorned the back of my work. If anyone had tugged at it, the whole thing would have come apart again.

I would have liked to make friends with Erna's little boy. I wanted to tell the five-year-old stories and play with him. With fair-haired Rolf, I would have liked to do what I couldn't for fair-haired Jörg, the Little Teuton. But the child did not react to me at all. He simply went on pushing his wooden railway carriages or cars about the floor, imitating the noises they made.

Even when his goldfish was seen one morning drifting upside down in its bowl of water, little Rolf did not seem much moved. While I was still wondering how to comfort him, he instantly realised that the fish was dead, and asked, 'Mutti, fry it for me.'

That revived a memory. I too had once had a goldfish, and found out one morning that it was dead. I had been five myself at the time, and I had screamed blue murder. My parents did not like screeching, crying and bawling at all. So my father took me for a walk, and we discussed the problem of death. That was the first time I heard of Socrates and the Book of Ecclesiastes. On the way back we turned to everyday subjects again, and went into a chocolatier's, where I was told I could choose a chocolate animal. I chose a lion. When we were at home my father unwrapped the lion, broke its head off and gave me the head to eat. I began crying my eyes out again. For a second or so my father's face was flushed with anger, but then he said, 'Well, that's enough crying for today. A chocolate lion isn't a living creature, so now eat it up!'

That was how I remembered my goldfish in Berlin. And now, in Magdeburg, Erna's little boy just said, 'Mutti, fry it for me!'

On 4 April 1943, a tiny package arrived by post from Johanna Koch to Johanna Koch, care of Erna Hecker.

'Well, well – a package for you?' asked Erna.

'It's my birthday today,' I explained.

The tiny package contained a hard-boiled egg, a small piece of cake, a few cigarettes and a letter. In the letter, phrasing it very cleverly so that the censor wouldn't understand it, Frau Koch told me about the recent Factory Action, the deportation of all Jewish forced labourers from Berlin. She also described the demonstrations in Rosenstrasse, and told me that my uncle Karl, my father's younger brother, had been arrested. However, he was set free again after five days.

In the evening we sat with Erna's neighbour Frau Krause, a nice, kind and entirely non-political woman. She knew the truth about me, and went to great pains to act as my protector. Since I couldn't go out of doors during the day, she took me for a walk round the block every evening, as if she were taking out a dog. On these walks, she linked arms with me in a friendly, almost affectionate way, and adjured me to breathe in and out deeply.

Generally, however, Frau Krause was to be found sitting at Erna's kitchen table with her hair in curlers and a towel round her head. The two women spent almost every evening together. I took care not to get in their way, but I knew that I was expected to contribute to the conversation. If the subject was recipes, I knew it would be tactless to discuss one for which the ingredients were not available in south-east Magdeburg. After much thought, I decided on the Yiddish dish containing prunes known as *Pflaumenzimmes*, although I didn't give it that Yiddish name. I said that my aunt Grete used to make a wonderful beef dish in a heavy pan, adding prunes to the meat.

I often longed not to have to plan my tactics all the time, and wished that for once I could say just what I was thinking, without weighing every word to see if it would suit the vocabulary of my partners in conversation, or whether it might hurt their feelings.

One day we went to meet the second of the Aernecke sisters at a café in the city centre. Elsbeth, known as Elle, was married to Erna's husband's brother, so her surname too was Hecker. Naturally she was another staunch communist, but she was intent upon leading a comfortable life. Constantly bewailing the Nazis' dissolution of the German Communist Party was not her style.

Her husband was in the army, and she had enough money to live on. Elsbeth Hecker brought out her white-flour coupons so that she could order each of us a piece of cake in the café. On Trude's instructions, she had also brought me a present: a little bag of sweets.

She told us that some time ago she had been summoned to the employment office, and told that she was to be sent to work in the armaments industry. Naturally this horrified her. She borrowed the most extravagantly outrageous items of clothing that her circle of acquaintances could provide, turned up at the employment office dressed to the nines, in a hat with a veil and garishly made up, and told the people there that she was an artist. If she had to do manual labour her art would suffer. That did the trick. The employment office never got in touch with her again.

Another day we went right through the city to visit Erna's sister Edith. It wasn't freezing any more, but there was a very cold wind. All the same, I enjoyed being out of doors again at last. In Magdeburg-Rothensee we had to walk for some way beside fields. The wind made our eyes water, and at that moment I was simply glad to be alive. The sight of the landscape, the factory chimneys on the horizon and the smoke rising from them moved me greatly.

It was the beginning of spring, and I wanted to bend down, pick up some soil from the fields and smell it. But I didn't want Erna thinking I was out of my mind, so I refrained.

'Oh, Erna, I've survived the winter – my first winter underground,' I said happily. She smiled, and I saw a couple of tears run down her cheeks. 'Wait a moment,' she said, and then she herself bent down, picked up some soil and held it out in front of my face, bobbing something like a little curtsey.

We were approaching one of the city's housing estates. Erna had packed up a couple of sweet cinnamon pastries, explaining that you could never be sure whether Edith was prepared to entertain visitors in wartime or not. Our reception was much as she had expected;

Edith was lying on the sofa in the living room wailing that she didn't feel well. Her two little daughters were quarrelling because they both wanted to use the potty at the same time. Erna quickly sorted everything out.

In the kitchen we saw several days' worth of dirty dishes encrusted with the remains of food. Erna and I soaked all the crockery in a large wash-tub, laid the table, made ersatz coffee and prepared supper together. Edith gradually thawed out, and when she realised that matters in her apartment were improving she rose from her bed of pain.

Our third visit was to Frau Aernecke, the mother of all the sisters. She was extraordinarily corpulent, and reminded me of a fat Buddha. She had enormous dark braids, and wore a long, dark brown, coarse cotton skirt. Her appearance amused me so much that I had to concentrate hard on controlling myself so as not to laugh out loud. But I felt very much at ease in her spotless kitchen. Containers of provisions stood on shelves in the little room, like tin soldiers lined up in order of size: flour, salt, sugar and so on, until last of all came sago. I liked the way it was arranged in the style of the last century.

Anna Aernecke knew my cover name, and in her deep voice addressed me as Hanna. She had the thick legs of all the Aerneckes, legs on which they bravely stomped their way through life as committed communists, uncompromising anti-Nazis and kindly human beings.

Almost the entire family was assembled that day: Elsbeth, Edith, Erna and Rolf were all there, and the sisters' younger brother Herbert happened to be at home on a few days' leave. He was the only one to have fiery red hair like Trude. A very large open pan stood on the stove with a ladle in it; ersatz coffee was ladled out of the pan and into our cups. Anna Aernecke, who spoke very slowly, made a solemn speech. Its contents were very simple; she said that from now on I was one of her family. I was greatly impressed, and in the invisible diary that I kept in my head I entered, in capital letters and underlined several times: Adopted into communist clan in the war year of 1943.

10

After almost exactly six weeks, in April 1943, I returned to Berlin from Magdeburg. As I learned much later, those six weeks had been among the most significant events in Erna Hecker's life. My hostess knew that she had done a fine thing in risking her life for me, and she had carried out that task with joy such as I have hardly ever seen in anyone else. I myself had felt very well in Magdeburg; it had been a time almost without fear. However, I was also glad to go back to Berlin, because it meant going to the Neukes.

At 13 Schönleinstrasse, however, the atmosphere was very tense. Trude had not yet found another refuge for me. Besides all her other anxieties – her sick husband, her own health, her difficult children, poverty and her constant fear of being arrested for her resistance work – she was saddled with me again.

All the same, on one of my first few days there Trude came home very cheerful. Frau Steinbeck had told her that furniture which had previously belonged to Jews was being sold cheap somewhere. Now she had bought a coat stand for the front hall, complete with umbrella stands and a shelf for hats, all for three marks. Hitherto the Neukes had had to hang their jackets on nails in the corridor. 'Do you think that's bad?' she asked diffidently. 'Those people have been taken away, and if I don't buy that piece of furniture someone else will.' I said she was quite right, yet I felt a curious pang in my heart.

Another small thing happened on the same morning. When Trude was going to send her son to the baker's he grumbled, 'Why me? We're feeding a stranger here, let her go and get bread.' 'You're right,' said Trude quietly, unaware that I had overheard the exchange, and she sent me off. Of course I didn't mind going to the bakery, but my feelings were ruffled by knowing that I ranked below Trude's teenage son in the hierarchy of the household.

The boy had just been putting on his Hitler Youth uniform. When he came into the kitchen a little later in his Nazi outfit, Trude apologised to me, saying she ought to have spared me the sight of it. For my part, I thought that was unnecessary. After all, I knew that all young people were forced to join such organisations. 'I'm afraid we have to beware of our own children these days,' she complained. 'You can't know what the boy says to his friends. Or what questions one of the leaders may ask him.'

I was now seeing Hannchen Koch regularly again. Once a week we met at a café in Köpenick, where she gave me a precisely calculated amount of bread, fat and sugar.

Unfortunately she had a tendency to keep emphasising how difficult it was for her to spare these donations from her own food rations. Trude was different; she always assured me, with exaggerated cheerfulness, that she was doing 'almost nothing' for me.

The two women, who never met, did not like each other. In talking to me, they both used words like 'nefarious' and 'unreliable' about one another. 'She's politically dangerous, she was always after your father, she's a secret schizophrenic,' Trude said of Frau Koch, who in turn called Trude a 'Red Nazi'.

At one of those meetings in the steamy atmosphere of that crowded café in Köpenick, I couldn't refrain from telling Hannchen Koch about my latest experiences in the Neuke household. Of course that was not very clever of me, but my description had a wonderful effect on Hannchen. It gave her a chance to talk about her rival, apparently understandingly and with an air of superiority. 'You see,' she told me, 'those people are political fanatics, but they're not really fond of you. They don't love you.' In a certain way I could see that she was right. 'I'm grateful to the Neukes, I respect them and I acknowledge all they have done,' I said, 'but I myself can't love them.' Hannchen Koch beamed at me happily, and I saw that her eyes were moist.

When we were sitting in the kitchen one evening, and as usual

Trude was raising her voice too much, Jule performed a mime act. He pointed up with his long arm and large, erect forefinger, then down, to right and to left, and laid his hand on his mouth. 'For heaven's sake, the neighbours!' he was signalling. But Trude just imitated him maliciously and shouted, 'You idiot! You fool! There's only Frau Steinbeck to hear us, and she knows everything anyway.'

'Are you out of your mind?' he asked angrily.

Red in the face with fury, she screamed, 'You're just a stupid working man!' That shook me. She, of all people, who was always delivering tirades against the bourgeoisie, and praising the working class as the secret of redemption, using 'working man' as a term of abuse for her husband!

It had been Trude herself who let her neighbour Frau Steinbeck into the secret that I was a Jewish girl, and must be hidden. Of course that had been very dangerous, but Trude had thought hard about it. She knew that her neighbour was materially well provided for, but terribly bored. Now she gave Frau Steinbeck something to do; she wanted her to keep an eye on her friend, a woman who held some kind of Nazi office in this part of the city, observe her, question her, and warn us of any danger in good time. It sounds like a crazy idea, but it worked.

In that way Trude's resistance group was also provided with detailed information about this Nazi functionary. I did wonder, however, what they could do with their knowledge. Sometimes it seemed to me as if all these meetings of tiny resistance cells were more like a large but wholly ineffective game, its real significance being to sustain the morale of the players.

Many years after the war, at an exhibition, I saw a presentation summing up the activities of the Saefkow-Jacob-Bästlein organisation, as Trude's group of that time was called. A small cord on a map, reaching from Berlin to Magdeburg, showed that there had been a courier service along that route. I realised that I had been that courier, and the leaflets that I had supposedly brought over had been rumbling around in my case.

Much about Trude was ambivalent. She was indeed innocent of

any trace of anti-Semitism, but her face distorted with hatred as soon as anyone mentioned the bourgeoisie. On the one hand, I was a persecuted Jew to her; on the other, a lawyer's daughter from the enemy camp, to wit that same bourgeoisie. Once, in the course of a vehement discussion, she snapped at me, 'You haven't a clue about politics!'

'I wasn't even eleven years old when the Nazis came to power,' I defended myself. 'How could I have had a political education?'

The truth was more complicated: in my parental home, politics and history had been very important from my early childhood onwards. But we were interested in Jewish history and Jewish politics. Even before I went to school, for instance, I was very well informed about the persecution of the Jews in Spain. And as a child I also understood something about the difference between those Jews who were Zionists and those who were not, and also about assimilated Jews; the CV; and the extreme right-wing Naumann Group.* I knew that among Zionists there was a faction true to the Law – in the sense of the Torah – and a faction that was not. However, I couldn't make such distinctions clear to the Neukes.

Sometimes conflict flared up among us over small things. Once Trude poured the ersatz coffee into a cup so vigorously that it slopped over. 'In Magdeburg,' she explained, 'we say a cup must be full to the brim.' Laughing, I agreed with her.

'I've found you out!' she cried. 'Caught you! You're lying. Your family were fine folk, and they never fill a cup more than three-quarters full!' I explained that I couldn't survive without adapting courteously to whatever were my current surroundings. 'That makes sense,' said Trude, and this time our reconciliation was unusually emotional. She even caressed me – for the only time in our entire relationship.

---

* CV is the abbreviation of the Central Verein = Central Association of German Citizens of the Jewish faith. The Naumann Group was officially the Association of Jews of German Nationality, and was in sharp opposition to Zionism. The leader of the organisation was Max Naumann.

Meanwhile, Trude's search for another refuge for me was becoming more and more desperate. She would often leave the apartment for many hours, leaving me alone. Sometimes I shut the doors of the front hall so that no one could see me, and did gymnastics there.

Once, in such a situation, I decided to celebrate Passover. However, I would not let myself conjure up memories of Seder evenings in Rosenthaler Strasse, with all the family faces gathered round the large table. I celebrated my own, modern Passover by repeatedly singing Dayenu, the Passover song. The word means, 'For us it would have been enough.' Or more precisely, 'If you had done this or that for us, it would have been enough.' In my mind, I gratefully went through everything that I already had behind me, and that I had survived. I was confident that Trude would find somewhere for me.

She came home late, exhausted and discouraged. Her feet were swollen, and she asked me to fetch her a footstool. Pale and shaken, she told me how she had been visiting many of her women Party comrades, people she hadn't seen for years. The women were startled to see Trude suddenly at the door, and they often let her in only reluctantly. Their menfolk had been in prison or a concentration camp for a very long time, and now they were being asked to take in a Jewish girl? 'For God's sake, we're in such danger, in such want and poverty – that's impossible.' That was the answer she heard again and again. She had fared no better than Lieschen Sabbarth's father in her search for shelter for me.

Then Trude leaned back, with half-closed eyes, and indulged in a fantasy of wishful thinking. She told me her fondest wish was for me to find refuge with the nobility. Graphically, she described a castle fit for Sleeping Beauty, surrounded by huge, tall trees and walls. She even described the flower beds. A cultivated old lady lived there, and my only task was to read French novels aloud to her. There was a small library that I could use to further my education. The old lady slept a great deal, and after her midday nap liked to be taken into the fresh air, but on no account was I to carry her out; there were plenty of servants who could do that in the castle. I was there only to read aloud.

Trude was alarmed when she realised what she had dreamed up for me. Normally she had nothing but contempt for the bourgeoisie – but in secret she still thought highly of the nobility, particularly its upper ranks.

It was Herbert Steinbeck, of all people, Trude's neighbour and a Nazi non-commissioned officer, who had the crucial idea. He had suddenly arrived in Berlin for a few days' leave. His wife, of course, had told him the sensational news of what was going on next door.

Soon she was at Trude's door, saying, 'My husband said that Jewish girl must go. But he also said he won't denounce you. After Stalingrad, who knows how the war will turn out, and whether we may not need the communists one of these days?'

And Herbert Steinbeck had also thought of a way to get rid of 'that Jewish girl' as soon as possible.

FIVE

I was the girl without a name

After 1943: Something Like a Normal Life

1

Trude Neuke called him the crazy Dutchman. Gerrit Burgers was two years older than me, about half a head taller, and really rather good-looking. He was slim, had thick, light brown hair above a high forehead, expressive eyes and a thin face. His crooked teeth were less attractive; his front teeth were speckled with small brown marks. Striking characteristics were his quirks and his strange behaviour.

Out in the street, he always wore a wide-brimmed hat. Although he was slender and well built, he let his upper body lean slightly to the left. He always had a briefcase with him, slinging it round his neck on a strap so that it lay across his chest, bumping with every step he took. 'An idiot,' was Trude's verdict, adding the contradictory comment, 'And an intelligent man; you can have a good conversation with him.'

She had met Burgers when he went to lodge with her neighbours the Steinbecks. He had come to Berlin as a foreign worker, and judging by what Trude said was being robbed blind by his landlady. They had agreed that she would do his food shopping and cooking, but she kept most of his allotted rations as a manual labourer for herself and her husband. Burgers also had to clean their windows, take out the rubbish and so forth when he came home after a long day's work. He put up with it because he wasn't used to anything else; at home in the Netherlands his mother had always bossed him about.

His friendship with Trude and Jule Neuke began when he turned up at their front door in tears one day: Frau Steinbeck had locked him out. Burgers was prone to uncontrolled outbursts of emotion, and that day he poured out his heart to Trude. He had come to Germany voluntarily in search of work, but he was an opponent of the Nazis, so he felt at home in the Neukes' kitchen. Even after he had moved to lodge with another landlady near the Oberbaum bridge, he regularly dropped in at Schönleinstrasse for a cup of ersatz coffee on a Saturday afternoon.

The Dutchman had never had a girlfriend in his life, because he simply dared not approach women. He had told Frau Steinbeck this before he knew anyone else in Berlin to talk to. She had made fun of him for it, in a mean, nasty way, and of course she had passed the information on to her husband. That had given Herbert Steinbeck the idea of getting him and me together.

Trude was to inform me of this plan, and seemed much embarrassed by it. What she was suggesting to me was by no means a fairytale castle set in a beautiful old estate. Clever as she was, however, she was quick to see the advantages of such an arrangement, which would be in the interests of both of us. And I would not owe anyone thanks, she added, in an obvious dig at Hannchen Koch.

When the Dutchman turned up at the Neukes' apartment for ersatz coffee on the following Saturday afternoon, Trude sent me out of the room at first. A few minutes later she called me back into the kitchen. She hadn't needed long to explain to Burgers what a chance of sexual liberation he had here. In addition, there was the prospect of a wife to keep house for him without stealing his provisions; his new landlady was no better than Frau Steinbeck there. He showed interest at once.

Trude introduced the man to me in her Berlin accent as 'Jerrit Burjers', but I knew how to pronounce his Dutch name properly as I greeted him politely and gave him my hand. I had gone to visit an aunt in Amsterdam on my fourteenth birthday, and had picked up a few scraps of Dutch. An inarticulate cry of delight escaped him, and he opened his mouth wide. Then, clumsily and with his mouth still wide open, he gave me a kiss on the cheek. It was a very wet, slobbering kiss, but it would have been tactless to wipe the saliva away.

He came from Nijmegen, a city on the Dutch border, and had already spoken a mixture of Dutch and German there. By now he had acquired a vocabulary that could be understood by anyone he addressed in Berlin. As Johanna was not my real name, he decided to call me Frauke, meaning 'little wife'. 'Frauke, let's drink up and then we'll both go home,' he happily announced.

We went on foot from Schönleinstrasse to the River Spree. I kept my distance from the Dutchman. I found his appearance embarrassing, and I didn't want either to attract notice or to have the passers by staring at me.

It was not far to the Oberbaum bridge, yet I had never been in this area before. I liked it very much at once. It had the typical atmosphere of Berlin. The Spree was my Spree, my river. I fervently hoped that this might represent a long-term solution for me.

The bridge led straight to a short street on the opposite bank of the Spree, where there were three apartment blocks in a row. We went into the middle one. I immediately felt at ease there, even in the front hall of the building. An old cardboard plate hanging on the banisters proclaimed that they were just polished, and I saw another such notice in the same hand, and like the first with spelling mistakes, informing everyone that when the air-raid warning sounded the cellar doors must be left open. I relished the phonetic reproduction of a genuine Berlin accent on both notices.

We went up the stairs. There was only one door on the first floor, with the name Knizek on it. 'Just one tenant here?' I asked Burgers.

'Yes, this is a narrow house between the two big corner buildings,' he explained.

'How nice.' I was pleased; the fewer neighbours the better.

A small handwritten card indicated that part of this first-floor apartment was occupied by a lodger. It read 'KiHel', a name that puzzled me. Later I found out that the man's name was Kittel, but the two letters T had been crossed very close together and rather too low down, so that they looked like a capital H.

Herr and Frau Grass, the caretakers of the building, lived one floor higher up. Luise Blase, the Dutchman's landlady, lived on the third floor. There was a fourth floor above that, but we did not go up there until later.

Before we left her apartment, Trude had taken me aside for a moment. 'I've told Burgers that you're half-Jewish, so you've had a lot of trouble and have had to go underground,' she whispered to me. As it was to turn out, this was a brilliant idea, and was to make my survival in my new environment very much easier. With a cover story like that, I at least half belonged to the people I wanted to accept me into their world; I was not so alien that I must at all costs be kept out of it.

Frau Blase was seventy-eight years old, half blind and – as Burgers had told me on the way – an enthusiastic Nazi supporter. The Dutchman went straight to the point: he told her he had found a woman who was coming to live with him at once. I would keep house for him, and he said I was also ready to lend Frau Blase a hand at any time. Since I was not racially impeccable, it would be better not to register me with the police, he added casually. That didn't seem to bother the old woman, but she immediately began haggling over the rent with Burgers. She wanted twice the original rent for his room if I was to share his broad wooden bed. The Dutchman thought that was too much, and finally they agreed to split the difference. With that, I moved in, and from the end of April 1943 my address was Number 2 Am Oberbaum.

I had liked the apartment when we first stepped into its roomy entrance hall, which led to the kitchen on the right, and on the left to the large, light front room occupied by Burgers. A connecting door led to a second room that was also rented out. A Pole and a Hungarian woman lived there, with their small child.

It was a few days before I discovered where Frau Blase had her own rooms. At first the way she sometimes just disappeared from the kitchen when I hadn't seen her in the hall was a mystery to me. Only then did I discover that a narrow door in the kitchen resembling the door of a broom cupboard led to another small hall, leading in its turn into Frau Blase's bedroom. There was a huge wardrobe in this communicating room. I was not to learn what precious treasures it contained until later.

On the day after I moved in, Frau Blase asked me to go shopping with her. She couldn't leave the house or carry her purchases on her own. Either her son Kurt or the caretaker's wife usually went with her.

She put on a good hat dating from the twenties and a pair of gloves, picked up a handbag and took my arm. She had dressed in her Sunday best for her first outing in a long time, which was also to be the last of her life.

The dairy lay on the opposite bank of the river. She introduced me to the milkman, one Herr Pofahl, as her new lodger. 'How is your wife?' she asked him. 'Not so good,' he replied briefly. When we had left the shop, Frau Blase told me that Frau Pofahl suffered from severe depression, and had been in an institution several times because of it.

Next time I went shopping on my own. 'My regards to your landlady,' said the milkman, 'and tell her that we're closing down on the first of next month. I can't manage any more. My wife is in hospital again.'

Luise Blase was greatly affected by this information. 'I won't be going shopping any more,' she announced, and gave me the ration cards for herself and Burgers, telling me to register them wherever I liked. As she saw it, the closure of the dairy marked the end of a section of her life. Gradually she handed over more and more responsibility for her housekeeping to me.

The first serious quarrel between Burgers and Frau Blase came as a complete surprise to me. The reason for it was ridiculous. The Dutchman had been washing himself thoroughly in the kitchen – as usual, and as I did too. There was in fact a bathroom, but the bath was full of coal.

Our landlady had tactfully withdrawn at first, and didn't come back into the kitchen until Burgers had finished. But he had accidentally left a boot in the middle of the kitchen floor. Frau Blase, who was almost blind, stumbled over it and got a shock. 'Only a filthy foreigner can be as slovenly as that,' she protested angrily. 'We Germans are neat and tidy!' Burgers responded loudly and indignantly, because he was deeply hurt. He had such a pronounced passion for cleanliness that he was constantly disinfecting the toilet. And now the two of them were hurling the most vulgar abuse at each other for quite a long time. It was disgusting.

Then the old lady went beetroot red in the face, her lower jaw began to tremble, and she threatened to throw her Dutch lodger out. Even worse, she said she would denounce his 'Jewish Dulcinea' (that was me) to the Gestapo so that there'd be an end of me at last. She described exactly how she imagined that end, too, mingling a lust for murder with pornographic notions fit for *Der Stürmer*. She had never read a book in her life, so where she got her ideas was a mystery. She gave vent to terrible and sexually perverse threats of murder, while he shouted wildly at her, stamping his feet like a small child in a tantrum, tearing his hair and addressing her as 'Mother' in loud and sarcastic tones.

My heart was thudding, and I was frightened to death. I wasn't to know that the quarrel would be made up a few hours later, without a word to explain it. Burgers and Frau Blase hated and loved each other equally.

Our landlady's attitude to me was no less ambivalent. On the one hand, I was a Jewish girl, and of course you had to be hostile to such people and exploit them. On the other hand, she had chosen me as a substitute for the daughter she had always wanted but never had.

When money came in for her, it was always a cause for celebration. Frau Blase was indeed blackmailing the Dutchman to get a higher rent from him, in return for her tolerating my presence in the apartment. But it wasn't clear to her that she was gaining only a ridiculously small sum, ten or fifteen marks a month. I had heard rumours that when those who had gone underground suddenly had to spend a night in one of the boarding houses on the Kurfürstendamm, they were now charged about a hundred marks for it. Frau Blase wasn't making anything like that kind of money.

When those few extra marks came in from Burgers, she would rub her hands, cackling in her ancient voice, and tell me, 'Here's money, dear daughter. You go down to the bar and get us a can of beer from Altermann. That's one in the eye for those Jews, dear daughter. So now there's money in the house, let's have a drink.'

She was curious too, of course. For instance, she wanted to know how my father had made his living. I couldn't say he was a lawyer; to her, the word suggested someone enthroned in the clouds. But it had to be something respectable. When she asked me, I happened to be standing by the big, bricked-in kitchen stove, one corner of which was covered with yellowed newspaper. My eye fell on an advertisement for the services of a house-painter in Köpenick.

'We had a little shop selling paints and varnishes in Köpenick,' I said.

'What was the address?' asked Frau Blase.

I quickly read out an address from another advertisement. Then she asked me more questions, showing a great interest in paints and varnishes.

Of course I didn't know the first thing about the subject. So the next time I had a chance, I went into a paint shop in Neukölln and asked the saleswoman a lot of questions about its wares, most of which were not in evidence. 'Where's your bombing certificate?' the elderly woman inquired. She meant a document in official jargon, to the effect that I had been bombed out and thus had permission to buy a given number of rolls of wallpaper or similar goods.

'I haven't got one,' I admitted.

'Don't you know there's a war on?' she asked, annoyed.

'Yes, of course. I just wanted to know what it used to be like.'

'What's all this nonsense in aid of?' The saleswoman lost her temper. 'No one's ever tried to annoy me like this before! It ought to be forbidden by the police!'

'Police' was a word that immediately choked me with fear. Of course I was over-reacting; the woman was just saying what came into her head, and would certainly not have gone to raise the alarm at once. But to me it was the signal for flight. I quickly said goodbye and left the shop. As soon as I had turned the next corner I ran for all I was worth. I was surprised by my own athletic prowess, for in sports at school I had been at best an average runner.

*

And then, one morning, someone really did ring the front doorbell. Old Frau Blase was still in bed, and Burgers was already at work. I told myself: if for some reason or other I've been denounced, it makes no difference who lets the Gestapo in. I'm here and they'll find me anyway. So I opened the door. There were indeed two police officers outside, with a warrant to search the place, but they weren't interested in me. It was about the Polish and Hungarian couple.

This wasn't the first time the police had come on account of those two. The man was considered work-shy, which in those days was a crime that could get you sent to a concentration camp or even sentenced to death. The officers took him, the woman and the child away, and the three of them never came back to the apartment.

I must admit that I was relieved. The couple had been curious about me, and suspicious, and had made themselves at home in the kitchen in an unbearable way. The child had cried a lot. We could never all have got along together in that apartment for long. At the time I hardly even thought about the family's ultimate fate.

After this incident Frau Blase said she really didn't want the police visiting her apartment, and she was never going to rent to such 'dirty foreigners' again. I was welcome to move into the empty room, she added, but she would need money for it. Burgers offered to pay a few more marks if she promised him to let the room stand empty. She shook hands on the deal at once.

The next explosion between Burgers and Frau Blase was because of the various bugs that infested the entire apartment. The Dutchman had already warned me about this problem when we were first on our way there over the Oberbaum bridge. Whole districts of the poorer parts of Berlin were plagued by insects, and at that time there was no really effective way to get rid of them. All three apartment blocks would have had to be cleared and then filled with gas to destroy the pests, because if only a few of them were killed the survivors would emigrate into the neighbourhood through cracks in the walls and would soon be back.

Burgers had tried putting the bugs down with disinfectant, but not very successfully. You couldn't even reduce their numbers; on the contrary, they increased and multiplied. Finally he took off one of his slippers and squashed them against the wall with it.

Frau Blase's son often came to see her, and she told him to inspect our room. Kurt Blase was an SA man, and a believer in the final victory. He was a textbook Nazi. He saw the bloodstains on our wall and reported them to his mother, who immediately kicked up a fuss. Instead of apologising for the bug infestation and lowering the rent, she wanted financial compensation for the marks on the wall. Once again she called Burgers a 'filthy foreigner'. Once again there were furious scenes, and I was terrified. But after a few hours it all passed over, nothing much was said about the row, and an odd sort of harmony set in.

When a similar scene threatened on another occasion, I went straight into the kitchen and talked to the old lady. 'Gerrit was going to clean your windows tomorrow. What with the air raids there isn't a window cleaner left in the whole of Berlin, but please don't make a fuss about it, you'll do yourself no good.' And I told Burgers, 'Oh, for heaven's sake! It's getting harder and harder to find a place to live in Berlin, and we've been lucky here. It's not worth quarrelling with the old woman at her great age. She's really very fond of you, you know.' And I took his hand, led him into the kitchen, and that was the end of it.

However, soon Burgers and I had our own first real, violent quarrel, and just because I was reading a light novel that Trude had lent me. The book was lying open on the desk in Burgers's room. He had finished work for the day, and we were sitting on the sofa. But I found talking to him terribly boring, so I kept getting up and taking a few steps over to the desk to go on reading my novel, which was no great work of literature but was very exciting.

'You're not to read when I'm at home,' he grumbled, at first mildly enough, but then sounding annoyed and then shouting. 'You're supposed to be here just for me.' I obeyed his instructions for a few minutes, and then went on reading from where I was on the sofa, quite a way from my book. When he noticed what I was doing, he felt so irate that he took off one of his boots and hit me on the head with it.

I had a black eye for some time afterwards. At first that embarrassed me a great deal, but then I realised that only now did I fit into my present surroundings. People didn't notice my black eye; indeed, it made me inconspicuous. It was local colour, so to speak.

I was horrified, humiliated, repelled, and angry with the invisible enemies who might ultimately have been to blame for my situation. I told myself that I was not just anyone, as my aunt Sylvia had put it. I was a lady, I had taken my school-leaving certificate, and I belonged to the middle classes, if only to the less prosperous part of them.

I set myself an allotted task to be done daily, and called it work. I would make myself maintain a dignified manner of everyday speech in line with the class to which I really belonged. I decided to write my internal, imaginary diary in literary German some of the time, and the rest of the time I would also write it in the most vulgar and improper Berlin slang. I determined that sometimes I would think in hexameters and write in an old-fashioned German style, but I had to give that up. I couldn't use the language of the eighteenth and nineteenth centuries correctly because I had no access to a single book of that period, which annoyed me very much.

2

When I was still lodging with the Jacobsohns in Schmidstrasse, I often used to feel fear and anxiety weighing heavily down on me when I awoke in the morning. That was the time of the deportations from Berlin, and I sensed nothing but unhappiness in the air. Now that I was living at Number 2 Am Oberbaum, however, I almost always woke in a good temper after a deep, refreshing sleep.

Burgers went to work very early. I got up when he did, but often went back to bed for another hour after he had left. If it was fine weather outside, I opened the window of our room later and did gymnastics, entirely naked. At first I didn't notice that our window was directly opposite the stationmaster's little office at the Stralauer Tor overhead railway station, so that he could see me from that vantage point. Once the elderly gentleman, who looked like a station-master from a picture book, greeted me from his office, smiling and waving to me with his signalling disc. I cheerfully waved back, but I remembered to pull the curtain over the window in future.

One morning in late spring I had a surprise visit from Trude Neuke. She brought me a tiny bunch of primroses. She had even managed to get them wrapped in the shop, although paper was in very short supply. Trude always set great store by conventions and proper behaviour. She unwrapped the flowers and gave them to me without any fuss, but with an elegant gesture. I was very pleased to see her, asked her in, and we sat on the plush-covered sofa in Burgers's room. I put the flowers on the table in a glass.

After a little preliminary talk, Trude asked me cautiously whether I found the relationship with Burgers tolerable. I could give her a positive answer, saying that we had begun to get used to each other. My influence over him was increasing, and Frau Blase and Burgers often said that they felt they were looked after better than ever before.

Gerrit Burgers, aged twenty-five,
in February 1946.

I had no particular trouble in adjusting to the Dutchman and his whims. For instance, just before Burgers came home in the evening I often poured some water over the floor and spread it around. That took about two minutes, but he was delighted. His countrymen, in particular his mother, as he emphasised, set great store by cleanliness, but he had never before met a housewife who washed the floor again in the evening. He was quite beside himself with delight.

The primroses that Trude had brought me lived for a long time. Often I just sat looking at them. Without knowing it, Trude had granted a great wish of mine. Despite all the less welcome aspects of my situation, I longed to lead something like a normal life.

However, there were still some terrible scenes between Burgers and me during the first six months at Am Oberbaum. For instance, when he discovered that Frau Blase was getting food out of me by blackmail, he reacted with a fit of rage. Every week I met Frau Koch, who always gave me a big black shopping bag full of food. When Frau Blase saw this, she wanted some of it, and gave me a second bag to take specially. I found this very disagreeable, particularly when I realised that Frau Koch was not simply dividing my rations in two but giving me some of her own sparse provisions, so that both bags would look as if they were half full.

Once I came back very late from one of these meetings. Burgers was home already, looked at the two bags, and saw me giving one of them to Frau Blase. As he had already put his slippers on, he didn't even need to take a boot off in order to give me another black eye.

The next quarrel between us flared up because he was extremely keen for me to share everything he had. In itself that was very nice of him, but unfortunately he insisted on it fanatically. His favourite dish was the wartime bread that he moistened with ersatz coffee and sprinkled with a thick layer of sugar. When he wanted me to eat some I declined, repelled by it. That led to another violent scene.

But then I did succeed in explaining that tastes differ, and he mustn't take it personally if I didn't like his bread and sugar. However, I had no objection to the fact that he smoked like a chimney and wanted me to keep pace with him. I was a heavy smoker myself.

Our relationship therefore gradually became easier. I could almost always avert his fits of fury in time. And unlike Frau Blase, he never threatened to denounce me or put me out on the street.

I often told myself that the bargain we had struck was not a bad one. Burgers did well out of it, but so did I. If we lived to see liberation, we would be quits and I would end the relationship at once. I had plenty of practice, after all, in escape and evasion – in short, in jumping off church towers, as the clairvoyant had put it.

But a time came when I became more and more aware of another question: how was I ever to pay off the duty of gratitude that I owed to Hannchen Koch?

In the end I often ate the food that Luise Blase made me give her after all, because the old woman ate like a bird. She offered me a taste of this and that from her meals increasingly often. That meant that it became a habit for me to keep her company at her midday meal and have some hot food myself. We often sat together for hours.

Luise Blase still had good posture and had kept her figure. Her sparse, snow-white hair had a few blonde strands in it. She wore it in long braids pinned up into an impressive nest. Where her scalp showed through her hair it was ash-grey to black, but her complexion was pink and her hands well tended.

She always sat at a little folding table that, because of her eye trouble, she was constantly moving to a place where the sun wouldn't dazzle her. This tiny item of furniture, light as a feather, was like an inseparable part of her. She spoke the kind of Berlin dialect, the accent of the metropolis, that had been usual before the First World War, and I liked to hear it. Frail as she was, and almost blind, she worked the whole story of her life into her conversations with me.

She had been born in 1865, the illegitimate daughter of a maid-servant. Luise Schieke – that was her maiden name – was at first brought up by her grandparents, but they soon died. Then she was passed on in turn to an assortment of relations, all of whom found her a nuisance. Meanwhile, her mother had risen in the world to some extent, and had married a man from the lower middle class.

'So now that she'd improved herself,' Frau Blase said, 'she had a proper apartment, she didn't have to go out to work.' And at last her mother took the girl in. When Luise was ten her half-sister Klara was born, followed ten years later by little Anna, the baby of the family.

Like her mother before her, Luise went to work as a maidservant, and had already left home when the last little girl was born. But she had very affectionate, almost maternal feelings for the child. Every few weeks, when her employers gave her a day off, she went to see her mother's family, although she had a chilly reception there. Her half-sister Klara showed particular dislike for her.

Once, she had bought a little bag of sweets for Anna out of her tiny wages. As she was giving it to the child, Klara struck the bag out of both their hands as hard as she could, then trampled on the sweets and told her little sister, 'You know you're not allowed to take anything from horrid godforsaken Luise!' After that, Luise and Klara were deadly enemies for the rest of their lives.

For many years Luise Blase had worked as a parlour maid for a Jewish couple who lived in a grand apartment on the Kottbusser Ufer. The father of the family wanted his two sons to be brought up in spartan style so that they would be good businessmen. As for his wife, the mistress of the house, Frau Blase described her as the quintessence of the fat, rich, Jewish social upstart. She settled herself rather more broadly in her chair and imitated her employer's screech of a voice. 'That's how the woman sat, stuffing herself with food,' she told me. She still remembered exactly what subjects were discussed at length when there were visitors, for instance where to get replacements if the lid of a dish or one of the good porcelain cups was broken.

The lady who stuffed herself with food had a sister who was not in the least like her. She was slender, blonde and blue-eyed, always on the go, doing this or that about the house, very nice to the servants and inclined to physical movement and laughter the whole time. This sister was also rich, and gave large parties. On such occasions she sometimes borrowed Luise from her mistress.

Frau Blase still remembered the woman with affection. She was the only human being who had ever been nice to her. When she had been sent to help her mistress's sister out, she was welcomed at the door with open arms and a beaming smile. 'Ah, here's our little Luise!'

Frau Blase described the dinners there down to the last pot-herbs for the soup. I had no difficulty in identifying the menus as kosher. The meal began with clear soup, then blue trout (so called because the poaching method made the skin look blue), followed by many other courses including delicious specialities. Large quantities of food were bought, so that the kitchen staff could eat the same as the invited guests. But that didn't suit the servants. 'Trout, no, never had that before,' and they somehow didn't fancy this and that, or would only try a little of it. As a result the cook had asked permission for them to cook themselves something different, said Frau Blase, a huge pan of potato soup. They had crackling on a lavish scale to go with it, and sat comfortably in the kitchen eating this thick soup, rich with fat from the crackling. They were promptly sick afterwards. And as the cook and another of the kitchen staff had to throw up at the same time, they bumped their heads painfully together over the kitchen sink. Old Frau Blase laughed until she cried at the memory; it was one of the funniest experiences in her life.

After Luise Schieke had worked as a parlour maid for a long time, she had to admit to herself that she was getting nowhere. Through the caretakers who lived in the building, and whose apartment was a centre of gossip for all the servants working there, she heard of a widower with two adolescent sons who was in urgent need of a wife. Old Frau Blase imitated, in the style of a caricature, the fine qualities that this good catch on the marriage market was supposed to have: he was a distinguished gentleman, well to do financially, dressed fabulously well, and so forth. In retrospect, her only comment on these advantages was a dry, 'Humph!' That said it all.

So Fräulein Luise arranged to meet this fine gentleman in the Hasenheide park. Soon afterwards she married him, and moved into his apartment at Number 2 Am Oberbaum, where she had now lived for thirty years.

Karl Blase was a clerk in a civil service office. He was a short-sighted man who wore pince-nez, much older than she was, pedantic, always finding fault, and generally repugnant. He was domineering, and treated his wife very badly. Frau Blase never knew why or when he would lash out at her. He insisted on having clean, well-ironed shirts, and she could certainly provide him with those. All the same, when she gave him a pile of freshly ironed laundry, he would put on his pince-nez to check that there were no little wrinkles or stains left anywhere. Once, Frau Blase lost her temper. She took a magnifying glass out of his desk drawer and handed it to him, so that he could inspect the shirts even more closely for himself. At that he beat her so hard that she couldn't sit down for several days.

His two sons were about twelve and fourteen when Luise Blase became their stepmother. The younger was a lout who was always making trouble for her, and even in his teens the elder was on the way to becoming a criminal. Frau Blase lived in constant fear of that heartless youth, whose unusual name was Fridot. He must have done terrible things that as a rule she didn't mention. But in some situations, for instance after a major reconciliation with Burgers when they had quarrelled, she would fall into a mellow and intimate mood, and say something about it. 'Fridot once went for his father with a knife,' she said on one such occasion, in a very different voice.

Money was always in short supply. One day, quite by chance, Frau Blase found out where her husband's earnings went. She was standing at a tram stop near Nollendorfplatz, and suddenly she saw him on the other side of the street, red in the face as he staggered out of a betting shop.

Her two stepsons left home early. The children that Luise Blase herself brought into the world hardly knew their half-brothers. The elder, her son Gerhard, had already fallen at the front when I moved into Frau Blase's apartment. I did know the younger, Kurt, because he regularly visited his mother. She had him very late in life; she was already around fifty when she noticed the baby's movements, and had thought she was well into the menopause. Whether at first she was pleased or horrified by this pregnancy she didn't say.

Even with two sons of her own, her role in the life of the family was a hard one. Her husband did pay for the rent and for gas, but he gave her hardly anything for the housekeeping. She took cleaning jobs to feed her family. Among other situations, she worked for years at a very good stationer's, and in a fine perfumery in the west of Berlin.

It was there that she accumulated the treasures she had hoarded in the huge, magical cupboard that stood in the hall between the kitchen and the bedroom. Half of it was full from top to bottom with top-quality stationery, notebooks and exercise books of all kinds, and cartons full of notepaper. The other half contained cakes of the finest French soap, hair lotions and shampoos. She told me, unabashed, how these things had come into her possession. She had always been regarded as a hard-working, thorough cleaner, and also as absolutely reliable and honest. The last bit, however, was not true. Over many years she had appropriated something particularly expensive almost every time she went to work at the stationer's shop or the perfumery.

In this old woman I recognised someone who, rejected by bourgeois society herself, took her revenge on it by breaking the law all her life whenever she could. Under the Weimar Republic she had even once hidden weapons in her home for a murderous group of paramilitaries.* 'Those gentlemen were so nice, they gave bigger tips than I ever had from anyone else in my life,' she was always telling me.

Her husband died in the middle of the 1920s in the bathhouse that he regularly visited to take what was called a Spanish bath, a kind of sauna. By the time a messenger arrived to tell Frau Blase that he had been found dead in a cubicle there, he was already in the morgue.

At first she had been frozen rigid with horror. A few hours later she began mourning the fact that she was now a widow. She was in torrents of tears until the first light of dawn, when she fell asleep at last – and woke with very different feelings. 'Then it occurred to me: my God, he's dead. I could have shed tears again, but what a change! I don't expect you've ever known anything like it. I thought to myself, this can't be true. Because all at once I realised: that bastard can't beat me any more. I'm free.' She rejoiced when it struck her that, while she would have less money coming in than before, because she couldn't expect more than a tiny widow's pension, there was no one to spend her money in the betting shop now. At last she would be able to live as she liked. And from that day on she brought up her sons on her own.

Sometimes Luise Blase's eyes were red-rimmed with weeping, and then I knew that she was mourning for her beloved son Gerhard. She often talked to me about him. Only after much vacillation,

---

* In the 1920s, many political murders were committed by nationalist German underground groups. The victims were usually so-called traitors from their own ranks.

however, did she show me an especially sacred treasure: his journeyman's piece made in the course of his training to work with stucco and gilding. It was a small wooden box thickly covered with stucco and decorated with very ornate roses, the whole thing finished with gold leaf even in the smallest cavities.

She also told me about Gerhard's birthday parties in every last detail. I learned exactly what cakes were baked, how much beer Frau Blase had brought in, and what a gigantic pan full of bockwurst had been served up as the crowning glory of the birthday meal. Groping shakily about, she brought the pan out to show me, and she described the huge dish of potato salad that was served with the sausages down to the separate cubes of gherkin.

No such stories were ever told of Kurt. He had always been considered stupid by his clever elder brother Gerhard and Gerhard's friends. He had left elementary school at fourteen, small, pale and still very childlike at the time. His mother had taken the boy to the Osram factory, a high-rise building close to the Oberbaum bridge. And it worked: Kurt was taken on as laboratory assistant to a Jewish physicist.

This man took a benevolent interest in the fatherless boy, who, while not very intelligent, was pleasant and well-behaved. He often patted his head and gave him presents at Easter, Christmas and for his birthday. In retrospect, Frau Blase still described the physicist as an angel, and was so moved that her voice rose to a squeak.

'What happened to the man?' I asked, with intentional naïvety. 'Does he still work for Osram?'

'No, that rich Jew didn't like Germany one bit, although he rose so high in the world here and made his fortune. Coward that he was, he went off to America,' she replied. Naturally, I made no comment.

I hated Frau Blase as a repellent, criminal blackmailer with Nazi opinions, yet I loved her as a mother figure. Life is complicated.

Kurt Blase was now twenty-eight years old. He had pale, fair hair, which he wore combed back and held down with pomade or sugarwater, a style typical of the Nazi era. He was always smartly dressed.

Even as an adult and the father of a family, he still had a decidedly childlike face, which appeared to be completely empty. 'If you were to compare his face to a railway station,' I said to Burgers, 'you'd have to put up a notice: No Trains In Service.'

Kurt had met his wife Trudchen in a greengrocer's shop. The young girl, who was very thin, with curly hair, was weighing out potatoes. Before it was his turn, a woman customer said to Trudchen, 'What a strong perm you have! The hairdresser must have worked hard over it.' To which Trudchen replied, 'I don't need a perm, it's all natural. And I never go to the hairdresser. I save the money instead.'

Kurt, who had never made friends or ventured to approach a girl, thought: a woman who doesn't need the hairdresser is the right wife for me. He made a date with her, took her to the cinema, took her to the cinema again and married her. They had three children within a short time.

Now and then the whole family came visiting. The children were out of nappies, but not old enough for school yet. They were pale, undernourished, backward and seemed to have been taught no manners at all. They rampaged noisily round the kitchen. I felt sorry for Frau Blase. Of course she wanted to love her grandchildren, but it wasn't possible.

Trudchen herself couldn't stand her children. She usually sat on the coal-box, smoking. She was probably much the same at home. The first time they came to visit we took part in the ersatz coffee party in the kitchen. The eldest child kept pounding away at his mother's lap and bellowing, 'Wanna go home, wanna go home, wanna go home.' Old Frau Blase's feelings were hurt. She was sad, and finally mimicked the child's cry of, 'Wanna go home, wanna go home.'

Suddenly Trudchen burst into a fit of lunatic laughter. Her mother-in-law groped her way over to the coal-box, crouched down, put her face so close to her daughter-in-law's that their noses touched, opened her own toothless mouth and maliciously imitated Trudchen's laughter. Kurt just sat there defenceless, looking desperate. It was not the way I had imagined an SA man.

Burgers and I took refuge in our room. A minute later there was a knock on the door: it was Kurt. 'Can I sit here with you two for a bit?' he asked. 'This is more than I can stand.' We talked easily for a while about everyday subjects, until Kurt and his family left. And we gradually began to make friends with each other.

3

When I left Zeuthen, Frau Fiochi had told me I would be welcome
to go to her youngest sister Miranda in Kreuzberg some time and
darn stockings. I would be warm there, would get something to eat,
and into the bargain I would be paid fifty pfennigs an hour – it was
all settled. Moreover, Miranda's husband, Camillo von Weissenfeld,
worked in the Ministry of Propaganda. I was horrified, but Frau
Fiochi reassured me at once: he would never denounce anyone, she
said; he was the best of the whole family.

So one day I went from Oberbaum to the address on the Kottbusser Damm that I had been given. You wouldn't have known that
Miranda von Weissenfeld had been an artiste and dancer in the past
from looking at her now. She had gained a lot of weight, and spoke
German very badly. I spent six hours darning a huge mountain of
stockings, until the master of the house came home. Camillo von
Weissenfeld knew very well who I was, and that embarrassed us both
so much that we made clumsy small talk about the weather.

Then Miranda asked us to clear the stockings away into the
bedroom. It was impossible to overlook the booklet entitled *How
Do I Learn to Speak German Properly?* lying on her bedside table.
'There, you see, you don't need anything like that even though
you're in such a difficult situation,' Camillo von Weissenfeld told
me, and blushed. Spontaneous understanding sprang up between
me and this slender man at a glance. With his attractive white teeth,
thin face and huge horn-rimmed glasses, he did not in the least
resemble the bloodthirsty enemy whom I would have liked to look
in the face just once.

I got home very late in the evening from this visit. Burgers was
back before me, and said it wasn't worth my while to go to work
for that meagre three marks. All the same, I would have liked to go

back there and get to know the milieu better, as well as Camillo von Weissenfeld, that member of the ministry headed by Goebbels.

None the less, I always had plenty to do during the day when Burgers was at work. I was now running the entire household. Simply doing the shopping and bringing it home took a good deal of time. I also resumed my long walks in the city. The area between the Oberbaum bridge and Görlitzer Station, Stralauer Allee and Treptower Park became my new preserve.

I felt a great need for intellectual activity, and wanted to read something worthwhile at last. So I asked Hannchen Koch to get hold of books for me, preferably from the library of Karl Jalowicz. I had not had any contact with my father's brother for a long time. It would have been too dangerous. But I knew that he still lived in Pankow, protected from deportation by his marriage to his non-Jewish wife Frieda.

I was sure there was no trash on Karl's bookshelves. And as Hannchen Koch was positively keen to be in touch with an educated middle-class Jewish citizen, who in addition was my father's brother, she happily agreed to my request.

But after she had brought the third or fourth large tome to the café in Köpenick where we met, she suffered a kind of breakdown. She wept so terribly that everyone there turned to look at us. She was ready to make any sacrifice for me, she sobbed, at the same time holding out the bread she had bought at a black-market price. The worst of it wasn't carrying the heavy books about. The worst of it was that she mustn't let Karl know who the books were for, so she had pretended to have discovered a passion for serious literature in herself, and now Karl wanted her to discuss the contents of every book that she brought back to him. It was just too much to ask her to spend her nights reading thick books of a kind to which she was entirely unaccustomed, when she was overburdened with so much else anyway.

I felt unspeakably embarrassed, and made haste to say that she must stop doing it at once. She dismissed that idea, of course. So I wrote a short piece about each book she was going to return: a few lines giving an opinion on the work as a whole, and saying enough about its content to make any further discussion unnecessary. She could learn those few lines by heart on the tram journey as she took the book back to Pankow, and she conscientiously did so.

After the war, Karl told me that he had always enjoyed these messages from me. 'I recognised your literary style at once,' he said. 'I knew that those assessments could only be your work.' But after a few weeks this exchange came to an end, because the journeys to and from Pankow were too much for Frau Koch.

Trude had another idea. She was an avid user of lending libraries; she simply registered me for one of the branches that she knew and paid the security pledge for me. However, the basic stock of these libraries was light fiction. Better than nothing, I thought, and decided to write a study of some length on that genre of literature. For I soon discovered that even in these cheap novels there were many passages of good writing, where the authors were probably describing experiences from their own lives.

One day a tattered volume by Theodor Fontane fell into my hands in the library. The spine of the book had been torn off and the last few pages were missing, but all the same I very much wanted to borrow the volume. 'That's here by mistake, it's not been cata-logued,' said the librarian. 'So you can't borrow it.'

'All the same, I'd like to read Fontane,' I protested.

'You know the name of Fontane?' asked the woman. She sounded distrustful. I was terrified; suppose she called the Gestapo because I seemed to her suspicious?

'I once heard it at school. Is he something special?' I asked, trying to sound as calm as possible. Then I returned my last book, but I did not borrow another. I got the librarian to return my pledge, and never set foot in the lending library again.

So now that source of books had also dried up. Still, I had already begun making notes for my study of popular literature. I wrote them in a handsome, fat exercise book on the best pre-war paper and with a wax-cloth cover; Frau Blase had taken it out of her magic cupboard as a present for me. Under the heading for each book, the name of its author, its title and its year of publication, I sometimes added a tiny letter E, standing for *Eigenes*, my own, and under it I noted down sayings by Frau Blase, conversations with Jule and Trude Neuke, and everyday observations that I wanted to remember. It was the only time that I dared to put my own experiences and thoughts down on paper.

Gradually I came to know everyone who lived in the building at 2 Am Oberbaum. Directly below us lived the caretakers, Auguste and Alexander Grass. Grass's wife was a few years older than him, and with her hair combed high on her head and pinned up in a bun at the nape of her neck, she looked like the figurehead of a barge. Her husband, so Frau Blase whispered to me, had had several convictions in the law courts. As a result, they both hated all authorities and felt much solidarity with me, the girl who had gone to ground. They were friendly people, if not ideal characters, and they were rather unpopular in the neighbourhood.

Alexander Grass's old, bedridden mother also lived with them. You never saw her, but an unpleasant, penetrating smell came out of their apartment and there was often shouting. Frau Grass abused her mother-in-law in the most vulgar language, and the neighbours in turn took Frau Grass for a Fury, letting a sick old woman go uncared for. Frau Grass also raged against the Nazis in equally vulgar terms, employing wonderfully graphic expressions.

The couple naturally addressed everyone in the house by the familiar *du* pronoun, including Burgers but with the sole exception of me. They always spoke to me formally, with *Sie*. I was the girl with no name.

The Knizeks, husband and wife, lived on the first floor. They were delighted when I said, 'I'm sure you must really be called Knížek, but the little mark over the letter Z has gone missing in German. Am I right?' The short, stout couple were Czech patriots who had lived in Berlin for many years, running a vegetable stall in the market.

Their lodger, Herr Kittel, did not fit into this environment. He was an old gentleman, very lonely, very well-groomed, almost excessively polite but extremely reserved. It was a long time before I realised that he too knew about me. From then on he always greeted me with a mischievous smile.

He was another of my friends and protectors. Although we all tried to keep as much warmth as possible in our rooms, with fuel in such short supply, he slept with his door to the front hall of the apartment open at night, so that he could hear whether anything threatening went on in the building. He was much too good-mannered to mention the fact to me, and I was sure that I would wake up of my own accord anyway and make my escape if I heard any unusual sound.

But then the caretaker's wife asked me one morning, 'What did you think of all that racket last night? Wasn't it terrible?' I had slept like a log, and hadn't heard anything at all. However, two or three drunken soldiers had come into the building, rampaging about, shouting and lying down on the stairs. Herr Kittel had woken at once, greatly concerned for me. He had put on his fireman's uniform and gone to wake the caretaker. Together, the two men had managed to remove the drunks from the stairs, and had thrown them out of the building so as to protect me.

The top floor was occupied by Frau Haase, a widow who was so deaf that she heard almost nothing. She simply smiled at everything I said, in a very friendly way, but she showed absolutely no interest in me.

Kurt Blase came to see his mother regularly. Now and then she sent him to check up on our room, and in doing so he once discovered the fine wires stretched across it.

Burgers had been given a cigarette packet by a colleague who was an enthusiastic radio amateur, and who had built a crystal receiver into it. However, to receive radio signals we needed some kind of antenna. We had stretched fine wires back and forth across the room for that purpose, and it worked: we could listen to news broadcasts from other countries, although we couldn't choose the transmitter precisely. And we were very keen to hear news from abroad, because we wanted to know the truth about the way the war was going.

The best time to listen to the radio was when an air-raid warning had sounded. Then, to quote Jule Neuke, 'those lying German newsreaders shut up' and the foreign transmitters could be heard loud and clear. I found it wonderfully exciting to hear the famous chimes of Big Ben over the radio from London. Once I also heard the voice of the German newsreader Walter Hertner, whose real surname was Herz, an actor who belonged to the Jewish Cultural League and had escaped to England. I had been a great fan of this actor before the war, and thought him extremely important.

My greatest radio experience, however, came one morning when there was an air-raid warning in broad daylight. I simply did not go down to the air-raid shelter, but sat in front of our crystal set. Suddenly I heard a distant voice: *Po Yerushalayim* (This is Jerusalem). I knocked on the wall above the receiver and cried, '*Chaverim* (comrades), I'm shut up here with an impossible Dutchman in an apartment full of bugs belonging to a Nazi woman called Blase! But I want to live! I'm fighting, I'm doing my best to survive! *Shalom, shalom!* Once again I heard a few scraps of Hebrew coming over the airwaves, but I couldn't make out whole sentences.

Of course Kurt understood the significance of those wires, and told his mother. There was another almighty row with Frau Blase, leading to angry words, threats, and finally reconciliation. We kept our radio.

In late autumn the weather turned damp and cold. When Frau Blase felt the stove in our room one day she realised that it was nice and hot, much hotter than hers. That was because, for one thing, we had a more modern stove, while the stoves in the other two rooms were practically antediluvian. They went right up to the ceiling and had kitschy stucco decoration, but only one opening for the fire, so that the fuel and the ashes mingled, and on account of their inadequate construction they never got really hot. For another thing, the fuel you could buy at the time was de-gassed and had very little heating power.

However, we ourselves were burning pre-war fuel, and it

happened like this. One of Gerrit's household tasks was to bring up coal. In doing so he had discovered many hundredweight of the very best pre-war coal with a black, greasy gleam stacked by the longer wall of Frau Blase's cellar. To this day I have no idea where all this fuel came from.

'This building is sure to be bombed sooner or later. Why let all that wonderful peacetime coal go to waste?' said the Dutchman.

'If you want to bring it up here so that we have a warm room, go ahead,' I told him. 'But I'm not taking someone else's property.' To me, it was a question of dignity; I didn't want to sink to the level of the German riff-raff. Burgers had fewer inhibitions.

Now Frau Blase told Kurt to find out whether, by any chance, we were burning her good pre-war coal. He asked us directly. 'This will make you laugh, Kurt; yes, we are,' said Burgers. 'Those stocks of coal will probably outlast your mother, so why should we freeze?'

'Ah,' said Kurt thoughtfully. 'And there am I shivering with cold at home.' He lived in Thaerstrasse in the Friedrichshain district, in a chilly apartment that couldn't be kept warm.

From then on we were in league over the peacetime coal question, and Kurt dropped in almost every day. Before going to see his mother, he knocked at the wall of my room from outside in the stairwell. I quietly opened the door, gave him the cellar key, he went downstairs, packed a briefcase full of coal, hid it somewhere or other, and only then did he ring the bell, visit his mother, and go away again with his loot. These regular visits greatly reinforced our friendship.

He liked me, and I liked him too. When he raised one eyebrow, as he often did, it always looked as if he were marvelling at something. And in fact he was, because he was learning the phenomenon of friendship for the first time in his life. Kurt never made remarks of any kind about National Socialism or about the Jews. Why he had become a Nazi and what he had thought about it I preferred not to ask. Thinking wasn't his strong point anyway.

Once Kurt Blase got a bonus of 200 or 250 marks for his

achievements at work. To him, that was a large sum. He told us that he wasn't going to let Trudchen know about it; he would do something for his own pleasure for once. Frau Blase was enthusiastic, and clapped her hands with glee; she hated her daughter-in-law like poison, and liked to think of Kurt going behind Trudchen's back. It turned out, opportunely, that he had gone on a little work-related trip to Frankfurt an der Oder, and on the journey had met two very nice girls. One was a nurse, the other an office worker. He had plucked up the courage to amuse himself with both girls and exchange addresses.

One of them had a birthday soon afterwards. He wanted to send her flowers, and went to some trouble to get them. His mother recommended him to get me to write a letter to send with them, perhaps in verse. I was happy to do that, and it impressed him greatly, particularly when the girl felt very flattered.

Kurt spent all the rest of his bonus meeting the two girls and inviting them to all kinds of harmless pleasures. Then he told me that, sad to say, he would have to break off contact with them, because the money had run out.

'Wouldn't you like to make real friends with one of them?' I asked.

'Get intimate, you mean? Nothing doing,' he said brusquely. 'If I get fun out of something, then judging by all I've known so far I'd be bound to ...' He didn't finish his sentence, began stammering, and finally collapsed on my breast in sobs. I had difficulty keeping a straight face, but I pulled myself together. So the two of us sat harmoniously united on the sofa. I put my arm round his neck to console him, and thought, with an echo of Goethe: *Happy is he who from the world can take his well-earned rest / without a grudge, while the SA is held against his breast,* simply changing the words *einen Freund* [a friend] to refer to the SA.

A few days later I had a very unpleasant experience. I was wearing a winter coat that didn't fit me properly, an ugly garment that I had inherited. I tried to make up for its shortcomings by belting it in round the waist. I also usually slipped my shoes on barefoot, since

I had no stockings. I would have needed clothing coupons to buy some, and I had none of those either. That day a woman stared at me in the street and then let fly. 'Ha, ha, ha – I never saw the likes of that before! Ever such an elegant coat –' she didn't mean that ironically – 'and no stockings!' She cocked a snook at me, and when I swiftly turned and walked away, feeling afraid of her, she followed that up with a torrent of abuse. Once again I felt unhappy with my decision to class myself with the poor, oppressed and exploited, or in Christian terminology those who labour and are heavy laden. I just didn't like the company.

'Wait a moment,' said Kurt, when I told him about this scene. He hurried off to his mother and came back a few minutes later, beaming, with her card of clothing coupons. 'I told Mother that I'd like to give those two ladies stockings, and if Trudchen knew she'd explode with rage.' He opened his wallet and gave me not only the card of clothing coupons but also money to buy stockings. I was truly moved. And Frau Blase was delighted about anything that was withheld from her daughter-in-law.

That also applied to the cigarettes that Trudchen chain-smoked. As neither Kurt nor Frau Blase smoked, she consumed their entire rations. It drove her mother-in-law to distraction. One day I heard her in the kitchen, coughing and making inarticulate sounds: at the age of seventy-eight, and after all the setbacks she had known, Frau Blase was smoking the first cigarette of her life. She hoped that she might yet become a smoker and thus use up her whole tobacco ration by herself.

4

In the winter of 1943–1944, Frau Blase fell severely ill. First she had a bad chill, then she caught a cough as well, and she stayed in bed all day. She did come into the kitchen to wash, she went to the toilet, and she also made herself something to eat. She didn't want me to look after her; she was well-disciplined and refused to spare herself, to the point of obstinacy.

But then her condition deteriorated. She ran a high temperature, wheezed as she breathed, was unsteady on her feet and had to hold on to the kitchen stove to keep from falling over. Several times I suggested fetching a doctor, although that was a near-impossibility, because most doctors were in the field with the armed forces. She refused. 'I can die without doctors, but I don't want to die and I'm not going to,' she announced.

One day, when I was busy in the kitchen, I heard cries for help. Of course the magic door was closed, but out of a presentiment that she might need someone she had left her bedroom door wide open, and in her feverish state, she had fallen out of bed and lost her sense of direction. With great difficulty I lifted her, put my arms round her and got her back into bed. I had never been in her bedroom before. Then I brought her a cup of tea.

She was over the worst of it now. Her temperature gradually came down, but she would never be really well again. Within a few weeks she seemed to age ten years. She was a case for nursing now, she had to lie down a great deal, and never came out of her bedroom before eleven in the morning again.

But the weaker Luise Blase was, the easier my own situation became: I was now solely responsible for the housekeeping, and I took the best care I could of the old lady, in need of nursing as she was. That way she could stay in her familiar surroundings and keep her independence.

*The Oberbaum bridge on a historic postcard. To the right of the picture, the
apartment block 1 to 3 Am Oberbaum. Number 2, the middle building, is where
Marie Jalowicz lived in Luise Blase's apartment from 1943 to 1945.*

She was deeply grateful to me for that, and so was Kurt. Now and
then she gave me one of those wonderful soaps or shampoos from her
cupboard; the mere perfume of them was a joy to me.

It was absurd: here was I, going into hiding with a Nazi blackmailer who lavished consumer goods on me, luxuries that even the
most privileged members of society could hardly hope for. When I
was alone in the kitchen in the morning, I would fill the wash tub
with water, put it over two gas rings and then manoeuvre it over to
two chairs placed opposite each other. Then I took a real hip bath,
splashing the water about and singing. Sometimes I felt so happy in
that apartment that I hardly know how to express it.

The situation with the Kochs was also rather easier now. Emil, who
by this time was over forty and extremely short sighted, had been
moved to another barracks, where they asked him what job he used
to do. He replied, as most people who were quick off the mark did
at the time, by saying that he had been a cook. He had no idea how
to prepare food, but his wife quickly taught him some of the basics.

From now on, Emil had access to considerable quantities of food. Hannchen made him a kind of wax-cloth vest to be worn under his clothes: an undergarment equipped with artificial kangaroo pouches. When, as was often the case, there was meat loaf or meatballs for the firefighters, she sacrificed their white bread coupons so that he could bulk out the minced meat to make it go further. He brought the stuff home by the kilo in those wax-cloth bags fitted to his body. He also regularly brought whole rye loaves back for us. I didn't have to listen to comments about the high price that a black-market loaf had cost me any more.

And now Hannchen Koch revealed to her husband what he had already worked out for himself anyway: I wasn't in Bulgaria, and my visit to that country had been a long time ago; I was back in Berlin. I had slept that one night in the Kochs' marital bed in their little wooden house in Kaulsdorf after my return. Emil Koch had found a hairpin of mine there, and made his own deductions.

One day, when I was sitting with Hannchen Koch in the Köpenick café, Emil suddenly came in. We greeted one another warmly, and after that we all three of us sometimes met there. He would buy me a glass of wartime beer and one or two cigarettes, but he never made me feel that I owed him eternal gratitude.

I was still getting pocket money of five marks a week from Hannchen Koch, and that did weigh on my mind. She earned less than a hundred marks a month, so it was really difficult for her to spare such a sum. And she went on telling me, at frequent intervals and in an affected tone of voice, 'I'm naturally given to self-sacrifice.'

I kept house as well as possible with the food available to us. No one starved, but our diet was often terribly monotonous, and short of vitamins. Frau Blase was all the happier with anything special that I could get hold of. For instance, you couldn't get salt and mustard on a ration card; you had to be known in the shop to buy such things, but I didn't want to be on very friendly terms with the shopkeepers in case they started asking me personal questions.

So I devised my own ways and means. Once, shopping in a

greengrocer's, I had been given fifty pfennigs too much change. I didn't notice until I got home; fifty pfennigs wasn't much, and money had no real purchasing power anyway. But I wanted to be honest, so I went back to the shop next day to return the money. The saleswoman was really touched to find that in wartime, when everything was so coarse and brutalised, there were still honourable people around.

Then I tried the same thing in several other shops. I would go in and say, 'I bought something here two weeks ago, and you gave me fifty pfennigs too much change. I haven't been around here again until today, but now I'd like to give it back.' The reaction was always one of pleasure and respect, and in that way, for instance, I came by three little packets of fruit paste off the ration, available only under the counter. Burgers was delighted, Frau Blase enchanted, and I gave Hannchen Koch the third packet.

Once I also went to the Rigaer Strasse indoor market in Friedrichshain. Frau Blase had once worked as a cleaner for a married couple who had a butcher's stall there. 'Look in on them and give them my regards,' she told me. To my surprise, after we had chatted for a little while she gave me a large ring of blood sausage for my landlady off the ration, and two small blood sausages 'for you and the Dutchman'.

I was taken aback. 'How do you know about me?' I asked.

'Well, it's obvious who you are. Kurt lives hereabouts, and he told me what a tough time you're having.' So people didn't keep themselves to themselves as much as I'd thought, but my luck held, and no one denounced me.

As usual when I had a message for Frau Blase, she was delighted to think that, as she put it, I'd been in touch with someone who knew her. In this cheerful mood, she told me that the butcher and his wife had always thought her very honest, but every time she went to work for them she had abstracted meat or sausage from the market stall under their very noses. That was her speciality.

You had to queue for a very long time, on average an hour, to make every purchase. For me it was twice that time, because for safety's sake I had registered the ration cards of Burgers and Frau Blase in different shops, in case some inquisitive shop assistant asked, 'Is your surname Burgers or Blase, and who's the other one?'

You were really supposed to enter your first name on the ration card as well, but I had put only an initial: G. Burgers.

'Shall I guess your name?' a salesgirl once asked me. 'Gerda!'

'Quite right!' I said, beaming at her. She filled in the name on the card, so from then on I was Gerda Burgers in that shop.

Waiting in line, I was quite often asked to change places temporarily when a couple of acquaintances wanted to talk to each other. That was how I got to know a pleasant woman who looked as if she were in her forties. This Frau Rose was telling her friend about her very old mother who needed nursing, and as the friend was very hard of hearing she had to raise her voice. So I learned that Frau Rose was always short of washing powder, because she had to re-bandage her mother's leg ulcers so often and change her sheets several times a day.

This was a case where I could be helpful. Frau Koch had given me a whole handful of crumpled coupons for wartime soap and washing powder. They came from customers at the laundry, and she should really have stuck them on their cards, but she didn't want the extra work. However, she couldn't exchange the coupons for anything, because it would have been obvious where they came from. So I went up to the woman in the queue, apologised politely for overhearing her conversation, and offered her soap coupons if she had anything to exchange for them.

'I have plenty of food rations, that's no problem,' she said. 'My mother hardly eats anything now. I can offer you bread coupons.' Then she told me her address, in a road off Stralauer Allee, and said that as a former dentist's receptionist she set great store by hygiene, adding, with a pause for effect, that she came from Tempelhof. I didn't know at once how I was supposed to react to this information, but then I made her a little bow, which turned out to be just the right thing: Tempelhof was a good residential area.

From then on I went to visit Frau Rose about every ten days. We exchanged coupons, and talked for a little while. I heard all about her mother's state of health on every occasion, and fortunately seldom had to say much myself. It was rather surprising, then, that one day, as she went to the door with me, she said, 'You know, I don't think our acquaintanceship can be called that any more; I'd say it's a friendship.'

We had so much bread available now that when Gerrit and I went to see the Neukes as usual every Saturday, we could take half a loaf with us as a present to our hosts. Finally, the Dutchman told me, 'You can cancel the order for bread.'

'What do you mean?' I asked.

'Tell your friend she doesn't need to give you bread any more. We have plenty.'

That remark showed that Burgers realised what a strain my relationship with Frau Koch had become. I wouldn't have credited him with such perspicacity.

It was extraordinarily interesting to listen to conversations in those long queues, where I learned a great deal about the political mood of the times. Once a discussion programme about Jews came yakking over the radio in a ground-floor apartment. A woman in the queue said, in quite a loud voice, 'As if we hadn't heard enough about that by now! They repeat it year after year. Goebbels said the Jews have all gone, so why don't they tell us when we'll be able to get smoked fish again and when the bombing will stop?' Everyone agreed with her.

On another occasion I heard two women talking about the Rosenstrasse demonstration of February 1943 by Aryans with Jews in their families, mainly women whose Jewish husbands and other relations had been interned in the Rosenstrasse community centre. That was over a year ago now. One woman said to another, 'Your cousin was there, wasn't she? Did you go too? What was it like?'

'Yes, I was there, and we called out, "Let our husbands go free!" They weren't going to shoot German women down there in the city centre, and finally they did let the men out.'

'Oh, I'm glad to hear that. If I'd known in time I'd have gone along too.'

'A lot of people did, just to show solidarity,' said her acquaintance.

But most of the women waiting in those long queues were complaining, for instance about the tiny amount of the fat ration, and the fact that everything else they really wanted to eat – especially fruit and vegetables – had disappeared from the shops. Even fully Aryan people in employment were undernourished. Well, I thought to myself, if you wanted to live normal lives, you shouldn't have elected Hitler and conjured up a war.

Once I spent four hours queuing in the freezing cold for horsemeat, which was a delicacy in wartime. The meat didn't come from tired old nags but from good horses that had died as the result of enemy action, and were now being sold for meat.

My legs already felt like lumps of ice, when a girl who had arrived long before me came out of the horse butcher's with her shopping and walked past the queue. Suddenly she stopped in front of me. She had recognised me, and I too now remembered seeing her from time to time in the synagogue yard. 'Hey, I know you! In the same boat, aren't we?' she said pertly. I unobtrusively nodded.

'So you're from a kosher household,' she went on, keeping her voice very low now, 'but all the same you're buying meat from the horse butcher?'

'Yes,' I said. 'I've decided that if you look at horsemeat in the right frame of mind it's strictly kosher.* And at this moment I'm the supreme rabbinical authority.' Then I had to laugh.

I was in luck that day. So much meat had been delivered that four times the normal amount of the meat ration on your card had been allotted. Instead of 500 grams of meat you got two kilos, and also marrowbones that made wonderful broth. Because the sale of the horsemeat had been announced in advance, I had three meat ration cards with me, from Frau Koch, from Burgers and from

---

*According to the religious dietary rules already laid down in the Torah, only meat from animals that are ruminants and have cloven hooves is kosher.

Frau Blase. They were all pleased and grateful, and praised me to the skies.

That wasn't the first time I had met people who, like me, had gone underground. When I saw someone in the street whom I knew from the old days, we usually made swift eye contact agreeing not to show it. Later I counted these meetings, and in all I had met twenty-two other people in the same situation as me.

The most important of them was Fritz Goldberg. He was the son of our former landlord's family in Landsberger Strasse, and was already over thirty. When we were lodging at his parents' house I didn't have much to do with him. However, when I ran into him at the Schlesisches Tor U-Bahn station, it was as if I were meeting a fellow countryman in the desert. From that moment on we were friends.

He was living with his fiancée Ruth Lachotzke in the back room of a dairy. At the time I had the impression that all Jews living illegally in Berlin were lodging in dairies. Fritz Goldberg was in touch with various small groups of those who had gone underground, and he told me where they met. At our very first meeting he asked me if I wouldn't like to belong to one of the fabulous barter exchanges.

'I don't have anything to barter or anything to sell,' I said, 'and I'd rather not be in touch with those circles. I'd be breaking all the rules of conspiracy.'

Fritz was aware of the danger. He knew the names of several Jewish informers such as Stella Goldschlag, called 'the blonde ghost', and Rolf Isaaksohn. He also told me about Ruth Danziger, daughter of the managers of Danziger's Diner. It was from him that I first heard the expression *Greifer*, literally 'gripper', for a police detective.

These informers frequented places where they could meet Jews who had gone to ground. Those who still had money might spend their evenings in such places as the State Opera House, and not a few of them were turned in at the end of the performance by informers waiting for them outside the entrance.

'Are you living near here?' Fritz Goldberg asked with interest.

'Yes, not far away,' I said.

'Where exactly?'

'Why do you want to know?'

I wasn't going to tell him. When we parted, I acted as if I were going the wrong way on purpose. I ostentatiously made for the building where in fact I really was living, but I gave him a conspiratorial grin; I wanted him to think that I was deceiving him and that was certainly not where I lived.

After that we crossed each other's path by chance now and then at the same U-Bahn station. If we had time we went for a walk in Treptower Park and sat on a bench there. As everyone was supposed to work, we had to be careful not to arouse suspicion. If someone passed we pretended to be lovers, leaned close together and smiled at each other. An old lady might give us a friendly nod.

Once, by chance, I went into the shop at the back of which he was living. As I was handing a new ration card over the counter to have it registered, the salesgirl pinched my hand. Only now did I recognise his fiancée, Ruth Lachotzke. I quickly withdrew the card, because I didn't want her to see the address, or the names Blase and Burgers. 'I just looked in to say hello,' I said, and left.

I knew that the relationship between the two of them was very difficult. Fritz clung to the girl because she gave him a sense of security. She was a blue-eyed blonde, as non-Jewish as you can imagine. But the two of them used to quarrel all night. Their mutual anger and hatred were enough to outweigh caution, and they stopped thinking about the neighbours. He said she was so demanding that she sent him crazy, always wanting him to get hold of butter somewhere instead of margarine.

As a forced labourer, Fritz had worked with the refuse collectors, and had a colleague among them who could indeed get hold of butter. But when he turned up at the refuse tip, the man warned him off. 'I know you,' he said. 'You're the one with the star. Better not come back here, there are Nazis around.' It was sheer madness that he did show his face there again, several times. Finally someone recognised the Jew who didn't wear a Jewish star in the yard, the Gestapo were called in, and that was the end of him.

Fritz Goldberg had literally sought his own death. I heard about it from Ruth Lachotzke. A few days after his arrest, I met her in the street during the midday break. 'They nabbed Fritz,' she told me. 'It's all very sad, but as far as I'm concerned they can torture him as long as they like.' Seeing the horror in my face, she went on, 'I'm sorry, I didn't mean it like that. Of course I cried my eyes out. All I mean is that he would never say that he was living with me, or where to find me.'

The loss of Fritz Goldberg as someone to talk to was very sad for me. He had given me important information, and I had been able to exchange ideas with him, as the only person I knew from my former world, about my situation and my fears and concerns.

Now I could only hold fast to the Jewish tradition. I don't know what will become of the Jews in the USA or Palestine, I said to myself, but I'm here, I'm a *minyan** in myself, I am all Israel and I'll do my duty. After that, I gave the park bench where Fritz and I often used to sit the name of Weissensee,† and for a long time I went there regularly to say the Kaddish. I wanted Fritz Goldberg to have a proper Jewish memorial.

Gerrit Burgers meant nothing to me really, yet he was gradually becoming a familiar figure in my life. If he wasn't in the middle of one of his fits of rage, he could be very pleasant, attentive and considerate.

We always had plenty to talk about. When he came home from work he told me what he had been doing, and on a day when there had been an air-raid warning we exchanged accounts of how and where we had spent the time.

Every day I bought the *Berliner Süden* newspaper, and Burgers brought the weekly *Das Reich* home. He took a great interest in politics, and had become something of an armchair strategist about

---

* In Jewish tradition, a *minyan* is the quorum of at least ten Jewish men required to hold divine service.
† One of the largest Jewish cemeteries in Europe is in Berlin-Weissensee.

the way the war was going. We had cut maps out of the newspapers. Gerrit marked out the fronts with pins, and we put our own interpretation on every new development. We read *Das Reich* aloud to each other and discussed what it said. He was well informed about geography, and could assess any piece of information at once. In addition he liked solving crossword puzzles, and was good at them; he could identify all the tributaries of any obscure African river, and all the operetta characters whose names consisted of four, five or eight letters. He had never heard the operettas themselves.

When the all clear sounded after an air-raid warning, Gerrit and I often went out into the streets. My thoughts were so graphic that I had to be careful not to say them out loud. So I developed my own ritual for the situation: while we saw the red firelight on the horizon, I sang in my head, to the tune of the Horst Wessel song, 'Qui sème le vent récolte la tempête' ['He Who Sows the Wind Shall Reap the Whirlwind'], a line that I had liked very much in my schooldays.

To me, these raids meant not defeat but victory. I'd have liked to tell the bombers, 'Keep going. This war could have been avoided, so let anyone who voted for Hitler feel the consequences.'

Now and then we also went to the cinema at the weekend, not of course to the palatial picture-houses of the west of Berlin, showing premières of films, but to the fleapits of Neukölln or the Görlitzer Bahnhof. When, towards the end of the war, Marika Rökk sang the sentimental song 'Im Leben geht alles vorüber' ['Everything Passes Over'], I thought: now they're really in a stew!

At that time, anyone who wanted could hear the language of slaves and the special kind of humour developed by people living under a dictatorship. I realised that one day when I was walking down Adalbertstrasse in Kreuzberg. I liked that street, with its enormous number of back yards; to me, it was the quintessence of a proletarian residential area.

On a blazing hot August day in 1944, I saw a few passers by gathering outside a small bakery there and laughing. I approached with caution, something always to be recommended on such occasions. A cake with the wording *Happy New Year* carefully piped on it in icing had been placed in the display window on this sweltering day in high summer. A cardboard notice beside it explained that this was the sample work produced by an apprentice hoping to qualify as a journeyman baker, and another notice explained tersely: 'Dummy'.

In the circumstances of the time, this amounted to a political statement – and an anti-war statement at that: no one could make a genuine cake topped with genuine icing sugar for want of the ingredients. It was, as expressly stated, a dummy or mock-up of a cake, and the comment suggested 'Happy New Year – in this heat?'

'Ooh, that's a good one, that is,' said an old lady. 'That's a real laugh.'

A few days later, I saw a crowd forming outside the same bakery again. A uniformed police officer broke it up and then went away. I stayed at a safe distance, and only afterwards did I go up to the shop and asked a woman coming out of it, 'What's been going on here?'

'The police wanted that cake and the two notices taken out of the window.'

'What's it to do with the police?'

'They said there were reasons, but they weren't allowed to discuss them because they could be misunderstood.'

Also in Adalbertstrasse, I saw another incident that made an even more lasting impression on me. A very long line of soldiers, like an army-worm, was winding its way along the street, singing. The repertory of its songs was always the same, and as so often the folksong 'Dark Brown Is the Hazel Nut' rang out. When I walked along beside a column on the march like that, I took great care not to keep time with the marching men, but it was difficult not to; the rhythm practically forced itself on you.

Suddenly I saw a decrepit old gentleman marching along beside the soldiers, doing the goose-step. He must once have been a singer, because he had a good voice and articulated the words very well. He wore a bowler hat, a red handkerchief peeked out of his coat pocket, and he was the kind of eccentric you don't often see at large.

This man was simulating the trumpet prelude to the Radetzky March in a very loud voice, and then he followed up the melody, in stentorian tones, by singing, 'So put your hand right up my arse, and I'll give you the Radetzky March.' Hundreds of soldiers stopped singing and laughed. And I marched along with them like a good girl, deliberately keeping time with the rhythm set by the old man singing his Radetzky March song.

I can't describe the fun of it all: the cacophony of the performance, discords from the idiotic song about the dark brown hazelnut mingling with the demand to 'put your hand right up my arse'. I loved the disharmony which, to me, expressed the essence of resistance.

I remembered the experience for a long time: the way a single decrepit old man, with a cord round his waist instead of a belt, had brought hundreds of soldiers to a halt, and nothing terrible had happened to him. I wondered: what might a properly organised resistance still do even now, when the war couldn't last much longer?

It's worth it, I thought. It's worth not marching in time. And it's been worth facing all the fear and unpleasantness. Because life is beautiful.

5

Our caretaker Grass was a gifted comic. And since the Nazis had no sense of humour – dictators never do – almost everything that could raise a good laugh was to do with resistance.

I was walking towards the Oberbaum bridge late one afternoon, a few steps behind Alexander Grass, when the local 'Golden Pheasant', as we called certain Nazi officials, came towards us. Grass suddenly began moving as if he had no backbone, raising his arm to the Golden Pheasant in the Hitler salute and at the same time, wriggling like an eel, bowing to him, while he came out with a verbal mishmash somewhere between 'Heil Hitler' and 'Good evening, sir!' The Golden Pheasant roared with laughter and, influenced by the power of suggestion, responded with equally idiotic jabbering. I laughed at that for a long time in retrospect.

It was a very good thing for me that Herr and Frau Grass were also in charge of the air-raid shelter in the cellar. With the aim of keeping everyone in uniform at a distance, Grass had even volunteered his services as assistant air-raid warden. There was not, in reality, any such post, or at least not officially. But he had made it clear to the real air-raid warden that people had to stick together in hard times, and he was therefore prepared to take full responsibility for the apartments at numbers 1 to 3 Am Oberbaum. He would make sure that everyone, including the old folk, got down to the cellar when the air-raid warning sounded. And after the all clear, he would check to see whether an incendiary bomb had fallen anywhere. He did all that just so that I could use the air-raid shelter safely. If a uniformed man did happen to look in, Grass was there at once, claiming all his attention and chatting away to him until he left again.

The inhabitants of all three buildings sat together in one large cellar that was the air-raid shelter. Many of them had brought their own chairs, others perched on the primitive benches that Herr Grass had made. Whenever the alarm went off, people brought their emergency kits with them. Stout Frau Grass stood in the middle of the room looking rather self-important as she showed everyone to their places; they all knew where to go anyway.

The young people sat together in a corner. Here we regularly met Grete Grass, the caretakers' daughter, who was an assistant in a food shop. Then there was a girl juggler who lodged in one of the buildings next to ours. She suffered from chronic conjunctivitis, and was being treated by the ophthalmologist Dr Martha Jun, who was well known as an anti-Fascist and a staunch opponent of the Nazis. The young performer told me once that she knew exactly who I was; an apprentice of the Kaufhold troupe in Zeuthen had told her about me. So there was a great deal of interested gossip, even though – or perhaps because – Frau Fiochi had tried to make a great secret of my origin. It is really astonishing that no one ever denounced me.

Another of the young people was Lotte, a prostitute who cheerfully admitted to her profession. I had a reliable protector in this vehement anti-Nazi. She would talk frankly and in the most ribald Berlin dialect about her work as a tart, using all the professional jargon of her trade. The average model would have been envious of Lotte's figure. Men called out *Beene wie Marlene*, after her, *legs like Marlene's*. But she had a huge conk of a nose, and jagged at that. It bent once sharply to the left and then sharply to the right. Lotte was always cracking jokes, and not just about her nose. Everyone roared, screeched, rolled in the aisles with laughter when she began talking. If I had a prize for brilliant comedy to award, I'd be hard put to it to decide between Alexander Grass and Lotte the whore. For a while I tried linking the two of them together in a double act, which I thought would be terrific, but it didn't work. They simply didn't interact with each other, and at the most exchanged banalities.

'Yours is really an excellent profession,' I once told Lotte, to show how much I liked her.

'But it wouldn't do for you if you survive,' she replied. 'I guess you'll study and get a "Doctor" in front of your name. That's your way, and mine is mine.'

Once, when I was climbing the stairs to our apartment, I heard a lot of noise in the attic. I was immediately terrified: was it the Gestapo? Nonsense, I told myself at once. If I were denounced they wouldn't be setting to work with hammers and pickaxes in the attic. But I had to persuade myself firmly of that to get my fear under control.

The same evening Alexander Grass told me what had in fact been going on up there: a gang of construction workers had been breaking through the thick firewalls between the separate buildings, so that people could get from one attic to another.

There had been similar openings in the cellar for a long time. If access to one cellar was blocked by rubble, then we would be able to get out into the open through another. Now our assistant air-raid warden had persuaded the man who was really responsible, the official air-raid warden, to do something like it in the attic storey. When he told us about their conversation, Burgers and I laughed out loud. 'You see, comrade, you have to think logically,' Grass had told the man. 'Where will people run to? If they've run down from upstairs to get away from the bombs, and then the bombs fall, they'll have to run up from downstairs again.' Grass had bombarded the air-raid warden with this nonsense at top speed, twisting and turning like an eel, until the man was worn down and agreed.

And our caretaker had done it especially for me. 'If the danger comes from downstairs, from the lowest riff-raff ever known, and that's the Nazis, you don't want to run down, you want to run up. Because there's usually one of them still standing outside the door. Then you can get into another building by way of the attics, and leave again in another street,' he explained. When I tried to thank him, he would have none of it. 'No need for you to thank anyone. On the contrary. What's been done to you and your people is monstrous. It's you we have to thank if we can help you.'

In the evening Lotte went fishing for customers in Altermann's bar in Mühlenstrasse just round the corner. I had to go there now and then myself. When Frau Blase was in a good temper she would hand me a green glass jug with a patent lid on it and send me to fetch draught beer from the cask. I didn't like the bar, or the wartime beer either. In addition I was afraid of losing control of myself if I drank alcohol; I wanted to be wide awake all the time with my mind clear. So I developed ways of quietly tipping the beer from the big jug down the kitchen sink without letting Frau Blase notice.

Once she asked me to give her regards to Altermann. 'Lads,' announced the landlord in a loud voice, 'any of you lot remember Full Bladder?'* A few old soaks who were drunk even in the afternoon explained to the others where the nickname came from. It was because she used to drink beer without stopping. There was much noisy shouting in the bar, and then one of the old soaks went from table to table, whispering something that had the drinkers in an uproar again.

Later, I learned what sensational news he had been spreading. Frau Blase often talked about the long and difficult time she had spent away from home, and how terribly sorry she had been for her dear children. It was some time before she admitted that she had been in a women's prison for a while, because she had been procuring prostitutes for Altermann, to improve her small pension and her earnings when she went out cleaning.

She had been found out only because she also tried to blackmail the elder of her two half-sisters, Klara Kalliwoda, whom she hated. Klara had risen to some prosperity working as a midwife in Wedding; she had scraped together the money, as we said in Berlin, by performing illegal abortions. When Frau Blase threatened to report her to the police if she didn't pay a certain sum, Klara Kalliwoda engaged a private detective. He quickly found out what criminal activities Luise Blase herself had been pursuing at Altermann's bar. And so in the end she was the one facing a judge.

Incidentally, Frau Blase spoke of her blackmail of her half-sister

---

*Blase is the German word for 'bladder'.

without the slightest moral scruples. She thought it no more than her right, while of course Klara, who had hired a detective to get Luise out of her way, was the nastiest creature in the world.

At first we laboriously took Frau Blase down to the cellar every time there was an air raid. But soon she said she wouldn't bother, because it was too much of a strain for her. That was a great relief for us. Burgers had enough to do getting our air raid kits down to the cellar, two cases in each hand, and I myself was busy taking old people's cases and helping them down the cellar stairs. There were hardly any able-bodied men in the building, and everyone agreed that the young lady (me) was so kind.

Once, when a bomb was dropped close to us, all the window panes broke. Burgers and I spent a whole Sunday standing out in the yard, in sunny weather, removing splinters from the frames, a horrible job. But the windows couldn't be reglazed unless all the splinters were gone. The old folk wanted to pay us for doing it, but luckily Burgers and I agreed that we weren't going to accept any money. Our neighbours were moved to tears to think that there were good-natured people around.

None of these neighbours of ours ever denounced me, but they were not opponents of the Nazis, let alone anti-Fascists in general. Some of them might well have reported an elderly man weighing 150 kilos who looked as they imagined a rich Jew would. I was never sure.

Once, when I came back from a long, refreshing walk, I found a strange woman in our kitchen. I disliked her at first sight. She was vulgar and primitive, dressed from head to foot in various shades of red. She was introduced to me as the new tenant of our empty room.

This woman, I discovered, wanted to be near her husband, an anti-aircraft gunner. One of those guns was mounted on a roof close to our building. I could see when the gunners had an approaching aircraft in their sights, and I felt like calling out to the British or American pilots, 'Go away, or they'll shoot you down.'

The woman had asked in all the surrounding buildings whether there was a room for rent anywhere. I hadn't come home yet when she rang our doorbell, and Frau Blase had been sitting in the kitchen. Feeling that she was asking an enormous amount, she had said she wanted five marks a day for the room. The woman, with peasant cunning, realised that she was talking to someone with no idea of present-day values. 'Rather expensive,' she said, 'but I can pay five marks.' Anywhere else many times that sum would have been demanded.

I was a thorn in her flesh from the first. She was a Nazi, suspicious by nature, and she had it in for me. Once again I wondered whether any tolerable situation that I had laboriously created for myself could last in the long run. But after a few days she appeared with her eyes red from weeping. 'I'm leaving, my husband is going to the front,' she said. And luckily that was the end of that.

'Mother Blase,' I said affectionately to our landlady, 'she was a harmless woman. But suppose you'd opened the door to a robber? The foreign workers around here are riff-raff, you're always saying so yourself! Someone like that could knock you over and rob you blind. You must never open the door again if I'm not here!'

Our landlady thanked me for the warning, and agreed that she had been lucky yet again. We decided on a way for Kurt to ring the bell showing that it was him. He reinforced her in her belief that she should take my warnings seriously. For all his love for his mother, Kurt was now loyal to both sides. He would never have done anything to hurt me.

Now and then Frau Blase received letters, although she never wrote to anyone. She couldn't, and not just because of her poor eyesight. For instance, on her birthday a card arrived from Anna Ziervogel, the little sister of Gerhard's fiancée, Gerhard being the son whom Frau Blase had loved so dearly and who had fallen at the front. The fiancée had obviously consoled herself with someone else in short order, and never got in touch again. Anna Ziervogel seemed very indignant about that, and even sent Luise Blase a poem that she had written herself.

In me, Frau Blase had someone who could reply to such letters, and so a lively correspondence developed between me and Anna Ziervogel. Of course I always replied on behalf of Luise Blase and signed the letters with her name. Once I even wrote a serious poem about the feelings and thoughts of an old woman. Anna liked it, and wanted to meet me – I mean the old lady – but she lived far away in Pomerania. Furthermore, she was a great admirer of the Führer and believed firmly in the Final Victory. As a farmer's daughter, she had no idea how dependent we were on our meagre rations of food in the city. So I sent her one of the wartime recipes that were good for nothing but making inadequate ingredients into barely edible dishes.

Soon after that a huge parcel full of the best cake arrived from Anna Ziervogel. Frau Blase was enchanted, not so much by the cake itself – she hardly ate anything these days – as by having it in her possession. Snatching things and owning them was in her nature, but so was giving them away, and she gave me half the parcel of cake.

I didn't touch it until Burgers came home, and then I let him taste it first. The cake was delicious, he said, but his wartime bread moistened with ersatz coffee and spread with sugar was even sweeter and just as nice.

After that I tried my first piece of cake, and I suddenly found myself in tears. 'What's the matter?' Gerrit asked me in surprise.

It was the only occasion in all this time that I had cried, and I was ashamed of myself. I hadn't even shed tears when my relations were taken away to the death camp. But now I couldn't keep back the tears.

'I'm crying for joy,' I said. That cake was a delicacy such as I couldn't have imagined any more. And that made me happy; once again, I suddenly felt how good life could be.

At first I meant to take Hannchen Koch a piece of the cake, but I wasn't going to see her until a few days later, and by that time it was almost finished. Perhaps it was better that she didn't know I had access to such luxuries. She was not free from envy; she wanted me to be poor, dependent and in need, so that she could caress and console me.

Frau Blase also told me a great deal about the time when she had been taken to the Virchow hospital because of her eye trouble. She described all her fellow patients and the nurses in detail. I felt a particular interest in one of them: a Frau Krause, obviously an inveterate communist who worked as a caretaker in Schöneberg.

When Frau Blase asked me to find out how this woman was now I was keen to meet her. It took me some time to find the entrance to her apartment, because the door was inside the gateway leading from the street to the yard of the building.

This would be a good place to hide, I thought. Then I rang the bell. No one answered it, but a few moments later a woman came across the yard, making for the door.

'Good day, I've come from Luise Blase and wanted to visit you and ask how you are,' I said. As soon as I said the name her face darkened.

'Thanks,' she said, 'but I don't have any time to spare. I have this huge building to look after.'

She was going to close the door in my face. 'Wait a moment,' I said hastily. 'I'm lodging with Frau Blase for a very particular reason, but I'd feel embarrassed for you to assume I share her political opinions, far from it!'

'Oh, come in, do. There's not really any such thing as having no time, you can always make some,' said the woman suddenly in very friendly tones. She led me into her kitchen, where I saw photographs of her husband and son, who had both fallen in the war. Once again I found myself sitting in a wicker chair, and then we had a long talk about politics.

'You're very trustworthy,' I said after a little while, 'so now I'll tell you my own story.' And once again I served up Trude's brilliant half-lie: I was partly Jewish, and had been in trouble because of that, so I had gone to ground in Frau Blase's apartment. The old woman clapped her hands happily when she heard that. She was happy as a child to think of that old Nazi Luise Blase helping someone who had gone underground. Then I plucked up my courage. 'If anything catastrophic happens,' I asked her, 'would you by any chance take me in here?' Frau Krause slapped her thighs enthusiastically with her fat little pat-a-cake hands. 'Why, yes! For a while, certainly, and then we'd find somewhere for you.'

Finally, she invited me to come and see her again soon. I went away in a good humour. In fact I felt so good that I caught myself hopping along on my way home. Grown-up people don't do things like that, I told myself severely. On the other hand, the Gestapo were hardly going to ask to see my papers just for hopping a few steps in the street.

6

I heard the first news of the events of 20 July 1944 from a foreign radio transmitter. I was standing by the crystal set on the wall of our room, and I got very excited. I kept close to the radio for hours, trying to find out more. But the foreign radio stations had only the same sparse information as German radio: there had been an attempted *coup d'état* by German officers, but they had not succeeded in assassinating Hitler.

At first the news depressed me deeply. For a moment liberation through the removal of Hitler had come so close, yet it had failed after all. Then I thought perhaps it was for the best. The officers planning the assassination had never blamed Hitler for starting the war; they blamed him now because he was losing it. They disliked him because he was vulgar and plebeian, and did not come from their own background of the old aristocracy and traditional army circles. They were not really anti-Fascists but conservative military men. I told myself that a successful attempt to end the war at five minutes to midnight would have been a lazy compromise. Germany must be entirely conquered, the Russians and the other Allies must march in, the Red Flag must fly over Berlin. When Burgers came home from work that evening we talked about it for a long time, and he saw it in exactly the same way as I did.

The only people with whom we could discuss such subjects openly were Jule and Trude Neuke. We were still visiting them every other week, and sometimes I was counting the days and the hours to our next meeting. Now our exchange of opinions was particularly important to me.

Without any forebodings and full of anticipation, I hurried up the steps of Number 13 Schönleinstrasse on the Saturday afternoon of our next visit. Julius opened the door in silence. Still silently, he steered us through the hall and into the kitchen. We waited in the doorway while he went over to the window, sat down on a chair, picked up a cobbler's anvil and hammered wildly away at a shoe. A warm summer wind was blowing in from outside.

Burgers and I looked at each other with a question in our eyes. Jule didn't say hello, he didn't ask us to sit down, he gave no explanation for his behaviour. His face had frozen in a kind of furious grimace. Only after a long, tormenting delay, during which we watched, baffled, as he worked away at the shoe on the cobbler's anvil, did he put his tool down and look at us. All he said was, 'Trude's been arrested.'*

It was like a bolt from the blue. There wasn't much to discuss, and Jule himself didn't know any details yet. What it meant to us was clear: we must keep away from Schönleinstrasse in the immediate future. Only after four to six weeks might Jule know more: whether their apartment was under observation, whether nearby buildings were being searched, and where Trude was. After that time Gerrit would go to see him alone to find out what he knew about the situation. Gerrit was not in as much danger as I, since he was in Berlin legally.

Later we discovered that Jule was not injured. Even when men came to arrest his wife they had treated him as if he wasn't there. 'Not you,' was all they had said to him. Trude had always told her group that she didn't want her husband to know anything about her political work. He couldn't stand the nervous strain of it, she had said, and in the end he would blame her for thinking of politics instead of making him Sunday lunch. Obviously the informer who finally denounced the group had believed what she said.

In the late autumn of 1944 we resumed our regular visits to Jule Neuke. He was in a wretched state, suffering from dreadful anxiety

---

* According to the charges brought by the Supreme Reich Prosecutor at the People's Court on 16 January 1945, Gertrud Neuke was arrested on 15 September 1944. It is possible that there may have been an earlier arrest, not mentioned in the records, or an arrest by the Gestapo before that date.

about his wife, from the responsibility for his two stepchildren, and the terrible pain of his leg ulcers. He was also in financial difficulty. There wasn't much that we could do for him except bring him half a loaf every time we visited.

Meanwhile the war went on. The newspapers were full of death notices, and I registered the different ways in which they were phrased. If the wording said that the son of a family had died 'for the Führer, the People and the Fatherland', then it was clear that Nazis had written it. But there were other notices, such as one from a family in Charlottenburg saying, 'The Lord God has taken our daughter from us.' The young woman had died in an air raid. The same death notice remembered a beloved maidservant who had been one of the family. Reading between the lines, you could tell that it contained a clear anti-Nazi statement, but phrased in such a way that the authorities could not take exception to it. I noticed the names and the family's address, and thought that if I were in need I would go to them. They would probably help me.

Luise Blase's two half-sisters, Klara Kalliwoda and Anna Zouplna, had also been bombed out. They both asked if they could stay in the apartment at Am Oberbaum – after years or even decades in which they had not been in touch with Frau Blase. The old woman got rid of them by saying that both her rooms were rented out, one to a foreign worker from the Netherlands and the other to a young woman.

One day, however, Kurt came to the door. The building where he lived had been completely destroyed. The whole family – father, mother and three children – were there in our kitchen needing new accommodation. And Trudchen was pregnant again. This time danger really did threaten; after all, Kurt knew that there was a vacant room in the apartment.

We immediately made eye contact with each other. He shook his head very slightly, and I responded almost imperceptibly myself: please don't, was the message. We both knew that if Frau Blase had to live with her detested daughter-in-law, who spent her time sitting on the coal-box smoking, the outcome would be disastrous. But it was likely that Trudchen would want to move into the Am Oberbaum apartment while the Dutch lodger was turned out to fend for himself. Burgers and I were already anxious enough over the rumour that foreign workers would no longer be allowed to live privately as lodgers, but should move into collective accommodation.

It was obviously difficult for Frau Blase to tell her son that she didn't have enough room for his whole family. But Kurt didn't mind. After that conversation he came to see me and ask me to write a letter to the Nazi Party, explaining that he had been bombed out, had many children, and was asking for preferential treatment in his application for another apartment. For the only time in my life, I signed off with the official 'Heil Hitler!' formula. And he did very soon get a new place to live, although once again it was freezing cold.

In spite of everything life went on, and even became almost a normal everyday round. I regularly visited Frau Rose and swapped soap coupons for bread coupons, and I met Hannchen Koch once a week. Burgers too had several acquaintances among his colleagues at work.

One of them was Erich Klahn. Soon after beginning to work where he was now employed, the Dutchman had made friends with him. Klahn was an anti-Nazi, and from the first had been particularly inclined to like Burgers, his only non-German colleague. They had soon found that they shared political opinions, and they trusted each other. That was how Burgers had also discovered that Klahn was a retired burglar. For years he had made his living by breaking into properties and stealing from them, and he had never been caught. Then he contracted severe stomach trouble, and now, after several operations, he could do only light, part-time work. That was the end of his career in burglary.

Because of his stomach trouble, Klahn could eat hardly anything. But he didn't want to take the sandwich he brought to work home again for fear of his wife's sharp tongue. So he often gave it to his

Dutch colleague, who was surprised and pleased. Burgers was always hungry.

Finally, Klahn was off work sick for a long time, and when he came back to collect his pay packet he told Burgers that he would like to meet me. He gave a curious reason: he wanted to learn how to solve equations with two unknown quantities, he said. Burgers had told him about me, boasting of my superior education.

Klahn suggested a bench in Treptower Park for our meeting, and when I arrived I was considerably taken aback. True, Burgers had always described Klahn in Dutch as 'the little man', but he hadn't told me that his friend was in fact a dwarf. He had a normal upper body and an intelligent face, but his lower limbs were tiny.

I was furious with Burgers for failing to warn me, but I quickly found a way to disguise my shock; I knew that there are *berakhot*, Hebrew blessings, to be spoken at the sight of a giant or a dwarf. I didn't know what they were, but I improvised with the usual introductory phrase of a Hebrew prayer, *Boruch atoh Adaunoi* – 'Praised be he' – and then went on, 'Praised be he who has made very small people.'

After that we got on very well. 'My friend Gerrit has hinted at funny things. He says you're not registered with the police; is there any special reason?' Klahn asked right at the start of our conversation. I gave him a vague, evasive answer.

'You know what they do to Jews, girl?' he asked, and then went on, 'They take them away to the East. And do you know what that means? It means murder.' He shook himself and repeated, 'Murder, yes!' At that I told him the entire half-truth; I was half Jewish, so I had had to go into hiding.

'Is the old woman, your landlady, happy about that?' he asked. And he immediately began thinking how he could help me. He was still in touch with men who had gone breaking and entering in his company, he said, but even in those circles you couldn't be sure you were safe from idiotic Nazi prejudices these days. So if I needed somewhere else to go, it would be better to say I had to disappear for a while because I'd been standing guard for a burglar breaking in somewhere.

Then, drawing in the sand with a stick, I taught him, as well as I could, how to solve equations with two unknown quantities. We met several more times in Treptower Park. The retired burglar turned out to be something of an intellectual; during his long stays in hospital he had read his way through whole libraries. It was clear to him that the Nazis made anti-Semitism the core of their ideology, and he had wondered: where does this hatred of the Jews come from? He had engaged the hospital doctors in conversation, borrowed books from their private libraries, and in that way acquired a good knowledge of theology and church history. He had come to the conclusion that the roots of anti-Semitism lay in Christianity.

Erich Klahn also told me a good deal about his life. His first marriage had been to a handsome woman of normal stature who ill-treated him shockingly. There was a son of this marriage, now grown-up and in prison. He too had been a professional criminal. He had joined a gang that specialised in breaking and entering, but also went in for robbery with violence. Klahn didn't like the latter at all. In a drunken state, his son's gang had once stormed a kiosk to get their hands on schnapps. When the police stepped in there had been an exchange of shots, a subject on which Klahn waxed morally indignant. As he saw it, breaking in was a legitimate way to acquire property, but he categorically rejected the use of violence. He hated the sight of blood, and almost fainted if he saw anyone even slightly injured. I had never imagined a criminal being so sensitive.

Klahn's second marriage was to a dwarf like himself, a brutish, dull-witted woman who hated her husband. As he kept wanting to meet me, I began to be afraid of the relationship's taking a form that would be very unwelcome to me. I was vulnerable to blackmail, and the idea that Klahn might become importunate was unbearable. In addition his Nazi wife could do me a great deal of damage if she found out the truth about me.

Burgers, usually very jealous, suspected nothing in this case. Cautiously, I had to make it clear to him that he ought not to force the relationship between me and his colleague at work to go any further. However, we did pay a visit to the Klahns, who lived near Görlitzer Station in a building with many back yards.

When we had climbed the stairs and were at their door, we heard a voice inside calling, 'Careful, we're opening the door!' Burgers knew the significance of this; one door opened outwards, and might easily have hit us on the head without that warning. Frau Klahn, who was even smaller than her husband, opened a second door to the inside of the apartment. She had a profile like a real witch, with a wry mouth and a malevolent expression on her face. Her life consisted entirely of cleaning and polishing the whole apartment to a high gloss.

We were taken into a dining room very much of the lower middle class, and we sat down. There was ersatz coffee, and a slice of bread spread with the usual almost inedible four-fruits jam available on the ration. I was relieved to find the hospitality here so meagre; no one was making sacrifices that called for gratitude.

When Klahn was talking, the Dutchman looked fixedly at me, with an expression on his face that said, 'Don't I have a fabulous friend?' When I was talking, he looked at Klahn in exactly the same way. His wife was getting angrier and angrier. I realised that this relationship really must be broken off as a matter of urgency; it was dangerous in the long run.

Later a neighbour joined us, a stout, common woman who wore a Nazi symbol on her summer coat. A terrible tug of war ensued. This neighbour wanted to fix a day to go picking berries in the Brandenburg Mark, and I was supposed to go with her. We would need a foraging permit to do that, and I knew why: deserters and Jews who were in hiding, people without ration cards, were correctly suspected of collecting wild berries and mushrooms to eat. Many foresters went hunting people who had no foraging permits, hoping to bring their beloved Führer the heads of those who had gone underground as trophies.

I defended myself with all my might against going on this exped-ition, explaining that I had no foraging permit and no money to buy one. Burgers failed to understand the situation and encouraged me. 'Oh, go on, it's not expensive, and it would be a nice outing for you! My God, it's so long since I ate blueberries! And as you know, people can pick huge cans of berries in a day.' I had no choice but to tread on his foot hard and painfully under the table, until at last he got the message.

Frau Blase spent all day listening to the radio, of course only the German stations that she received on a primitive People's Radio set. One of her enthusiasms was for the Romanian prime minister Ion Antonescu, who led one of the most ardently fascist of Hitler's satellites. I once gave her a picture of Marshal Antonescu from an illustrated magazine that had come my way as wrapping paper. She was delighted, and gazed admiringly at the portrait photo, without noticing that she was holding it the wrong way round. Then she put the picture on her bedside table, and gave me a lovely cake of French soap from her magic cupboard by way of thanks.

One day, in the autumn of 1944, she told me in blissful excitement, 'The final victory will soon come! The Führer is going to force a change in our fortunes; he's called up the Volkssturm.' Only instead of saying *Volkssturm*, she had understood the term to be *Volks-Turm*, and she also told me that each of the soldiers would be armed with a *Panzerfrau*, whereas she meant *Panzerfaust*, an anti-tank weapon that could fire a single shot.* Burgers and I amused ourselves hugely over this misunderstanding. Gerrit enjoyed broaching the subject again and again, and talking about the People's Tower and the armed woman.

But soon my laughter died away. One afternoon a strange sight met my eyes in the hall of the apartment. I had just come home, and had not switched the light on yet. Then I saw that Frau Blase had manoeuvred two legs of her folding table into the dimly lit hall; the other two legs of the table were still in the kitchen. The old woman

---

* *Translator's note*: The Volkssturm (People's Storm) was a territorial force set up by the Nazi Party. *Volks-Turm* means 'people's tower' while *Panzerfrau/faust* means 'armed woman/fist'.

was sitting at it, waiting for me. I realised that she wanted to tell me something. Still in my coat, I went up to her.

'Good evening, Mother Blase, what is it?' I asked, rather uneasily. She didn't reply, but I saw that she was crying. She had never before shed tears in front of me. She groped about on the table top with her right hand, until she found mine, took it and pressed it. 'Kurt has been called up to the Volks-Turm,' she said at last. 'Now I shall lose the last person, the last thing on earth that I've loved, and my own life is over. But it has to be done for the Führer.'

At that moment I felt respect for her, as she understood the consequences of a frame of mind for which otherwise I had not the slightest sympathy. I had never been able to see why this old woman, who knew nothing about history or politics, loved the Führer so much, and had closed her mind all her life to any decent way of thinking. But for that brief moment I did respect the attitude with which she was already mourning her son.

There was nothing to be discussed. I tried to encourage her with phrases about the darkest time coming before the dawn, and I used the word *Volks-Turm* as she did, so as not to make her feel silly. I asked when Kurt was going to be called up. Then she sobbed. 'He's just been here with his armband on.'

Kurt Blase fell fighting with the Volkssturm, as I learned only after the war.

7

After the beginning of February 1945, there was no more just staying in bed after an air-raid warning had sounded, turning over and comfortably going back to sleep. It had sometimes felt as if sitting in the icy cold for hours was worse for our health than being hit by a bomb. But all that had changed now.

These days, there was no subject of conversation but the war in the long queues at the shops, and I too was exhausted by constant lack of sleep, with my nerves on edge. I shared the fate of all the people of Berlin, yet at the same time I didn't share it. For unlike almost everyone else, I was not afraid of what was coming, I hoped for it. And that hope gave me strength.

One night when we were down in the cellar again, we heard a frightful crash overhead. Soon it was obvious that our building had been hit by a high-explosive bomb. However, we hadn't been buried. We had only to move a little rubble aside to get out into the open. The three buildings that comprised Am Oberbaum were still standing, but the façade that they all shared had been torn away and fallen to the ground. You could look into the separate floors like so many stage sets. The stairway was hanging askew, and one banister rail was missing.

Soon after the all clear the firefighters arrived, as well as paramedics and air-raid wardens. Frau Blase was retrieved from her bedroom. She was confused, but only slightly injured. Furniture had fallen over and scratched her face while she lay in bed. Frau Grass padded a wicker chair with sofa cushions for her. She was placed in it, had a couple of plasters applied, and that was that.

Alexander Grass came down the stairs weeping; his mother was dead. A wardrobe had fallen on her bed and a chair had flown through the air. In death, she was still clutching a chair leg in her hand. Grass's wife was about to make some silly, inappropriate remark when I interrupted her. 'Frau Grass, your mother-in-law is dead. Do please be kind to your husband. You can see how miserably sad he is.'*

'You're right,' she said, and she quietened down.

Burgers ventured to climb up to our bombed-out apartment once more to retrieve a few things. We had most of our stuff with us, in our air-raid emergency kits. I couldn't and didn't want to go up there myself. I was afraid of the climb. The desk – my desk – was partly hanging outside. I asked Burgers to bring my wax-cloth notebooks down for me, but he refused with obvious malice, laughing gleefully. That was his personal revenge on me, because he had always hated the desk and my reading and writing.

I regret the loss of those notebooks to this day, for they were an important record of my memories and observations. At the time, however, I thought: the war is nearly over. The main thing is to come out of it alive. Nothing else matters.

Even that morning, Burgers set off punctually for work, and he did so on the following days as well. We camped in the cellar, and I went out shopping from there, trying to provide for us somehow. It was still dark. The only light was from a naked electric bulb hanging from the cellar ceiling. Frau Blase spent day and night alike in her wicker chair, taking in very little, and hardly reacting to what anyone said. Her complexion had turned an unnatural raspberry hue, and she just said, now and then, 'Yes, yes, bombed out.'

What was going to happen to me now? I discussed it with Frau Koch when I met her in Köpenick one Thursday afternoon. The obvious thing to do seemed to be to join one of the bands of refugees trekking in from Silesia, Pomerania or East Prussia that

---

* Marie Simon cannot date the bombing of the building precisely from memory. However, the death of Friederike Grass is on record. Her funeral certificate runs: 'Salvaged from her destroyed apartment at 21.15 hours, on 9 March 1945.' The apartment building Number 2 Am Oberbaum was bombed that night. The destruction of the Stralauer Tor / Osthafen overhead railway station, which stood immediately opposite the building, is recorded on 10 March 1945.

kept arriving in Berlin that spring of 1945. I could have had myself registered as a refugee, and would then have had a right to accommodation, ration cards and work. But that wasn't what I wanted. I was afraid, for instance, that someone might ask me what street in Königsberg I had lived in. Or that some official might recognise me from the past. Frau Koch reduced it to a formula that I could accept at once, because it occurred to me at the same moment: don't go to the authorities if you haven't been summoned. That was just how I felt. I had gone underground, and I wanted to stay there until the end of the war.

One fine spring day, I suggested a walk to Lotte. I was still wearing my old winter coat, although I hated the sight of it by now. 'Listen,' Lotte told me, 'I'm getting a certificate saying I was bombed out. No one knows I saved my entire wardrobe.' The bathroom wall in her apartment had fallen in, but the contents of her wardrobe were indeed lying safely in the tub. None the less, she had a right to a whole new set of clothes.

She bravely climbed up inside the building, brought down her winter coat and gave it to me. It was brown fake fur, very good quality. While I was still trying on this fine coat, she picked up my old black one and threw it into the ruins, where it fell deep into a bomb crater. I laughed, although for a moment I'd felt cross: its fabric was so indestructible that I could still have made a skirt out of it.

'I've got an idea,' said Lotte. 'I know someone, a colleague of mine, we sit in Altermann's every evening' – another prostitute, she meant – 'a really nice person, she lives quite close.' This was when we were moving away from the cellar. An air-raid warden could come along at any time to check our papers.

Lotte's colleague and her two small daughters by unknown fathers were living in a street off Stralauer Allee. Her apartment had a large front room that she used solely for professional purposes. Lotte said that her friend could just as well work in her bedroom and rent Burgers and me the front room. Just in case her colleague objected to that idea, Lotte had another plan: she would send a man in the uniform of a postman, a soldier or a railwayman along to commandeer the room for us. Lotte knew plenty of men.

Late in the afternoon, when Burgers came back from work, the three of us went there. Our new landlady received us in the kitchen. On the stove, where a blazing fire was burning, stood a pan full of children's underwear or nappies. The lid of the pan rose again and again in a certain rhythm, and a brief glug-glug was heard. Then the soapsuds boiled over and the lid sank again. Lotte's friend never thought of moving the pan aside a little way to moderate the heat.

The woman agreed to take us in at once. I was still so young, silly and fond of adventure that I was a little sorry; it deprived me of the pleasure of seeing the room commandeered by a postman. I had imagined holding a whole company spellbound with that story some time after the war.

Lotte's colleague, a very nice and spotlessly clean young woman, had called both her little girls Veronika. She was so dim that no other name had occurred to her. And it was not forbidden to give several children the same name. When someone went to register a birth, no registrar was going to ask, 'Do you already have any other children of that name?'

I was almost asleep on my feet, but as soon as we were in our room, I said to Burgers, out of sheer curiosity, 'Those two children are sitting on their potties outside – do go and see whether she addresses them differently.' Burgers went out as if to do something in the hall, came back after a while and said, 'No, there's no difference at all. She calls them both Veronika.'

There were constant air-raid warnings by day now; you couldn't plan anything ahead. I was always relieved when Burgers came home safe and sound in the evening.

People described it as an inferno. I didn't call it that myself, of course, but it was not paradise either. The situation was chaotic, and I was afraid myself. The idea that I might yet perish in the war was terrible. When others complained of the present state of affairs to me, I civilly agreed with them. It was part of my masquerade. But little as I wanted to march in time with the columns of soldiers, I could not share the opinions of the population still hoping for the final victory. In my mind, I kept my distance.

Every night we found ourselves, sooner or later, in a large cellar that served as an air-raid shelter for several buildings. An especially strict air-raid warden often came round to check our papers. He was mainly interested in the men, since there was a truly hysterical search on for deserters. I inconspicuously slipped past him and managed to avoid showing my identity card.

After a few days our new lodging was also hit by a high-explosive bomb. Everything above us collapsed with an enormous noise. The cellar shook, but its ceiling stood up to the blast. Many of us were screaming. I ducked in fear and horror, and covered my eyes and ears.

Then calm returned again, and a kind of snowstorm began: the mighty shock of the explosion had loosened the whitewash from the walls. My eyes were inflamed for quite a long time from being in that vast cloud of dust.

'Bombed out!' several people who had lived in these buildings cried in horror. So far as they were concerned, their whole world had collapsed. I had only lost the part of the city where I had been living. 'We're buried alive!' was the next cry to go up. The entrance through which we had got into the cellar was blocked by rubble. Men in uniform picked up the tools ready for use if that happened, and began hacking another way out. Burgers helped them.

I sat calmly on my improvised bench and waited. Several old women were in tears. After about an hour there were shouts of, 'The way out is clear!' We left the cellar to find ourselves facing great mounds of rubble from which nothing could be salvaged, not a piece of furniture and no personal possessions.

Burgers looked at the time. It was early morning, when he usually went to work. As ever, he was aware of his duty. We stood in the road, discussing our situation. Even now we were talking nonsense.

'Right, listen,' said Burgers. 'This is what we'll do.' And that was the end of it; he had no idea what to say next. 'No,' I said, 'I have another suggestion.' But in fact I had no suggestion at all, and we went on talking like that for some time. We were baffled, and had no idea what to do next.

He looked at the time again, and seemed nervous and fidgety. 'I'll have to go now,' he said. 'I don't know whether there's any transport to use or if I'll have to go on foot. I must tell them at work that I've been bombed out, and then they'll find me a place in shared accommodation for foreign workers. We won't get another furnished room.'

And so we went our separate ways. 'Goodbye, the war will soon be over!' we told each other, adding, 'See you again after liberation.' It couldn't have been a less dramatic parting. If one of us had gone off to buy a loaf of bread, expecting to be back a few minutes later, it would have been just the same.

SIX

I didn't have to surrender
The War Is Over

1

I was amazed. I had expected the last, chaotic days of the war to be full of loud noise, but instead a curious, positively eerie silence reigned in Berlin.

I was also amazed to find how easy it was to get to Kaulsdorf.* Contrary to all expectation and my experience to date, there was a regular, fast suburban train line running to Wuhlheide.

After I had said goodbye to Burgers and walked through Berlin for a few hours, I had set off in search of the Kochs. I felt it would be apposite to see in the first days of liberation where I had spent my first night after going into hiding. This was the end of March 1945, and I wasn't to know that it would still be several weeks before the war finally came to an end.

As I walked along the footpath through the wood, I composed a few sentences in my head for Hannchen and Emil: I wanted to thank them for everything. I was going to say that it was they who had really helped and saved me, it was they, more than anyone, who had given me the courage to go underground, because they had shown me that there were people who would come to my aid. But I kept thinking that the tribute I was composing in my head was too long and too stilted, and I tried to devise ways of expressing myself more briefly and precisely, less pompously.

As I approached the little house that had once been my family's holiday home, several different voices spoke up inside me. I hope nothing's gone wrong, I hope the house hasn't been bombed or damaged and the Kochs are all right, said one voice. You're lying, another voice contradicted the first, you really hope the place is

---

*The actual place name of the area in which Number 13 Nitzwalder Strasse lies is Kaulsdorf Süd. Wuhlheide is a meadow and the nearest S-Bahn station.

in ruins with the Kochs buried under them, and then you'd stand there crying your eyes out, but so far as you're concerned that would be the end of it, and you wouldn't have to be grateful to anyone. But that's horrible of you, said the first voice, you have to hope the Kochs are all right, even if your relationship with them is difficult. And so it went on back and forth for quite some time. At a loss, I sat down on a tree stump.

Frau Koch looked terrible. She was worn out, utterly exhausted. She had her daily work in the laundry, she also had to look after her house and garden, her husband and her old parents. She was spending her nights in what was called a slit trench, not an air-raid shelter but an open trench in a zigzag shape dug out on a large meadow near the Kochs' house. It was open to the sky, and you sat in it on improvised wooden benches.

But I sensed that Hannchen Koch was not just exhausted, she was also angry and hostile. She was not a bit pleased to see me. 'My parents have been bombed out,' she told me, 'and now they're living here too.' In fact only her father was in the house. As it turned out later, he couldn't be said to have been bombed out. He simply hadn't known how to look after himself, and had made up the story about the bomb damage because his wife was mentally sick and in a state of total confusion. She had been going out on the streets stark naked in all seasons, and often couldn't find her way home again. Hannchen's father therefore broke a window pane that had been cracked for years, smashed some empty glasses and tipped the china cupboard over: that was the full extent of the 'bomb damage'. He hadn't broken the empty bottles on which he could get a deposit back, but stacked them carefully in a corner. It was an unintentionally comic spectacle staged by a desperate man.

As the old man was convinced of the merits of natural healing, after moving into Hannchen's house he had turned for advice to Professor Paul Vogler, director of the Naturopathic Hospital. He had come back from seeing him very disappointed: there was no herbal remedy to cure his wife's condition. Committing her to the

Wittenauer Heilanstalten* could no longer be avoided. The certificate to that effect was still lying on the table, and I read it too. It said, straight out, 'Frau Guthmann is completely demented.' Since then Adolf Guthmann had been regularly visiting his wife in the asylum, although the way to Reinickendorf was long and difficult.

Herr Guthmann was as unenthusiastic about my arrival as I was to see him there. He was a staunch Nazi, although he had always been too miserly to join the National Socialist Party, and he was also a very unlikeable character who was constantly afraid of not getting his due. From the first moment, when we shook hands with friendly smiles, there was a deep mutual antipathy between us.

He also thought it was only natural for his daughter to look after him, and often pointed out that he was, after all, living in his own daughter's house. Nazi bastard, I thought, this is really my house, and you've only Aryanised it.† I must confess that I was wrong there, and full of hate as I was I did him an injustice. I had to try very hard to stay humane, because survival means not sinking to the level of your enemies.

Of course the old man was an anti-Semite. That was part of his ideology. He told a story of how, as a child, he and some other boys had cut sticks to size, smeared them with birdlime to catch flies, and gone around the local farms praising the virtues of their fly-catching sticks, but he was the only one to express himself grammatically. A rich gentleman who looked like an entrepreneur or a businessman happened to pass by, praised his correct manner of

---

† Only when Marie Simon dictated these memoirs in 1998 did she find out that she had been wrong in thinking the Kochs had Aryanised her parents' property. Hermann and Marie Jalowicz had sold their summertime house to the Kochs in September 1938 for 6,400 Reichsmarks. The larger part of the purchase price was to pay off debts that Hermann and Betti Jalowicz owed to various relations of theirs. The sum corresponded to about the market value of the property at the time. Hermann Jalowicz received 500 Reichsmarks in cash for furnishings and household goods. In February 1940 the Kochs, probably with the help of Hermann Jalowicz, drew up a will naming Marie Jalowicz as their heir if they died without having children of their own. Marie Simon was surprised to inherit this legacy when Johanna Koch died in 1994.

speech and bought all his fly-catching sticks. 'He was a Jew,' growled Hannchen's father. He made a face, showed the same revulsion as old Frau Blase in her reaction to that word.

'So he wasn't nice to you?' I asked, pretending to innocence. The old man was surprised. 'What a question! And you an intelligent person at that! No, he wasn't just nice, he was charming. It was really moving.' There was no way to argue with the man.

A few days after my arrival in Kaulsdorf a telegram came from the hospital: sad to say, the patient Elisabeth Guthmann had died of heart failure. It was obvious to me that they didn't want to go on feeding someone incurably ill. I knew already that murder was committed in psychiatric hospitals, even after the end of the Nazis' 'euthanasia' operations.

It was 4 April 1945, my twenty-third birthday. Frau Koch was very ruffled. 'You'll understand that I can't give you a birthday present in these crazy circumstances,' she told me aggressively, adding, 'It's as much as I can do to wish you a happy birthday.'

'Of course I understand entirely. And many thanks for your birthday wishes,' I replied. She was in a terrible situation, and so was I.

The house was very crowded. There was just a small living room, with a door into the bedroom, as well as a verandah and a stuffy attic to be reached only by climbing a kind of chicken-house ladder. That was where I slept.

During the day I had to hide. I sat in a corner of the room that had once been my parents' bedroom as if nailed to the spot. I couldn't be seen from outside there, even if anyone had looked straight through the window. I was condemned to total inactivity, and could do nothing to occupy my time but read the books I found in a Biedermeier-style glass-fronted cupboard in that room. Frau Koch would probably have liked to slap my face. She was worked half to death, and exhausted. Going shopping meant hours of torture, now that permission had been given for people to use all the coupons on their ration cards. 'Buy what you like, as long as the supplies in the shops hold out,' we were told. Hoarding was the order of the day.

Sometimes I saw Hannchen Koch turn pale and hold on to a piece of furniture to keep herself from falling over. 'No, it's nothing,' she groaned when I ran to support her. I was ashamed of myself for being unable to help her, but I also thought it was not of the least significance to keep all the floors sparkling clean in these topsy-turvy circumstances. Even sand crunching underfoot wouldn't have bothered me.

There was no wood available either, and thus no coffins. None the less, Frau Koch had taken it into her head to give her mother a dignified burial. She went all over the district to see if she could find a coffin somewhere. 'Oh God, I'm so sorry about all this,' I said dutifully. 'If only I could help you by going on some of those trips myself.' But of course she could tell that, secretly, I was thinking: we are near the end of the most terrible war and the greatest murder of the Jews ever known in human history, and it is relatively unimportant whether a woman who has been mentally ill for decades is buried in a coffin or not. It seemed to me ridiculous for Hannchen Koch to be wearing herself out looking for one, cycling all over the place to see acquaintances of acquaintances, and now and then having to go into other people's shelters because the air-raid warnings kept sounding.

Once, we had potato dumplings and roast rabbit for Sunday lunch. That was a banquet by the standards of the time. Frau Koch had asked a neighbour to kill a rabbit for her. Her father, who hadn't really been looked after properly for years, fell on it avidly. He talked about almost nothing but food anyway. The potato dumplings were a good size, he said, although they ought really to be as big as babies' heads. In his greed he didn't use cutlery but ate with his bare hands, swallowing a dumpling to the accompaniment of disgusting sounds. Emil was sitting at the table too, showing proper table manners and making a few remarks in his kind, friendly way. At that Frau Koch, whose temper was no longer in a normal state, told her husband off, suddenly rose from the table and kissed her father on both cheeks.

I often thought that getting away from that place at last would be another kind of liberation. But I was dependent on the Kochs, so I sat on my chair and let Hannchen make poisonous comments: 'I only wish I could just sit about reading!'

'Hannchen, please try to understand me. What can I do about it?' I tried desperately to explain my situation to her. But she knew it herself. She simply no longer had her anger under control. I felt like an elephant compared to this delicate and utterly debilitated woman.

Only gradually did I come to see that something else was troubling Hannchen Koch: when the war ended, so would my dependence on her. The splendid role of resistance heroine that this shy woman from humble origins had been playing for years would be over. She would be tending her garden, like the neighbours to right and left of her, and she would live without the fear of air raids, but also without any prospect of exciting events.

At that time her wishes and dreams and mine, our thinking and feeling as a whole, were diametrically opposite. I longed for the liberation that she was bound to fear. That was why Frau Koch infuriated me, and that was why she couldn't stand my presence.

There was not only a slit trench in the large meadow opposite the Kochs' house – it used to belong jointly to a Jewish community who had equal interests in it – but also several huts for prisoners of war and women forced labourers.* Most of the prisoners were

---

*The land at Number 90 Kaulsdorfer Strasse belonged to Felix Walter, a Jew from Erkner. At first the 'administration' of it went to the German Reich, which then confiscated it. The camp erected on that land served first as a transit camp for German settlers from Volhynia, then as a camp for French prisoners of war. After 1942, over 1,000 prisoners of war and forced labourers, including many women and children, were accommodated here and had to work for German Railways. In the winter of 1943–1944, the camp was destroyed in an air raid, but then partly rebuilt. After the end of the war it served as a point of assembly for prisoners, forced labourers and foreign workers of various nationalities before they were repatriated. Today there is an exhibition by the Marzahn-Hellendorf Museum on the spot, recording the history of the camp.

Ukrainians, and they must have suffered much mistreatment. Their screams could be heard again and again, but most of the neighbours preferred not to notice. I had personal experience of the way they organised this failure to hear anything.

A hit song that was often played on the radio at the time ran 'My Sweetheart Takes Me Sailing on a Sunday', sung by a woman who had a good soprano voice but lisped badly. One day the windows of the nearby houses were all open to let in the early spring air, and that song rang out of living rooms from all sides. Then, however, the screams of the tortured inmates of the prison camp were also heard – and all the windows closed at the same time as if by previous agreement. No one's sweetheart wanted to take her sailing on a Sunday any more. Those were the same people who claimed, later, not to have known any of what was going on.

Long before I arrived in Kaulsdorf, however, Emil Koch had been talking to the guards stationed at the fence of the camp. He had pointed to an old Ukrainian with a large moustache and said, 'That old boy looks as if he could chop wood well. Can you send him over to me some time? I'm a German, I don't have to do it for myself.' And he had given the man on guard a couple of cigarettes. So the Ukrainian, whose name was Timofei, came over to the Kochs' house. He didn't speak a word of German, but they communicated somehow or other. Emil saw that he limped, and his face was distorted by pain. The Kochs got him to lie down on the sofa, took his shirt off, saw the bloody weals on his body, cooled them and gave him something to eat.

From then on Emil often gave meatballs to the guard by the camp fence; Hannchen made them from the minced meat mixture that he smuggled home from his work with the fire brigade in the wax-cloth pouches of his vest. In exchange, the guard let him have the Ukrainian, allegedly to chop wood. Timofei was so grateful that he could be prevented only with difficulty from kneeling down to kiss the Kochs' feet. He kissed the hands of everyone in the house.

Two Polish women, Krystyna and Halina, also visited us regularly.

They were forced labourers, and must have felt it was a miracle; they knew Germans only as slave-drivers, but here were friendly people who welcomed them warmly, gave them food and drink and respected them as human beings. Sometimes a French prisoner of war called Legret came visiting as well, and on occasion all four were invited at the same time. It was very cramped in the Kochs' little living room then.

Naturally I was present at such times myself; I was part of the household, and helped to pour the ersatz coffee while Hannchen Koch served potato cakes.

One day Krystyna, who came from Krakow and had studied at a conservatory there, went over to the piano – the instrument that had come from my parents' apartment. 'You piano play?' asked Frau Koch, in the way one addresses foreigners. 'You "Chopsticks" know?' Krystyna blushed. No, she didn't know 'Chopsticks' and didn't want to. Instead she played Mozart's A major piano sonata. Our eyes met, and then I quickly looked away, because I didn't want to put anyone to shame. But for a brief moment I had felt the strong bond that exists between people of culturally similar backgrounds.

What future, however, was there for poor Frau Koch, overworked and worn almost to a skeleton? She, the resistance heroine now entertaining international guests, was to go back to the wallflower existence that had once been hers.

Unfortunately, Hannchen Koch had an irrationally great and, as I saw it, totally disproportionate fear of bombs, and insisted on our going, every evening, to the bunker used as an air-raid centre in the next village but one. We couldn't occupy the slit trench together while I was hiding in her house. With a scarf pulled well down over her eyes she set off with me, always taking care to avoid going close to houses where fanatical Nazis lived.

It was several kilometres to this bunker, and we were always in a hurry because first she had to wash the dishes, mop the floor and go round with a duster. I could have slapped her for this pedantic good housekeeping. By the time we finally left the house she was panting with exhaustion. I had to drag her along behind me, hauling and half carrying her.

The bunker had two separate entrances, but she insisted on our marching in together through the same one. Luckily, the checks at the entrance were only perfunctory; no one looked hard at my identity card with the faked photo and the other card certified by the postman, or it would have been obvious that the details given in the two identity cards were the same apart from the altered date of birth.

The whole thing was an attempt at combined murder and suicide, since Hannchen Koch didn't want her days of heroism to come to an end. And I thought: she is cancelling out all the fine things she's done for me. It was much the same when she invited Else Pohl for a cup of ersatz coffee. That was in the last days of the war, when the approaching sound of battle had become our constant background music.

Hannchen never usually asked women friends in; she didn't have any. She was only on distant terms with her neighbours and her colleagues at work. Emil, however, had a few acquaintances, including Richard Pohl, Else's husband, whom he had known since his schooldays. Else was mad about the paranormal. She devoured books on astrology, black magic and psychology, and just like Hannchen Koch had a love of anything mysterious, irrational and not subject to the dictates of reason. But she was also an avid Nazi, so you had to be careful if she came into your house. And now Hannchen Koch was inviting this of all women into hers.

'I'll just go into the cellar and read a book,' was my suggestion for the duration of her visit. But for some senseless reason or other this simple solution was rejected. Hannchen had another plan; she banished me to a place only a little way from the small coffee table in the living room. The bedroom contained two beds that could be folded up lengthways, with a cleverly designed surrounding structure of my mother's devising that acted to take lights and a bedside table. I was to get behind the curtain beside the beds, and make sure it didn't bulge out by flattening myself against the mattresses. Hannchen insisted on leaving the connecting door between the bedroom and living room open, alleging that closed doors aroused suspicion.

Else Pohl made it clear at the beginning of her visit that she was surprised by the invitation: people really had other things on their minds just now, she said, but since Hannchen Koch had asked her so nicely she thought she'd just look in. I was about three metres away, behind the curtain, hardly daring to breathe and forbidden to clear my throat, which of course made me want to cough. The conversation between the two women was about almost nothing. Frau Koch kept saying how nice it was for the two of them to be sitting there together. Her guest made several attempts to leave, but was persuaded to stay a little longer. The whole thing was staged to torment me. I stood behind the curtain, cursing to myself: silly cow, silly cow, silly cow.

On another occasion Frau Koch had to busy herself at the smoking stove, stirring up the fire with twigs to make soup. There was no gas now. As she did so she sang, unmusically and out of tune, the line from the former Austrian national anthem, now adopted by Germany, 'Gott erhalte Franz den Kaiser' ['God save Emperor Franz']. She couldn't remember any more of it, but then she began lamenting the downfall of her fatherland. This uncompromising anti-Fascist fighter who had sacrificed herself to her beliefs for twelve years was not her usual self at all.

Emil understood that and apologised to me for his wife; he forgave her everything and loved her with all her eccentricities. He himself had another problem. Before the Nazis came to power he had been a fireman, and he hoped to go back to that job after liberation. But he would have to choose the right moment to jettison his present uniform. Naturally he didn't want to be taken prisoner by the Russians in a barracks under the command of German police. However, he mustn't make his move so early that he might yet be reported to the field police or the Gestapo as a deserter. At just the right time he must cycle home, burn his uniform, find some old clothes to put on and then, limping a little, hope to pass muster as an old civilian. He did it, too.

A kind of no-man's-land period of time began. The camps on the big meadow began breaking up. One day the camp guards had simply gone away. The inmates could have walked out, but they didn't know where to go.

Then Emil said he had seen the marks of tank tracks in a woodland clearing. One tank must have arrived ahead of the others, although the Soviet army had not really reached the suburbs of Berlin yet. Emil told me where the place was, beside a small birch tree. I went there, found the tracks – and was greatly moved. I sat down calmly on the woodland floor and thought: this is a place where everything changes. This is where hope turns to confidence.

I was very glad, but not stupidly cheerful or foolish. Saying goodbye to hope was sad, too. Hope had kept me going for years. Now fulfilment of that hope lay ahead. What would it bring me?

When the war reached its very last stage, there were air-raid warnings almost continuously. I no longer hid from the neighbours. We didn't go away to the bunker but lay in the slit trenches. I often sat there on one of the rough-and-ready benches for hours. My bones hurt. Frau Koch clung to me, and people talked a lot of stupid nonsense. In a rather foolish way, I was annoyed to see the war ending in so tediously banal a way, and finding that I was not part of the turmoil of battle.

And then the moment came. Someone said, 'It's over. The Russians are here. We'd better come out.'* They all clambered out of the trenches with their hands up. I raised mine only slightly, because I was thinking: I didn't have to surrender. I stood formally by the side of the defeated, but my feelings were with the victors.

The Russian who faced me first was a picture-book example,

---

*The Soviet armed forces arrived in Kaulsdorf/Mahlsdorf on 22 April 1945. The forced labour camp at 90 Kaulsdorfer Strasse was liberated by Soviet soldiers on 23 April.

a pock-marked Mongolian. I embraced him and thanked him in German for liberating us. This simple solder looked rather shocked. And I admitted to myself that I had been putting on a theatrical performance.

I was free, the war was over, the Red Army had won. I would have liked to weep for joy and relief, but I felt no emotion at all.

2

The Polish women from the camp stormed through all the houses, breaking china and snatching up anything they could take with them. A pack of them was ransacking our house – but Krystyna and Halina suddenly appeared, stood protectively in front of Frau Koch, and quickly spoke to their countrywomen in loud voices: resistance fighters lived here, they said, people who had done good for years to Poles as well as others, and their house should be spared.

It was like a witches' sabbath. One of the women pulled Halina's hair, another struck Krystyna in the face with both hands. I saw all this as if from a great distance, like a spectacle that was nothing to do with me.

Then the Soviet soldiers came into the houses. A gigantically tall and corpulent man perched one of Frau Koch's ridiculous little hats on his head, put on the tasteless, showy plush jacket that she had made for herself and went away in it. That struck me as immensely funny. But her father howled 'Thieves!' out loud like a child, his mouth wide open. You bloody Nazi, I thought, you and your like voted for Hitler, you backed him when he started this war, you obeyed when you were told to hold out. And now you get upset about a silly little hat. But of course I kept my mouth shut.

Another soldier stormed into the cellar where old Guthmann did a trade breeding laboratory animals. He had trained as a purse maker, he later worked as a coal merchant and a park keeper, and now he supplemented his pension by selling white mice to the Charité hospital. He delivered the mice he had bred once a week.

I was standing by the open cellar door when the Russian saw all the cages and immediately opened them. With solemn gravity, raising his hands as if in blessing, he kept repeating the word *Ozvobožhdenie* in a singsong voice, as if conjuring up a spirit. It meant 'liberation', and he was performing what seemed like a childish magical act. Then he began liberating the preserved fruits from the many jars on shelves along the cellar walls. He kept solemnly saying, '*Ozvoboždenie*', as he smashed jar after jar. The mice rolling round in cherry and strawberry compote were dyed red, and I could hardly contain my laughter. But Hannchen's father was howling and shouting out loud. I felt like smashing my fist into his face.

The bad part was that the Soviet soldiers also rampaged through the houses raping women. Naturally I was among them. I slept in the attic, where I was visited that night by a sturdy, friendly character called Ivan Dedoborez. I didn't mind too much. Afterwards he wrote a note in pencil and left it on my door: this was his fiancée in here, it said, and everyone else was to leave her alone. In fact after that no one else did pester me.

I heard from the floor below hysterical screaming and screeching: they had got to Frau Koch as well. Looking out of the window a little later, I saw a tall, slender and dazzlingly handsome man of Mediterranean appearance leaving the house. This Soviet soldier was clearly high-ranking, probably even an officer.

That single, involuntary act of sexual intercourse had consequences, as it turned out weeks later. For decades Hannchen Koch had done her utmost to get pregnant, and now it had happened with that Russian.

Perhaps part of the strange state of mind in which Hannchen Koch found herself just after the war was due to her hormones. She was obsessed for a while with the idea that she ought to take food to the Kochs' neighbour, the worst and most dangerous Nazi in the whole area. After all, she reasoned, he must now be in terror of pursuit and punishment. In her crazed condition, she started making light conversation with this wholesale butcher on such subjects as the weather.

'Oh, save your breath,' said Emil, when she was talking to him about it. 'You're out of your mind. Those people have threatened and tormented us for twelve years. They've committed terrible crimes.'

'But our Saviour ...' objected Hannchen. Then he simply picked her up and carried her into the bedroom. 'Now, you lie down on the bed and discuss it with your Saviour. I'm sure he'll agree with me.' And he closed the door behind him.

After a few days news began coming in from the liberated concentration camps. We heard the first numbers of the monstrous murders committed there. That brought even Hannchen to see sense, and she reverted to being the reliably anti-Fascist woman she had always been at heart.

She clung to me in a way that troubled me very much. Once, when we were both in the kitchen, she dug the nails of all her five fingers into my flimsy summer dress. 'Oh, do let go, don't tear the clothes off me! I don't have a spare set!' I cried.

'You're my child. Promise you'll never leave me, promise you'll always stay with me and not push me back into the misery I came from,' she begged.

'Of course,' I replied as calmly as possible. I couldn't say no to her, but I felt terrible, because I was making a promise that I had absolutely no intention of keeping.

Our liberators also came to our houses to get the white bands they wore inside their collars like cravats washed and ironed. It struck me that while I didn't mind performing that service, did it well, and ought to regard it as a small way of thanking the Red Army for its great sacrifice in the fight against the most bloodthirsty regime of all time, I had not expected liberation to take exactly that form. After all, those who were really guilty could do such lowly tasks, I thought.

Some of the men were very helpful, touchingly kind to children, and showed respect for the old. One fair-haired Russian who came to us to get his neckwear laundered particularly impressed me. He could speak a little broken German, and was intelligent and forthcoming; he came from Moscow, and in civil life was a chauffeur. I tried to tell him that I was very glad of the Red Army's victory. He shook his head and said, 'Nix good. Gitler kaput – Stalin *toshe* (also) kaput – democracy good.'

Once, as I was walking through Kaulsdorf, I was picked up from the road along with several other people. The Russians handed each of us a rake, took us to a clearing in the wood and told us to rake it. I was furious: couldn't I wear a notice round my neck saying that I was not one of the conquered Germans? All the others went on pointlessly raking the woodland floor for hours. I just propped my rake against a tree as soon as the Russian supervisor turned round and went away. If I'd been caught, I would have said I had to answer a call of nature. But no one was watching me, and that was the Russian way of doing things; if I didn't get the work done, someone else would be told to do it instead.

I don't know who got on my nerves most, Frau Koch or her father. The hierarchy in the household was as follows: she was at the top, with her husband as her assistant. The two of them formed a pair. Then came her father, and I brought up the rear. Adolf Guthmann and I also comprised a couple, and had joint tasks to perform. For instance, we were sent off with a damask tablecloth to offer it to farmers in the east of the Brandenburg Mark in exchange for a sack of potatoes. We set out very early, since we had to go about twenty kilometres along woodland paths. I was afraid that horrible old man might make improper advances to me on the way, and preserved a civil but cold and uninviting distance. But he left me alone.

However, on meeting acquaintances as we were still close to our own village, he shouted right across the road, 'Saved her!' He struck his chest with his fist, pointed his forefinger at himself and then at me. Since the people he was addressing had no idea what he meant, he added, pointing to me again, 'This is a Jewish girl. I saved her and I've been hiding her.' I found it a great effort not to punch this repulsive creature in the mouth.

We were supposed to share another job. Frau Koch had a kind of washing machine, although it didn't run on electricity. It was a large, drum-shaped boiler that you put over the heat, turning a crank to keep the laundry on the move as it simmered inside, and it was very hard work. I had offered to do the laundry on a washboard instead, but Frau Koch didn't like that idea. It was a very hot day when the old man and I had to keep twenty or thirty kilos of wet laundry on the move, turning the crank all the time. After sharing that torment together, we felt far less hostile to each other. We took over from one another every few minutes and ended up dripping wet all over.

Soon the forced labourers were sent away. The Polish girls and women marched out of Kaulsdorf in a wide column. The procession passed the Kochs' property. I was surprised to see how many Poles had been held in that camp.

Earlier, there had been a warm farewell from Halina and Krystyna. But now Frau Koch staged a highly embarrassing scene. The long column was just turning the corner of the road. We had been waving to it, and our two Polish friends had kept turning to wave back. Now Frau Koch, just a few seconds too late, pretended to faint away. She cried, 'Never forget Germany,' and with a little sigh let herself drop to the ground, closing her eyes. However, I could see that she was peering out from under her eyelids so that she could take in her surroundings and all that went on around her.

Emil impressed me greatly at that moment. He had seen exactly what was going on, but in a serious and very masculine style he gave me a glance that told me not to laugh. He was sorry for his wife, but couldn't quite keep a note of irony out of his voice as he said, 'Oh God, Hannchen's fallen down in a faint. Now we'll have to get her indoors. I'll take her head, you take her legs.' And so we carried her into the house.

The hunger was hard to bear. At first there were no ration cards at all for the three suburbs of Biesdorf, Kaulsdorf and Mahlsdorf. Because the word *Dorf* means village, and there was still a kind of village centre in each with a church and a few fields nearby, the Soviet administration initially assumed that they were self-sufficient and could provide their own food. It was only after a couple of months that a German of Russian descent, a committed communist from Kaulsdorf, managed to explain the situation, and at last we got ration coupons.

The Soviet soldiers were enormously amused to see the people of Kaulsdorf eating spinach and rhubarb, which was all that grew in their gardens early in the summer. They were unacquainted with those plants, and thought they were not food for human beings but animal fodder. On the other hand, they confiscated everything that anyone tried to hide. The wholesale butcher next door, for instance, had stored large amounts of processed meat and sausage in a small, walled-up enclosure. A soldier stormed into his cellar with an axe and broke it open. I felt as if he had marched from the Urals straight to that hidden supply of food. It was all taken away in a truck. The Russians went through the gardens with long sticks, and unearthed several buried crates containing valuables or uniforms.

After the inmates of the camps had left, local people rushed in to see if there were any provisions left. Emil Koch brought home two drawers, one full of flour, the other containing a yellowish powder which Frau Koch made into a strong, sharp-tasting roux without any fat. As Emil then found out, it was a wartime blancmange powder of poor quality. We were half-starved, so we ate the roux as a sauce with the tiny agaric mushrooms that grew in the fields. They were not a poisonous species, but not really nice to eat either. I munched dandelion leaves and ate the tiny apples, no larger than marbles, that fell from the tree in early summer. 'You're eating all my fruit crop,' said Frau Koch venomously. We were both under great strain.

Some people did starve to death in those first post-war months. Emil kept us alive. When the Russians set up an improvised bakery nearby, he immediately volunteered to help as an assistant baker, and he was rewarded for his hard work with a loaf of dark brown bread.

Diarrhoea was rife. Half-starved people couldn't really afford to suffer from it, but old Guthmann and I both contracted the infection. It lasted only a few days, and in normal circumstances could have been cured by a couple of pills. But I had to go to the toilet every five minutes, and that primitive character Guthmann came beating on the door with both fists. 'Tell that foreign girl to come out at once, this is my shithouse.' I took to spending most of the day in the woods, equipped with rhubarb leaves, which made excellent toilet paper.

I was nothing but skin and bone, and so thin that I felt I was floating rather than walking, as if I weighed nothing and the wind was blowing me forward. I had a great need to sleep. Once I was shocked to find that I didn't wake up in my attic room until the sun was high in the sky. I had no watch, didn't know how late it was and hastily climbed down the henhouse ladder. Old Guthmann was standing at the bottom of it, mocking me as a lazybones. It was humiliating.

I told Emil about his rudeness, and from then on Emil climbed up to me every morning and woke me at a time when I wouldn't meet the old man.

Early one morning, I was in my attic when I heard a horribly familiar voice calling, 'Frauke!' from the garden fence. I hadn't expected ever to see Burgers again in my life. I had never told him Hannchen Koch's name or where she lived, and in the Blase household she was referred to simply as my friend. But he must have searched my handbag, found the identity card, noticed the name Johanna Koch, and discovered her address.

'Emil, get a pitchfork and throw him out,' I called crossly down from my attic. 'That's the man I was living with, and he gave me a black eye more than once.' But immediately I felt ashamed. This is no way to behave, I told myself, I want to be back in civilisation.

'Well, he won't be giving you a black eye now, not after liberation,' replied Emil calmly. 'And that's no way to say goodbye to someone you lived with for nearly two years. There must have been good times, too.'

'You're right,' I said in a small voice, and climbed down the ladder. Burgers was standing there in the suit he had been wearing when I first met him, with his crazy wide-brimmed hat and the briefcase slung round him, knocking at his chest with every step he took. He looked at me with large, sad eyes.

'Sorry I sounded so cross,' I said. 'I'm under a lot of strain. Let's talk for a few moments.'

He told me that he was living in shared accommodation hardly an hour's walk from Kaulsdorf, and said that the Dutchmen were about to go home very soon.

'Go to where he's living and you can say goodbye at your leisure,' Emil advised me. We set off and sat down in the woods together. I hadn't expected what came next, but it was heart-warming, and very nice. 'Come to Holland with me,' Gerrit asked.

'No, I want to stay here in my home …' I began, and then corrected myself; I didn't really want to claim Germany as my homeland. 'I want to stay in Berlin where I was born. I may still have some acquaintances here, and I know the language. But I'd like to thank you for all you did for me.'

We talked for at least an hour, and felt that there was a bond between us. He wept, and I wanted to shed at least a tear for him, but I couldn't manage it. As a souvenir he gave me a little metal box with footballers in relief on it.

'It's not nice to be laughed at,' I said, 'and it's hard to bear it when other people are triumphant. Don't tell anyone back in the Netherlands that I didn't want to come with you. Just say you don't know my name and address, I got caught up in all the confusion of wartime, and I can't get in touch with you because you never thought of giving me your home address.'

'You're right,' he replied. 'That's what I'll do.'

Then he said something that I'd never have thought possible. 'You must get away from those Kochs,' he said. 'It must be terrible for you.'

'What makes you think that?' I asked. 'She's the friend who gave me her papers.' I enumerated all that Frau Koch had done for me.

'And whenever you came home with food, you talked like a schoolgirl,' Burgers remembered. 'It was as if you were reciting a poem you'd learned by heart, saying what good people your friends were. But all the same it must have been unbearable for you.'

So I told him how I felt bound to Hannchen Koch by my promise, and said that I couldn't just abandon someone who had acted as she did. He offered to help me, saying he would tell the Kochs that I was going to Holland with him, and then I could go to other acquaintances. 'I can't do that,' I said. 'I want to stay here; I'm not emigrating to Australia. I'd be bound to cross their path sooner or later.'

It was some time, after all, before the column of Dutchmen set off to march home. Gerrit and I met two or three times more and went walking together. In the end we said a warm goodbye, and wished one another luck with genuine goodwill.

I took every opportunity to get out of the house and do something useful, so I thought of gathering rabbit food. I went out with a large bag; I could go for a nice, long walk, and be praised when I came back with dandelion leaves to feed the rabbits. One day, unfortunately, the rabbits were all stolen – everyone would steal from anyone else at the time. But after a few days Emil bought some new young rabbits, and I could go back to collecting food for them.

Once, when I was doing that, I came upon several groups of Frenchmen sitting at the side of the meadow. They were assembling here for the imminent trek back to France, and they were busy throwing their German money on bonfires: at home, the notes wouldn't be worth anything.* Jokingly, they called out something to me in French. They probably didn't expect me to understand it, because I was barefoot and looked like any simple farmer's daughter. Wouldn't I like to lift my skirt, they asked, collect the money in it and take the notes away before they burned them?

They were surprised when I shook my head and replied with something amusing in French. They repeated their offer a couple of

---

*After 1943 the German Reichsmark was worthless on the international foreign exchange market, and could not be converted to any other currency.

Johanna (Hannchen) Koch, who lent Marie Jalowicz her identity for three years, c.1945.

times, but I decided I would rather go on filling my bag with rabbit food than lift the hem of my skirt. So I watched the banknotes, which would have been legal currency in Germany for some years yet, go up in flames.

Later I was very cross with myself for not taking the money. At the time a bread roll or a cube of margarine cost hundreds at black-market prices. Only a few months earlier, when I was still living underground, such a decision would have put me in mortal danger. But looking on the positive side, those times were over.

Hannchen Koch had always wanted a baby, and now, for the first and only time in her life, she was pregnant by that one act of sexual intercourse with a Russian. Many women of child-bearing age soon felt the same consequences.

In our neighbourhood there was a practising doctor by the name of Hering, and the residents all went to her. This doctor, an ardent supporter of Nazi principles, was of course a passionate opponent of abortion. But now she was carrying them out as if on a conveyor belt: German women must not bear children by the enemy – such was the ideology.

The doctor performed these operations two days a week, with a younger male colleague as her assistant. Afterwards, the women were taken home by their husbands in padded handcarts.

Frau Koch applied to her when the necessity became obvious. On the morning when Emil took his wife to the doctor, I knew that this would not be a good day for me. I must be at Emil Koch's disposal – and I hoped to God for the last time. For in spite of the friendship between us, he identified me with the Russians whom I loved as my liberators. I must pay for what they had done to his wife.

It wasn't the first time. The relationship between Frau Koch and my father, many years ago, had been extraordinarily hard on Emil. And I had already paid for it then. He was the first, when I was still going to school and my mother was alive. I thought it was horrible. He had always proved to be humane, totally anti-Fascist and faithful to us, but I had paid the price, and I secretly hated him for that.

None the less, Emil was much more normal than his wife, and he was a decent human being. When it was over, he asked, 'Why did we do that? I felt as though we had to, but it was no fun for me, and I don't suppose it was for you either.'

'That's the way life sometimes goes,' was all I said.

3

Emil Koch heard a good deal that wasn't in the newspapers from his acquaintances, and they in turn heard more from theirs. People who worked as truck drivers or canteen waitresses quickly learned what was going on among the higher functionaries and in the administrative departments. And so, once the Americans and British had moved into Berlin at the beginning of July, Emil found out that the municipal authority had set up a new translation service and needed people to work for it. He suggested that I should apply. Well, I couldn't go on picking rabbit food for ever.

There was a bus running from our suburbs to the city centre now, although I had to walk for a long way through the woods to reach the bus stop. The buses themselves were crammed full, with people hanging from them like bunches of grapes. I let several buses pass before I ventured to board one and make the journey; after all, I didn't want to risk my life at this late stage.

I was pretty well exhausted when I finally reached the city council buildings. The translation service's office was near Klosterstrasse. I was seen by a British or American lieutenant. As it turned out, he was a German Jew who had emigrated at the last moment.

He was just finishing his breakfast, and had a half-empty cup of coffee in front of him – real coffee, made from coffee beans – as well as a plate of sliced bread. I had to bend my head so as not to show that my mouth was watering. It was white bread, white as snow, the kind I hadn't seen for ages, buttered and even with another spread on top of the butter: an unimaginable delicacy.

We spoke a bit of French together first, but when he changed to English I dried up. I was so hungry that everything was going black in front of my eyes. At that moment a maid put her head round the door and asked if she could clear away now. With a nasty grin he tipped the contents of an over-full ashtray on the remains of his beautiful breakfast and said, 'Yes, take it away, I've had enough.' I could have screamed and slapped this officious character's face on both cheeks. A man who acts like that, I thought, should be tried in an international Jewish people's court and given a severe sentence.

Smiling unpleasantly, he helped me out with the English word that I hadn't been able to find. 'So you speak a little French but hardly any English,' he said, adding in a very superior tone of voice, 'And if my idea of you is correct, you can't touch-type either; I guess you use two fingers.'

'You guess right,' I said. But ultimately none of that mattered to him. I was to start at once, and I was paid at once too. I was to sit at a typewriter in a large room typing out French and English texts. My colleagues were two or three young girls who had been to language school. They talked and giggled the whole time, and said that as we were all getting on so well, shouldn't we call each other *du*? 'No,' I said rather brusquely. 'I won't be staying long.' I couldn't simply fraternise so easily with these girls, or whatever the equivalent is with sisters, not when they might have been members of the League of German Girls only a few months ago.

When they took out their sandwiches they asked where mine were. I replied brusquely again, hoping to get them to call me by the formal pronoun *Sie*.

'But mothers always send one to work with something to eat!' said one of them.

'I don't have parents any more. I'm entirely on my own,' I explained. They looked at me sadly, shocked.

I arrived late on every one of the few days I spent working there. I got up very early, but then I had to wait ages for a bus that wasn't overcrowded with passengers. I typed very slowly and made a great many typing mistakes. I could see for myself that my work was a dead loss for my employers, who were throwing money away. So I soon went back to the lieutenant and asked to end our agreement.

However, I had been earning pretty well, and at last I could repay the Kochs some money. I didn't tell them that I had given in my notice. I went on starting out early in the morning, and then lay down in the woods to sleep for another hour or so. Then I went into the city centre. I desperately wanted to find out which of my friends and acquaintances were still alive, and how I could find my way back into a normal, legal life. I was particularly interested to know whether the university still existed and if you could enrol there again.

Once, before the bus began running again, I had gone on foot to the city centre. Then I had taken the U-Bahn, or the part of the line from Alexanderplatz towards Pankow that came back into service in May 1945. My first visit was to be to my uncle Karl Jalowicz. I wanted to find out whether he had survived as soon as I could.

Even from a distance I saw that his house at Number 2 Berliner Strasse was still standing. I raced excitedly up the steps. And then I saw him in the doorway: Karl was just saying goodbye to a woman patient who had had a dental appointment with him. Although he had had to use improvised methods, he had reopened his practice immediately after the end of the war.

'Mariechen!' he cried when he saw me, with delight such as I'd never known in anyone before. Not only was his whole face beaming, the whole stairway seemed to be brightly lit all of a sudden. It was wonderful.

I was also anxious to register myself as soon as possible with the Jewish Community at Number 8 Oranienburger Strasse.* On the way there I met Mirjam Grunwald at the Alexanderplatz U-Bahn station. My former classmate – the one who had borrowed Eva Deutschkron's husband – had also survived. She had jaundice, she was yellow in the face, and I felt terribly sorry for her. The hope of seeing her mother again had kept her going all those difficult

---

* The questionnaire that Marie Jalowicz filled in there when registering herself on 23 July 1945 is preserved in the archives of the New Synagogue Berlin Foundation – Centrum Judaicum.

years. And then the first news to reach her from the United States was that her mother had just died. After we had exchanged a few friendly words, Mirjam smiled her familiar bitter-sweet smile and said, 'You're still the same as ever.'

'What do you mean?' I asked.

'Untidy, untidy, a strand of your hair has come loose,' she said reprovingly, tugging it. 'If I had a pair of scissors I'd cut it off.' I made haste to say goodbye.

Only a little way further on, the next person I met was Edith Rödelsheimer. The musicologist with whom I had done forced labour at the Siemens works was coming towards me in Münzstrasse. When she saw me she simply dropped her handbag in the road. We hugged joyfully. Edith and her husband had been hiding in a summerhouse belonging to non-Jewish friends. She told me that during the week, when the owners of the allotment garden and its summerhouse weren't there, they hardly dared to move, and they couldn't cook anything for fear of steaming up the window panes on the inside.

A villa belonging to the most powerful Nazi in this residential area was in the immediate vicinity of the summerhouse. Sometimes they had seen people going into and out of the house late in the evening or early in the morning, and feared that they were under observation. Only at the end of the war did they discover that half a dozen Jews who had gone underground were living in the supposed Nazi's villa. These Jews, in their turn, were terrified of the people hiding in the summerhouse.

Feeling very excited, I soon went to Kreuzberg to find out what had happened to Trude Neuke and her family. When I turned into Schönleinstrasse, I breathed a sigh of relief. There were no gaps in the row of buildings. I ran up the steps to the door of the Neukes' apartment, but there I had a terrible shock. I leaned against the wall, weak at the knees. The Neukes' familiar oval porcelain nameplate was gone, and there was someone else's name on the door.

I could only ring the Steinbecks' bell. Trude's former neighbour

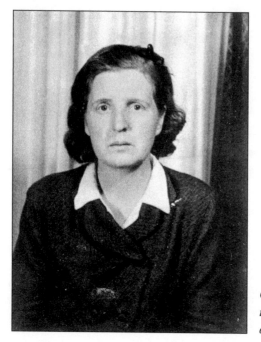

Gertrud (Trude) Neuke, aged thirty-eight, in the summer of 1945.

opened the door. 'Hello. I'm glad to see you haven't been bombed out,' I said politely. 'Can you tell me what's happened to the Neukes?'

'She came back. They're in the grandest part of Kreuzberg now, they're living in Urbanstrasse,' she replied in unfriendly tones. That was the way such people thought: in the old days the Neukes had been at the bottom of the heap and the Steinbecks at the top of it, and now it was the other way round.

I hurried to the address that Frau Steinbeck had given me. Even on the stairs I could hear Trude's voice. 'No, no, not pink! You can't wear a pink blouse with such a pale grey. It's a pretty two-piece suit, a strong, sunny yellow would be just the thing!' She was standing in her front hall saying goodbye to a neighbour. Before she could close her door I called, 'Leave it open, Trude, it's me!' And then we were in each other's arms. That really was a great, wonderful moment.

There were huge expanses of parquet flooring in Trude's new apartment, all polished to a shine. The familiar old pieces of furniture looked rather lost in these spacious rooms, as if a bird had left a few droppings around – here the desk, there a sofa. 'And here,' she announced, after we had seen round the front of this grand apartment, 'are my children's rooms.'

When I saw her again, a little later, she was already saying, 'I must have been out of my mind. I've been toiling like a slave, keeping those floors polished. What are we to do with a great big riding stable like that? We need light, air and sunshine.' The Neukes soon moved house again, and they went on moving at frequent intervals to the end of their days.

My best friend Irene Scherhey and her mother had also survived, and were still living in Prenzlauer Allee. After our first joy at our reunion, however, Irene was something of a disappointment: we couldn't establish the old, close connection between us again.

Irene had always been hyper-nervous. She talked very fast, kept interrupting herself, and wouldn't let anyone else get a word in edgeways. After the end of the war she had worked for a few weeks as an assistant teacher. Then she got a job with the Americans, and soon became attached to a GI. From then on she would speak only American English so as to practise the language, which infuriated me. 'Can't we talk in German?' I asked her several times. After all these years, there was so much that I'd have liked to discuss with her. But she only smiled and replied in English. Irene was crazy about all things American, and her heart was set on emigrating.

Soon after the end of the war, a delegation from Hannchen Koch's laundry went to see her to make her an offer. The managing director of the laundry, a man called Birkholz, had been a Nazi and was to be dismissed. Frau Koch was known to be a campaigning anti-Fascist and a reliable member of the laundry staff, and the delegation had picked her as his successor.

I was sitting in the next room when the endless discussion took place, and I couldn't help hearing it all. Hannchen Koch didn't want to accept. 'I want some peace at last, I want to recover and be a housewife,' she kept saying. When the delegation had gone, I tackled her on the subject. 'Hannchen, I think you're taking the wrong path.' And I added, as a joke, 'You may yet be Minister of Laundries.' Then she broke down in floods of tears, and this time they were genuine. 'I don't want all that any more, I don't want a job or a career. I want to bottle fruit and have a good sleep,' she sobbed. 'I want to get my strength back, and I want to do some nice needlework in bright colours.' At that moment I felt so sorry for her that I was really moved.

The managing director of the laundry had been one of my father's clients, and he was not an anti-Semite. He had worn the Party badge only because his career meant he had to. It was he who had provided the hundred marks of travel money that I had kept in my shoe on the way to Bulgaria, the money that had made it possible for me to return to Berlin. Later, through Hannchen Koch, he asked me to certify in writing that he had helped me. I made out a testimonial for a W. Birkholz, and Hannchen added his address.

Later on I heard from Trude Neuke, who was now living in a little terraced house in Britz. 'Who'd have thought it? There's a fellow who was once a really dangerous SS man called Birkholz living just round the corner from here. A Jewish woman actually gave him a testimonial saying that he had helped her in the war. And the bastard was denazified.' That man was also called W. Birkholz, but he had a different first name; he was Werner instead of Walter, or the other way around. And he had come by his denazification dishonestly, through his brother or cousin – in fact, the man who really had once helped me.

I once went back to the building where I had lived for almost two years. The Czech greengrocers who had been our neighbours were still lodging in the first-floor apartment, which had suffered least from the bomb dropped in the air raid. Frau Knížek told me that Kurt Blase and Alexander Grass had died fighting with the Volkssturm territorials at the very end of the war, and that Frau Grass had suffered a stroke and was now in a care home in Mariendorf.

I was particularly upset by the news of Alexander Grass's death. He had done so much for me! And at last the hard shell that I had

grown round my feelings broke apart. In a terrible kind of simpli-
fication, I had had only friends or enemies over the last few years.
The great danger, and thus the general criterion by which I judged,
had been the Gestapo. I hadn't minded who died or lived in the war.
At last I understood how much undeserved suffering the war had
brought to non-Jews and Jews alike.

It was Emil Koch who finally put an end to my difficult situation
in Kaulsdorf. He had made friends with a couple of physicists,
husband and wife, who lived in a rather better residential district
on the Müggelsee, Berlin's largest lake. He had probably been going
round there offering his services as a handyman or a gardener; he
went all over the place looking for work at this time. Anyway, he
discussed the awkward state of affairs in his little wooden house with
this couple.

From now on his constant refrain was 'The physicists said' this,
that or the other. The physicists had also looked at Adolf Guthmann's allegedly bombed-out house, which heartily amused them.
They and Emil made a plan together: first *Vadder* must have his
house put in order, and then *Vadder* needed a new wife. Emil already
had his eye on someone.

There were some Romanian refugees camping unofficially on
the attractive meadow outside our door. He had been looking for
a woman among them who was the right age for his father-in-law.
She was to cook for him, live with him and share his pension. From
a distance, he showed me the woman recommended to him. She
wore long, colourful, full skirts that looked like part of a national
costume. He introduced her to his father-in-law and the two of
them lived together for the rest of their lives.

Emil also knew about my promise to his wife. With the help of
the physicists, he devised a way to get me out of it. One evening,
when I was standing in the kitchen doorway, he began giving me
directions from where he was in the garden. 'We're going to do
something amusing. You go a little way to the right and then walk
forward.' After that he took a run up, lifted me from the ground

311

and whirled me round in a circle. 'And now I'm throwing you out,' he said, laughing.

Then we went for a little walk together. 'That was only a joke, of course,' he explained. 'But I'm the head of this household, and if I throw you out I'm the higher authority and you don't have to keep your promise. Of course you can take all the time in the world over leaving.' I was secretly jubilant. 'I'll go off tomorrow and look for a place of my own,' I told him, although he was sceptical about my chances.

When we came back, he told Hannchen, 'I've thrown Mariechen out, and now the two of us can have some peace and quiet again.' His wife reacted surprisingly sensibly. All she said was, 'That's all right. Things have to go back to normal some time.'

4

The house where I had grown up was no longer standing; 19a Prenz-lauer Strasse had been razed to the ground. So where was I to go? I knew that Pankow was one of the few parts of Berlin that were still largely intact. Not many bombs had fallen there. While the streets and pavements in other districts were still covered with rubble, you could walk round Pankow for a long time without even noticing that a war had been going on. Furthermore, it was the home of my only living relation, Uncle Karl.

So I set out on the journey to Pankow next day. The housing office for that district occupied a single large room, where the clerks sat at several large tables. Among them, to my surprise, I saw Tati Kupke, my aunt Mia's sister. She was considered an anti-Fascist who had proved her worth, and so although she had really been a manual worker in the past she was co-opted into this improvised office. We were both very glad to see each other again. At this moment, what had happened between her husband Willi and me when Tati gave me shelter for a few nights didn't matter. It was three years ago; she didn't mention it, and nor did I.

'I'd like to move to Pankow,' I told her. 'There are no apartments in Berlin itself, and Uncle Karl at least lives here.'

'I'm afraid there's a rule that you can only claim residence where you used to live before,' she told me. She fell silent for a moment. We were not alone in the room. Then she went on, 'But of course that applies to you.' And in a whisper she told me the name of the only street in Pankow that had been mainly destroyed, and the numbers of the buildings in it. I would have to give one of those addresses to get a permit to see apartments to let in Pankow. No one would be able to check whether I had ever really lived there.

Then she went to find her boss and ask him to let me have the permit at once. I was from Pankow, she told him, I was Jewish, I had gone into hiding to survive the war, and had been bombed out.

'I badly need peace and quiet,' I added. 'I don't just want a room, I want an apartment of my own.'

'Out of the question,' said Tati's boss. 'You're a nice girl, young lady, and you are certainly a victim of Fascism. But there are whole families who can't get anything but emergency accommodation here – just a single room, furnished or unfurnished.'

'Even if it's only a stable or a shed, I want to be on my own,' I repeated desperately. These words struck a chord of some kind in the man. 'How sad,' he murmured, and repeated several times, 'A stable or a shed.'

'Don't you at least have something the matter with your lungs? Do you suffer from tuberculosis?' he asked me.

'Not that I know of,' I said regretfully.

In the end it turned out that Tati couldn't offer anyone an apartment anyway. But she gave me a number of permits to view accommodation that I could show to prospective landlords, and I set off with those.

I went through all the addresses, and they were all useless. They included, for instance, a room with a wall badly damaged by a shell. It had a hole half a metre wide above the bed. The landlady was delighted when I turned up. 'I sleep on the other side of this hole,' she said, 'so now we can say good morning and good night every day. I get very lonely, you see.' Then she hurried round to the other side of the hole in the wall and called, 'Cuckoo!' through it. She obviously didn't have all her marbles.

'No, that won't do,' I said firmly. 'I need a room with its walls intact.' To get out of this difficulty I said untruthfully, 'My boyfriend would be practising the trumpet here.' I had trouble shaking the woman off, and had to be impolite to get away from her.

By the end of that very hot day, I was exhausted. The sun was already low in the sky, and I had only one viewing permit left, for a room in Binzstrasse. I went there and rang the bell, but no one came to the door. Through a ground-floor window, however,

I could see a man sitting down and shaving himself. Later I found out that his name was Levy. He was a Catholic, but he had Jewish forebears.

'You can ring until Easter and Whitsun fall on the same day, she's stone deaf,' he told me. 'What do you want with the old lady?' I showed him the viewing permit and told my story.

'Maybe you'd better ask Rühle the architect. He has his office right opposite, and the whole corner building belongs to him,' said Herr Levy. 'Rühle was always against the Nazis, and he's helped a lot of people. Perhaps he'll have something for you.'

I went to the architect's office and met him right away: an elderly gentleman with a fine-featured, clever, kindly face. Briefly, I explained myself. 'What luck that it's not too late to help you out,' he said, for he had an idea. He told me that one of his single-room apartments was rented by an old lady who had spent the whole war out in the country. She had come to Pankow only once a year to make sure that the building was still standing. 'Since she's made herself at home in her village for so long,' Rühle decided, 'she might as well stay there, and you can move into the apartment. I'll make sure it's all right with the housing office.'

Then he climbed to the top floor of the building with me to show me the little corner apartment. It consisted of a bedroom that was all peculiar angles, and a kitchen that could also be used as a living room. I was delighted.

'When could I move in?' I asked. He handed me the key and said, 'Right away. We'll draw up the agreement later. For now, let me wish you peace and happiness here.' I clutched the key, wondering if I was awake or dreaming.

Back in his office, he asked me to tell him a little about the time I had spent in Berlin since going underground. I was happy to do that, because it was a relief to me to talk about it. In return, he told me this and that about his own life, and something odd happened: he several times used the subjunctive mood in indirect speech. It was three years since I had heard that grammatical feature of educated High German, and I had to turn away to hide my emotion. I was moved to tears to meet with the kind of language that was familiar to me from my parental home and my schooldays.

Then it was high time for me to set off back to Kaulsdorf. On the way I held the bunch of keys firmly in my hand, looking at it again and again as if it were a precious jewel.

The Kochs welcomed me warmly. 'Back so late?' I had only just managed to return before curfew.* At first Emil could hardly believe that I had actually been successful. I had an apartment of my own, and I could move in at once.

I moved out of the Kochs' house next day. This time I had to go all the way from Kaulsdorf on foot, since I had a handcart to push. I had found a pair of sandals, but they were uncomfortable because they didn't fit properly, so I decided to walk barefoot to the former capital city of the German Reich.

'I'm going to equip you as if you were my own child,' announced Frau Koch, packing a quilt, pillows, bed-linen, cutlery, a whisk and other household items into the handcart. As she did so, she kept enumerating all the things of which she was depriving herself so that she could give them to me. I felt annoyance secretly rising in me: in spite of all this fuss, after all, she was giving me only a tiny fraction of what had once been my parents' household goods.

Two silver teaspoons also went into the cart. 'We've always been poor,' Frau Koch told me, 'we had only these two solid silver spoons. I've treasured them since my childhood, and now I'm giving them to you as your dowry.' That was total nonsense: the initial of our family's surname was unmistakably engraved on those spoons!

The full extent of her delusions was clear yet again at that moment. For years she had tormented me by announcing again and again, in a solemn voice, 'We are one and the same being, because we bear the same name and our birthdays are on the same day. Your soul belongs to me.' On the one hand she had lent me her identity,

---

*The curfew introduced on 14 August 1945 by Allied Command ran from 2300 to 0500 hours.

and on the other she had identified completely with my family; in her mind she was not Johanna Elisabeth Koch, née Guthmann, but a Jalowicz and therefore Jewish. However, I had never before heard anything so remote from reality as the nonsense she was talking now, at the moment of farewell. And at last it was quite obvious: this had to be the end of our association.

'I'll bring you back the handcart at the weekend,' I said, trying to sound affectionate and naïve. 'And of course you'll always be like foster parents to me. I'll come and see you every Sunday.'

'Never mind all that. I know what life is like,' said Emil, grinning. 'You'll come two or three Sundays running, then once a month, then once every six months and after that never again.'

I had planned to do three things on the long walk ahead of me. The first was to think of how, all those years ago, my parents had been given those silver spoons as a wedding present by Aunt Hulda, my grandmother's sister.

Second, I had decided that I would spit. I had been obliged to spend the last three years in places where many people spat in the street, and finally I had adopted that disgusting habit myself. Society had spat me out, so I spat back, but always with the proviso that I would stop it if I survived the war.

I was going to spit for the last time on the border between Kaulsdorf-Süd and Biesdorf-Süd. Only I didn't know exactly where that was. So I spoke to a man who was weeding his garden: could he tell me just where Kaulsdorf ended and Biesdorf began?

'What do you want to know for?' he asked suspiciously.

At that moment I said to myself: stop! I don't need to run away now, I don't need to duck, I have genuine papers in my bag, no one can do anything to me. A civil human being answers a question instead of responding with another question.

'Do you know or don't you?' I asked the man brusquely. He admitted that he didn't know for certain. After I had gone a little further, someone else was able to tell me that yes, I was right on the border. So I gathered all my saliva in my mouth and spat lavishly on the road. After that I felt better. I was out of what the people here called 'our colony' at last.

Point number three on my programme was that I would make a mental list of everything I wasn't going to do any more. I wasn't going to spit, because that was uncivilised. I was never going to sit in a wicker chair again. I was never going to marry a man who wasn't Jewish. I'd rather be on my own than with a partner who didn't have any higher education. I would be honest, as my parents and my other forebears had always been honest. I wasn't going to be on familiar terms with any Tom, Dick or Harry, as you usually were in bars. I was never going to be rude about the Germans again without differentiating between them. I was never going to be unjust and ungrateful to people like the Kochs, who had helped me. And so on. My list was a long one.

Between Lichtenberg and Weissensee I noticed a young woman ahead of me, looking very elated as she walked along. She was wearing a pale blue dress, and holding a huge enamel basin on top of her head. As I found out later, it contained a tiny piece of margarine that she had acquired somewhere.

When the girl turned round I recognised Ursel Ehrlich, a friend of Irene Scherhey's. She too had gone underground during the Nazi period and had survived. We greeted each other warmly, stopped to rest for a while and told each other how we had managed.

Ursel had found a source of spare pieces of leather somewhere, had used them to make bookmarks and other small items, and then went round selling them – in garden cafés in summer, in bars in winter. 'My best customers were in Altermann's bar,' she told me.

'Altermann in Mühlenstrasse! To think we never met there!' I said in surprise. Then I admired her dress. 'You're so elegant!'

'You have to do what you can,' she said. She had dyed a sheet blue, made herself a dress out of it, and applied the pattern at the hem by a batik method. It suited her very well.

She looked at my feet. 'You can go about barefoot in the country, but there's rubbish and splinters of glass everywhere in the city. Don't you have any shoes?' she asked.

'I do have a pair of sandals, but they don't fit, so I can't really walk in them.'

Of course we were speaking in Berlin dialect. I had learned to love it in the last three years: it was the language of helpful people. Correct High German, on the other hand, had not proved its worth; it was the cultured and educated upper middle class that had failed the test.

About an hour and a half later I opened the door to my apartment in Pankow. I had laboriously dragged the handcart containing all my household goods up to the third floor. I couldn't risk leaving anything out in the street; it would have been stolen at once.

My feet were hot and sore. I put two chairs side by side in front of the sink so that I could sit there comfortably. There was no gas or electricity on, but there was running water. 'Hello, dear water-tap,' I said cheerfully, but much moved at the same time. 'I'm all alone here, but I'm not really alone. I have you. And I have the great good luck that no landlord or landlady, no one else at all can disapprove of me sitting comfortably here on two chairs, running cold water over my feet.'

And that was what I did.

Afterwards I lay down on the floor, stretched out full length, and immediately fell into a deep sleep.

Afterword

'Do you seriously think I would not be intellectually capable of writing down the story of my life if I wanted to?'

My mother, then aged about seventy, shouted this question down the phone in a stentorian voice, as if she were standing in front of her students in the lecture room.

At the other end of the line, the recipient of her forcefully phrased inquiry was a journalist who wanted to publish interviews with survivors of the Nazi period. 'That's the last thing I want,' added my mother, turning to me – I happened to be visiting my parents, and was thus by chance a witness of this phone call.

Much as I understood her, I thought it a great shame that her story might never be written. I was more or less familiar with it, but I was far from knowing all the details.

Before 1997, my mother had never really told the dramatic history of her survival. Now and then she had mentioned something in the family circle, but never as a consecutive narrative, and always out of the blue. You could hardly ever tell what set such reminiscences off.

One of my childhood memories is of a family friend who repeatedly tried to persuade her to write or, better still, dictate her story. 'Yes, yes,' my mother would tell her, only to add at once that this, that or the other was more important and must be dealt with first.

Once – I was still at elementary school – my class teacher asked my mother to talk to my fellow pupils about her life in the years just after 1933. She agreed to that request. The lesson set aside for the talk passed quickly, and she still hadn't really said much, apart from describing relatively minor incidents in the years when she had been in hiding, although she certainly made them sound exciting.

As she grew older, however, she became increasingly willing to talk about the details of her life. For instance, I managed to persuade her to tell the historian Carola Sachse about her experiences doing forced labour for Siemens, and she gave her an interview, under the pseudonym of 'Gerda B.', on 22 April 1993. She was very anxious that her real name should not appear in Sachse's book.*

At the same time she went along with my wish for her to give an interview to the Berlin historian Raymond Wolff, who was working on the history of the Neukölln doctor Benno Heller, and then to answer his questions at length. However, as she had emphasised to me, she didn't want to tell him all she knew about Heller, even though it was her opinion that 'all omissions do considerable damage to the truth'. Again, she does not identify herself in that interview, but calls herself 'Frau Eissler'. In the case of a woman who had given her shelter when she was on the run, she was also anxious not to identify her by her real name, or to tell Wolff what it was; he did not learn from her that 'Frau Rademann' was really a woman called Gerda Janicke, who plays a not inconsiderable part in my mother's memories.†

In June 1993 she also said she was prepared to give a lecture at a conference in Eisenstadt, at the invitation of the University of Vienna, on the subject of 'The U-Boats – Individual cases of resistance' (U-Boats being a name that those who had gone underground in the Nazi period gave themselves). Significantly, this lecture was not published because – and I am sure of this – my mother didn't want it to appear in print. She had given away a good deal of herself in it, probably more than she had intended. This was the first and last time that she spoke in public on the subject.

In the lecture she confined herself to 'Survival in Berlin', adding, for the benefit of her audience: 'This has ... the advantage of my

---

* *Als Zwangsarbeiterin in Berlin. Die Aufzeichnungen der Volkswirtin Elisabeth Freund* [*A Woman Forced Labourer in Berlin. Account of the economist Elisabeth Freund*], ed. and annotated Carola Sachse, Berlin, 1996.
† Häftling Nr. 124868 [Prisoner No. 124868], in *Neuköllner Pitaval. Wahre Kriminalgeschichten aus Berlin* [*A Neukölln Case. True crime stories from Berlin*], Rotbuch-Verlag, 1994, pp. 79 ff.

being able to draw on my own experience, and where I quote others I can also criticise the sources from an insider's point of view.'

She devoted a good deal of space in her lecture to Dr Benno Heller and his wife Irmgard, and will have been directly influenced by the interview mentioned above, which she had given only a little while earlier.

I would not admit, being a historian myself, that I couldn't get my own mother to talk about her life, and so on 26 December 1997, without any warning, I put a tape recorder on the table in my parents' apartment and said, 'You've always been meaning to tell your story – go ahead.'

Rather taken aback, but also excitedly, my mother began recording her memories up to May 1945 on seventy-seven tapes in chronological order. The recordings followed strict rules; they were continuous, and I did not interrupt her narrative with questions. The clarity of structure was remarkable. My mother could pick up the thread of her story precisely, going on from the end of a previous session that had lasted sixty or often even ninety minutes. In parallel, I did my own research to check her facts. I always told her about it, especially when I came upon several people of the same name, and sorting them out was difficult. She found this extremely interesting, and was particularly glad when my research confirmed what she herself had said.

Our sessions, although interrupted again and again by time that she spent in hospital, went on until 4 September. Some of the recordings were even done in hospital; the last was only a few days before her death. Marie Simon died on 16 September 1998.

It is particularly obvious in the last recordings that her powers were waning, and one can sense the effort it cost her to dictate her memories.

Next the tapes had to be typed out, and then the transcript – some 900 pages – lay fallow for some time, because the copy had to be compared with the sound recordings, and I could not face that directly after my mother's death.

The writer and journalist Irene Stratenwerth, with whom I have worked for many years on various projects for exhibitions, finally, and with sensitive feeling for the original, turned the long transcript into a self-contained text, the manuscript of this book by Marie Jalowicz Simon. I can hear my mother's voice in every line of the present work.

Preparing the manuscript entailed not only identifying the most important of the astonishing wealth of details and characters that my mother had remembered, and finding the narrative thread that was always present in my mother's mind, however far she sometimes deviated from it. The events that she described also had to be exactly reconstructed. Now and then, for instance, she either did not know a precise date or had forgotten it.

The places, names and characters that featured in her memories were to be found in old address books, or the files of a number of different authorities. Many people helped to search various archives. Often it was only through this work of reconstruction that we understood 'the whole story' she was telling – and at the same time we kept acknowledging, in retrospect, that Marie Simon was right, and really had said all that was necessary on a given subject.

In the fifteen years since her death my own researches into hundreds of names, addresses and lives have shown that my mother remembered almost every detail correctly. I concluded my research work just before writing this afterword; only a part of what I found is included in the index of names. Describing the course of my research would make a book in itself, including, for instance, the account of how I found the descendants of Hans Goll, who helped my mother in Bulgaria, and those of 'the Dutchman'.

I would have liked to know more, and in more detail, about the time immediately after the liberation, and also about my mother's life in the 1950s, but she was not prepared to talk about those periods. That time in her life was not so easily recalled as the preceding years, and by the time she reached it in her account, her strength was failing her.

I still wonder why she left it so late to put it all on record. 'If I tell you something,' she said once as she was dictating her story on tape, 'then it has to be the truth, and there's a lot that one can't talk about until half a century later.' Her dictation did indeed sound as if it were a story that she was reading aloud, and a session often lasted as long as a lecture.

In the course of dictating her memories, and in contrast to the lecture at Eisenstadt mentioned above, my mother deliberately avoided using books already published as sources, and comparing her memoirs with those of other people, either printed or from archives. On that subject, she said, 'I didn't really want to draw on any sources other than my own memory, because if I had, they would have modified what I remembered … What is entirely subjective, if it is honestly presented, is of greater objective value than alleged objectivity that misses its mark. In other words, to use an image: a frog should describe its experiences from the froggy point of view. For all the limited nature of the depiction, for all the colouring of the picture presented, it is then of objective value as the object of its subjectivity. The frog ought not to act as if it could fly and see things from an eagle's point of view.'

However, she had thought of putting her memories down on paper even during the time when she was in hiding; she kept a diary in her head without paper or pen, and edited the entries again and again to make all her experiences after 22 June 1942 shorter and more precise.

It was on that date, 22 June, a Monday, that my mother escaped being arrested by the Gestapo, and from then on she was living 'illegally'. I give the word in inverted commas on purpose, because she repeatedly told me that she regarded the idea of illegality as extremely questionable, 'because the technology of the worst mass murder in the history of mankind was illegal; we must surely grant everyone the right to life. The Nazis were illegal, not me.'

It is interesting that the term had to be used at times by those who had gone underground themselves, for instance by a friend of my mother's, Fritz Goldberg, after his arrest.* She herself used it

---

* 'Declaration of property' of 23 July 1944; under the heading Residential Address,

when, at the beginning of October 1945, in a CV accompanying her application for recognition as a victim of Fascism, she wrote, still under her maiden name, 'I eluded arrest. I was not among those whose well-filled wallets allowed them to prepare well for a life of illegality.'*

This 'illegality' was to last almost three years; my mother's 'normal' life did not begin again until she left Kaulsdorf Süd at the end of August 1945, barefoot and with her few possessions on a handcart, to walk by way of Lichtenburg and Weissensee to Berlin, finally reaching Pankow, where she moved into her own apartment at No 7 Binzstrasse. On this long walk of almost twenty kilometres, she had made many resolutions for the future; it was a long list.

She was never going to marry a man who wasn't Jewish. She would rather be on her own than with a partner who had no higher education. It was important to her to be honest, as her parents and other forebears had been honest. She resolved not 'to be on familiar terms with any Tom, Dick or Harry, as you usually were in bars', and 'never ... to be rude about the Germans again without differentiating between them', for after all she had come upon many helpful non-Jewish people.

After her school friend Heinrich Simon heard that his friend Marie had survived (they had taken their school-leaving certificates together at the Upper School of the Jewish Community of Berlin in 1939) he came to see her at the end of January 1946. He had emigrated to Palestine, and was later to be my father, but at this time he was a British soldier, and paying such a visit was almost impossible, but my mother fixed that too.

She wrote British HQ a deliberately naïve letter, along the lines of, 'Dear Headquarters, please, please let my fiancé come and see

---

Fritz Goldberg is given at 'C2, 32 Landsbergerstr. [...] to 6 February 1943, after that living illegally.' (Brandenburgisches Landeshauptarchiv Rep 36A Oberfinanzpräsident Berlin Brandenburg [II] No. 11552.)

*Account of life of Marie Jalowicz of 8 October 1945, Landesarchiv Berlin, classification C Rep 118–01 No. 2754. On the attached questionnaire she writes, 'I eluded the Gestapo and lived illegally for three years.'

me.' She had worked it out, correctly, that a letter had to stand out to be noticed at all, because applications of all kinds came into that office every day. No doubt her letter was passed round the entire British office staff, amidst laughter, and met with a positive response.

Later on, when I asked my father after my mother's death whether they were both serious about being engaged, and whether she had really envisaged a life with him at that point, he couldn't say. 'At first it was just role-playing on both sides.'

On 29 January 1946, when she was not yet twenty-four years old, my mother had already written to a mutual friend of hers and my father's, Ahron Fritz Kleinberger (b. Berlin 1920; d. Jerusalem 2005), later to be a professor of education, explaining at length her reasons for wanting to stay in Berlin. First the young woman drew up a balance sheet: 'I'm alive, I am sound in mind and body, I am beginning my university studies and am happy with life (apart from some inhibitions deriving from the presence of my conscience).' On her decision to stay she wrote,

> Please don't be surprised if I tell you that I feel I've emigrated already. I have emigrated from Hitler's Germany to the Germany of Goethe and Johann Sebastian Bach, and I feel very comfortable there. In other words, I'm minded to stay. My reasons are as follows:
>
> 1) I was born and grew up here, so logically this is my home (perhaps I should add 'unfortunately', but there's no altering the facts).
> 2) I'm a little battle-weary, and I fear that if I have to come to terms with entirely new circumstances and all their difficulties, I won't get on with my studies or find the peace I need so much.
> 3) I can live here without having to make demands on anyone. The idea of facing a void as a refugee or beggar is more than I can bear, after all the years of pointless, mindless wandering in

terrible living conditions that are now, I'm glad to say, behind me.

And at this point I mustn't forget ... to say that I am enjoying many privileges here that make it possible for me to live more comfortably ...

4) I'd like to defuse the usual argument that pride doesn't allow us to live in the land of the gas chambers. Do you think that the mob anywhere else in the world, if their worst instincts had been cleverly aroused, would have behaved any worse than the mob in Germany? Germans have murdered millions of Jews. But many Germans, risking their lives, made great sacrifices to help me.
[...]
Do you remember how you once brought razor-sharp arguments to bear on my Zionist enthusiasm? *Tempora mutantur, nos et mutamur in illis ...**

If one doesn't want to perish, the only solution is probably to adapt to circumstances as they are.

I don't want my reasons for staying here to be taken as propaganda for Jews to come back to Germany. And I'm certainly not trying to influence you in that way, in fact I think the chances of my success would be low. All these thoughts of mine were purely egocentric. I don't believe in any final answer to the Jewish question, only individual answers. So I'd say the best thing is for us all to stay where we feel most comfortable.
[...]
I have the courage to be what I am: a German Jewish woman, and on my own if need be.

Of course you won't feel homesick for the accursed country of Germany – how could you? But if you ever, purely in the line of business, come here, even with contempt in your heart, don't

---

*Times change, and we change with them.

forget to visit me. I like to get visitors from Abu Telfan on the moon,* and will be waiting patiently for all my friends. Here I have an illusion that might melt away in the heat of Palestine: may God gather us in from all four corners of the world ...

So my mother stayed in that 'accursed country of Germany', more precisely in Berlin, and even more precisely in Pankow, moving only once, in 1952, into a larger apartment at 59 Wolfshagener Strasse.

My parents lived there for the following decades, and it was there that my late sister Bettina (1952–1989) and I (b. 1949) spent our childhood.

On her twenty-fourth birthday, 4 April 1946, she officially enrolled at the University of Berlin to study philosophy and sociology. She had already been able to attend lectures. In the questionnaire that she filled in to register at the Jewish Community on 23 July 1945, she wrote under 'Profession': 'Before 1933, schoolgirl; now, student.'

'I have now matriculated at Berlin University,' she wrote not without pride in a CV written for the Committee on Victims of Fascism, Department of Victims of the Nuremberg Laws, on 23 October 1945.† At the same time she was working at the G. Fritz translation and teaching bureau in Binzstrasse in Pankow. Because of that, she sometimes gave her profession as 'working student'. At the time she was also trying to find out what had become of several friends and acquaintances who had helped her in the past, but fundamentally all she wanted was to look to the future.

---

* Referring to a nineteenth-century novel by Wilhelm Raabe, *Abu Telfan oder Die Heimkehr vom Mondgebirge* [*Abu Telfan, or, Return from the Mountains of the Moon*].
† Two applications by Marie Jalowicz to be recognised as a victim of Fascism have been preserved, one of 8 October 1945, in which she wanted to be recognised as a political campaigner (now in the Landesarchiv), and the second of 23 October 1945, to the Department of Victims of the Nuremberg Laws, for recognition as a persecuted Jew (now in the Centrum Judaicum). The second bears a handwritten comment: 'Politically acknowledged'. I know of no parallel case of a persecuted Jew applying for recognition both on political grounds and also as a victim of the Nuremberg legislature.

*

She was not happy with the studies she had chosen; she tried this and that, for instance going to lectures on Slavonic studies. 'I joined some Bulgarian course or other, and very soon left again, finding that I'd done it for purely emotional reasons. But Bulgaria was over, I'd left it behind me, and the language that had fascinated and interested me so much didn't matter to me now. I listened to philosophical lectures and thought: you idiots, if you can't say what's chance and what's fate you might as well take a running jump. I got nothing out of all that, I didn't enjoy it, and sometimes I thought maybe there was no point in studying,' said Marie Simon half a century later.

On 2 November 1946 she wrote to my father saying that she went to lectures 'only very occasionally. Neither the intellectual level nor the distinctly Nazi attitude of most of the students is what could be expected of a cultured person.'

A few months earlier, on 5 July, she had said to him, on the same subject,

> You must understand that there's too much behind me, I'm too mature and too aware of myself to attend university uncritically, like a good little schoolgirl, particularly knowing that this state of things will improve, and with my qualifications … I'll be able to tackle the quota of work for two semesters in one. You know me, you know that discipline was never my strong point, and it won't be difficult for you to guess what conclusions I drew: I've been going to lectures as industriously as I used to go to handicraft lessons back at school (i.e. not at all).

Those days of persecution and deprivation had, of course, not left her unaffected; her body finally rebelled. She suffered a complete breakdown in the autumn of 1946 and was sick for two months. 'It was a matter of life and death … I felt very clearly that it was up to me whether I came through or simply fell asleep.' She wrote this to my father in November 1946. But at that time she was already past the worst, and getting a good deal better.

It was not the first time she had collapsed; she had already said to him, in January 1946, 'I got through my mental breakdown after the end of the war – it would have been unnatural if I had escaped one – and I recovered well.'

The return to normality was particularly difficult for her – she says that she could find no way of 'really coming to the surface again'. She also suffered from the fact that friends and acquaintances emigrated. 'Those terrible partings continue.' After all, she had lived with partings for years, 'in fact from 1933 onwards'.

'Coming to the surface' entailed the rejection of anything temporary and provisional. 'Because if you're living only for the time being you develop a chronic sense of discomfort, and it has to be counteracted.' She described herself as 'anti-provisional', and asked my father in August 1946 to share her view of the world. At the time he was still in Palestine; after demobilisation he was employed by the Jerusalem post-office administration. My mother, who had been vehemently in favour of staying in Berlin in the letter to Fritz Kleinberger quoted above, changed her mind at the end of 1946. In view of the difficult economic situation, and the poverty and misery suffered by the population of Berlin, she now wanted, whatever happened, to join my father in Palestine, in Erez Israel.

'I can no longer advise you, with a clear conscience, to come back to Germany,' she wrote to him on 2 November 1946, giving as her reason the fact that '[r]eactionary forces have the upper hand, and are greatly favoured by the powers that are now pursuing colonial policies hand in hand with Germany, and whose political aims are free of any idealism because they pay homage to capital as the ultimate principle. We are mud, just as we used to be. Those who weren't Nazis before have to turn Nazi now. What luck that I'm living in the Russian zone.'

My father did not take her arguments seriously, since he could not imagine the conditions in Berlin. My mother, on the other hand, could not form any idea of the difficult conditions in which my father was living in Palestine. At least, he did not let himself be

Marie and Heinrich Simon as a
newly married couple in 1948.

persuaded to change his mind, but left Palestine on 21 September 1947 to return to Berlin, where my parents married in March 1948. They had finally decided to make Berlin the centre of their lives.

Living on a provisional basis was over now; my parents' lives ran on well-ordered lines. They were both studying at Berlin University, which changed its name to the Humboldt University of Berlin in 1949.

Marie Simon concluded her studies with her doctoral degree on 14 February 1951. 'In my dissertation,' she wrote in 1972, 'I dealt with the border area between philosophy and classical philology that has remained my field of research.'*

In 1956 she became acting lecturer in the department of the history of philosophy in classical antiquity. Only when she had

---

* CV of Marie Simon dated 16 October 1972. Personal file in the archives of the Humboldt University of Berlin.

Marie Simon, née Jalowicz, aged sixty-two, at an occasion in the cultural room of the East Berlin Jewish Community, in 1984.

taken the examination for the next academic rank up, in 1969, was she promoted to full lecturer, and her appointment to full professor of the literary and cultural history of classical antiquity followed in September 1973, relatively late. She was fifty-one years old by then.

My father (1921–2010), who gained his doctoral degree at the same time as she did, became a lecturer a good deal earlier, and with effect from 1 December 1960 was initially professor of classical Arabic and Arab philosophy at the same university.

While my mother retired from her professorial chair in September 1982, she remained active at the university until the middle of the 1990s.

Thousands of students must have heard her inspiring and fascinating lectures. Among other subjects, she lectured to classical philologists on the philosophy and religious history of classical antiquity and to philosophy students on the history of philosophy (classical antiquity to French materialism); she gave archaeological students an introduction to Greek philosophy; she lectured to cultural scientists on the cultural history of antiquity, the Middle Ages and the Renaissance and to theological students on the history of Greek philosophy.

None of these students knew the details of her life; I have asked many of her former students about that.

Around 1970, however, when my mother did once mention, in a seminar on classical poetry with very few participants, that as a forced labourer working at a lathe she used to recite all the poetry she knew by heart to take her mind off the tedious work, the students were so surprised that they asked for no further details.

One of my mother's former students, the classical philologist and well-known journalist Detlev Lücke (1942–2007), said that Marie Simon gave her students stability and a sense of direction in difficult political times. In the weekly newspaper *Der Freitag*, where he was an editor for a long time, he remembered: 'What was so impressive in Marie Simon was the extraordinary clarity of her arguments. To me, her lectures were something special ... They were so well attended because she provided richer and more profound ideas than was usual in the standard compulsory lectures for social scientists.'*

Lücke describes her, his academic mentor, who 'showed no sign of her bourgeois origins' as 'a very modest, honest woman. Anything extravagant was part of her nature. She arrived to give lectures with a cigarette in her hand, and noticeably well dressed, which was rather non-German and therefore, of course, wonderful. Her searching look from under her eyelids went right through you.'

During my own university studies I would very much have liked to attend my mother's lectures, but she wouldn't let me – or rather, she asked me not to do so because my presence would make her nervous. So unfortunately I cannot say what distinguished them at first hand. As well as communicating her solid knowledge of

---

* '"Telling the Whole Truth at the End of One's Life." In Conversation: Hermann Simon and Detlev Lücke on Marie Simon, who as a Jew living in Berlin had gone to ground and survived the war', *Freitag*, 19 May 2000, p. 17.

their subjects, they must have contained political allusions to the circumstances of her times. My mother, typically, kept at a critical distance from those circumstances. Detlev Lücke summed it up by writing, 'She confined herself strictly to her scholarly context, which in itself was interesting enough. Others in the Institute ... tried to demonstrate that, from the historical viewpoint, the Soviet Union was the third Rome, but Marie Simon never indulged in such comparisons.'*

She was not afraid of the authorities, for one thing because over the decades she had come to enjoy something of the status of a veteran, having joined the Communist Party on 15 November 1945, and after the union of the Communist Party of Germany and the Social Democratic Party in 1946, an event that she welcomed, she was a member of the SED, the Social Unity Party of the German Democratic Republic.

I never asked her whether she thought of herself as a communist. She would probably have replied that politically she was on the left. Being a member of the Jewish Community and running a fundamentally kosher household did not represent any contradiction to her.

An important aspect of her work on philosophy was her study of Utopias, particularly the question of how long they remain utopian and what puts an end to that state of affairs. In her opinion, all Utopias ending in -ism, socialism and Zionism alike, had failed.

At the university, she was one of that 'honourable circle of scholars and university teachers who, with their wealth of expertise and courage in defending the truth, withstood doctrinaire impositions, and who taught and exemplified the ideal claim of a new society rooted in solidarity against the distorted image of the illiberal, authoritarian social state.' These were the words of her colleague, the philosopher Gerd Irrlitz, in an obituary of her. He went on, 'In discussions ... I appreciated Marie Simon's persistence in defending

---

*Ibid.

the criteria of scholarly criticism and rejecting officious politicisation – and I saw how disappointed she was by the turn that events had taken.'

She had not been thrown off course by the fact that the country for which she had consciously decided no longer existed; the old Federal Republic of West Germany was never a viable alternative for her. Yet the huge political changes after the fall of the Berlin Wall made her uneasy. In addition, there was a family tragedy: my sister, three years my junior, who had just taken her doctoral degree and was following in the scholarly footsteps of my parents, died of an incurable disease on 27 November 1989.

My mother bore this blow of fate with her characteristic strength, and shared her mourning only with my father. She did not talk about it to other people.

However, her grief over my sister's death may have been one of the reasons why she went along with my wish for her to dictate her memoirs. It is absolutely certain that if she had not wanted to, no one in the world could have made her change her mind.

In the course of the long time I have spent working on the story of my mother's survival, I have often wondered how far the experiences of wartime persecution determined her life after it. Can anyone really function properly after all that? What fears did it leave behind?

In looking at that question I must, of course, be careful not to see all my mother's characteristics as the result of what she had experienced. All the same, I will mention a few later consequences.

My mother was on friendly terms with everyone she knew, but kept her distance; she had hardly any close friends. Yet there were exceptions, such as the historian of classical antiquity Elisabeth Charlotte Welskopf (1901–1979).

The two women retained a formal mode of address in public, calling each other *Sie*, but they were intimate friends. My mother's friendship was not just with the university professor, but with her alter ego, the successful writer who published her novels about Native Americans under the name of Liselotte Welskopf-Henrich.

The basis of their friendship was that both, in their very different ways, had fought against the Nazis, and if necessary they continued to fight at the university.

My mother couldn't stand either protracted goodbyes or late arrivals on the part of her family and friends. It was taken for granted that until her death I phoned her several times a day.

Finally, her experiences caught up with her after a major operation, when she had not fully come round from the anaesthetic and was firmly convinced that the Nazis were torturing her with sharp-edged cannulas.

Only today do I fully understand some aspects of her behaviour. As a child, I was never allowed to wear a ski cap, although I would have loved to look like the other schoolchildren. But on the grounds that ski caps were 'Nazi headgear', I was given a fur cap instead. No explanation was forthcoming, and I had a feeling that I had better not ask for one.

Nor did anyone tell me why Trude Neuke, who lived in our neighbourhood, always called my mother 'Hannchen' when the two of them happened to meet in the street. I did know, however, that Marie Jalowicz had once gone under the false name of Johanna Koch.

Her relationship with the 'real' Johanna Koch, whom Marie Jalowicz Simon describes at length in all her ambivalence in her memoirs, was to play a part in my mother's life once more after Frau Koch's death.

On the whole, my mother succeeded in looking back at her past life soberly and with composure. Frau Koch is an exception in that my mother never really got over their relationship, and sometimes was overcome by panic, thinking that Johanna Koch might unexpectedly come to our door.

When Frau Koch died on 20 January 1994, a will of 18 February 1940 suddenly came to light. In this will, Emil and Johanna Koch left their entire estate to 'Fräulein Marie Jalowicz as their heir'. Towards the end of her life, then, my mother got her parents' house in Kaulsdorf-Süd back. She never set foot in it again; she gave it to me soon after the legacy came through, although not without asking the family's lawyer to go to see her in hospital, where she had to spend a good deal of time at that point.

In front of the lawyer, she told my wife and me that she would make the gift only if my family immediately sold the property that weighed on her mind so much, and we did as she wanted.

When we were clearing the house in the early summer of 1994, my father turned up unexpectedly. He went into what had been the Kochs' bedroom, and with the air of someone who knew what he was looking for opened a drawer in the bedside table and took out a number of documents. They included a passport made out in Bulgaria and my mother's identity card, both in the name of Johanna Koch.

Shortly before my mother left Kaulsdorf for Pankow at the end of August 1945, Johanna Koch had simply taken these documents out of her handbag on the grounds that they were her papers.

I assume that my father was acting on my mother's behalf. When he was about to take them away with him, I protested and asked him to let me have them. At the time, I was already forming a decision to preserve the life story of Marie Jalowicz Simon.

My mother was always convinced that chance had allowed her to survive. In a lecture of 1993 on the 'U-boats' who had survived the Nazi period, she generalised on the subject in these words:

> The justifiable wish of the scholar or serious literary writer to establish rules leads us to neglect what, as I see it, is the deciding factor of chance. But what is chance?
>
> According to Spinoza's definition, it is an *asylum ignorantiae*. 'Chance' is an auxiliary word, and like all auxiliary words really shows the helplessness with which we naïvely define the obscure. The survival of every one of those who went on the run from the Nazis rests on a chain of chance incidents that can often be called almost incredible and miraculous.

I will not call such chance incidents dispensations of providence, which would be unscientific and indeed blasphemous, for that interpretation implies knowledge of what cannot be known, the supposition that one has explored what by definition is the highest of all decrees, which would be both foolish and presumptuous. Would the survival of determined individuals be a blessing or a curse if it depended on predestination and divine guidance, in view of the murder of a million children? We have to come to terms with the fact that we cannot solve the riddle, we must content ourselves with admitting to our ignorance and grant it an *asylum* by using the word 'chance', and establishing that it is the deciding factor in all stories of survival.

Hermann Simon
Berlin, September 2013

Index of Names

Sylvia Asarch (b. 1882) was the daughter of *Doris Schapiro*. After her arrest in Berlin in 1942 her fate is unknown.

Max Bäcker (b. 1889) went underground in 1942. After a suicide attempt he was taken to the Berlin Jewish Hospital in 1943, and deported from there.

Luise Blase (b. 1865). The date and circumstances of her death are unknown. Her sons **Gerhard Blase** (1909–1942) and **Kurt Blase** (c.1915–1945) fell in the Second World War.

Georg Blumberg (b. 1923) was deported to Auschwitz in 1943.

Gerrit Willy Burgers (1920–1983) returned to Nijmegen in 1945, married and had four children.

Dr Ludwig Dahlheim (b. 1883) was deported to Raasikau in 1942, with his wife **Thea**, née **Toller** (b. 1899) and his sister Hildchen (Hilde) (b. 1888).

Ruth Danziger (b. 1920). The fate of the daughter of the café proprietors after 1945 is not known.

Leo Davidsohn (b. 1873), a relation of Marie Jalowicz on her mother's side, was deported to Theresienstadt in 1942 with his sisters Friederieke (b. 1865) and Julie (b. 1866).

Eva Deutschkron (b. 1918) emigrated to the USA after the Second World War, and died there in 2011.

Arthur Eger (1879–1938), brother of *Betti Jalowicz*.

Betti Eger see *Betti Jalowicz*.

Herbert Eger (1882–1953), brother of *Betti Jalowicz*, m. **Marie (Mia) Lindemann**, and had two children with her: **Kurt-Leo** (b. 1925) and **Hanna-Ruth** (1928–2007). The whole family emigrated to England in 1939.

Jacob (Kiwe) Eger (1838–1903), grandfather of Marie Jalowicz, m. **Marie Eger**, née **Wolkowyski** (1851–1919).

Leo Eger (1873–1923), brother of *Betti Jalowicz*.

Margarete (Grete) Eger (b. 1878), sister of *Betti Jalowicz*, was deported to Litzmannstadt in 1941.

Camilla (Kamilla) Fiochi, née Schenk (b. 1889) died in 1970 in Deutsch-Wusterhausen.

Recha Frankenstein (b. 1876), cousin of *Betti Jalowicz*, was deported to Theresienstadt in 1942 and from there travelled to Switzerland in February 1945.

Karl (Carl) Galecki (b. 1892) died in Berlin-Tegel in 1965.

Carl Goldberg (b. 1879) was deported to Auschwitz in 1942 with his wife Margarete (b. 1880). Their daughter **Ellen** (b. 1915) was also deported to Auschwitz in 1943 with her husband Alfred Guttmann (b. 1910). The Goldbergs' son **Fritz** (b. 1909) went underground, was arrested in 1944 and deported to Auschwitz.

Dr Hans Goll (1909–1989) was stationed in Sofia in 1942, and was responsible for sending Bulgarian workers to Germany. He was called up for war service in 1943, and was in a POW camp in 1945. Later he was active as a lawyer in the Federal Republic of Germany.

Else Gottschalk (b. 1903) emigrated to the USA in 1941. Her father **Gustav Gottschalk** (b. 1864) was deported to Theresienstadt in 1942.

Alexander Grass (d.o.b. unknown), caretaker in the apartment building Am Oberbaum, fell in 1945 in the last days of the war. His mother **Friederike Grass** (b. 1855) died in the air raid of 9 March 1945. His wife **Auguste Grass** died shortly after the end of the war following a stroke.

Dr Helene Gutherz (b. 1890) took her own life in Berlin in 1943.

Christine Hansl (b. 1898) died in Berlin-Spandau in 1977.

Paul Hecht (b. 1897), cantor of the Jewish Community, was deported to Theresienstadt with his wife and daughters in 1943. He survived, and died in the USA in 1984.

Dr Benno Heller (b. 1894) was first imprisoned in Berlin after his arrest on 23 February 1943, and then deported to Auschwitz. He was moved to the Sachsenhausen concentration camp in autumn 1944, and then to the subsidiary camp of Lieberose-Jamlitz, where he was last seen in mid-January 1945. His wife **Irmgard Heller**, née Strecker, died in Leipzig in 1943.

Rosemarie and Hannelore Herzfeld (b. 1923) were deported to Litzmannstadt in 1941.

Ruth Hirsch (b. 1921) was deported to Auschwitz in 1943.

Inge Hubbe (1927–1999) and **Wolfgang Hubbe** (1929–2004), the children of *Trude Neuke* and Rudolf Hubbe.

Franziska Jacobsohn (b. 1891) was deported to Theresienstadt in 1943 with her husband **Siegfried** (b. 1886). Her son **Werner** (b. 1930) and daughter **Hildegard** (b. 1925) were also deported from Berlin in 1943.

Moritz Jacoby (b. 1883), guardian of Marie Jalowicz, was deported to Riga in 1942.

Betti Jalowicz, née **Eger** (b. 1885), mother of Marie Jalowicz, died in Berlin in 1938.

Dr Hermann Jalowicz (b. 1877) died in Berlin in 1941.

Gerda Janicke, née Haße (b. 1911), died in Dortmund in 2001.

Dr Karl Jalowicz (1879–1952), Hermann's brother.

Dr Antonie (Toni) Kirschstein (b. 1898) was deported to Riga in 1942 with her son **Wolfgang** (b. 1924).

Ellodie (Ella) Klaczko (b. 1972), née **Eger**, sister of *Betti Jalowicz*, died in Riga in 1939. Her daughter Edit Rabinowitsch (b. 1904), disappeared without trace in the Second World War, together with her husband and daughter.

Johanna (Hannchen) Koch (b. 1905), née **Guthmann**, died in Berlin in 1994. Her husband **Emil Koch** (b. 1900) died in 1983.

Herbert Botho Koebner (b. 1891), cousin of *Ernst Wolff*, was arrested in Berlin in 1942, and deported to Auschwitz in 1943 with his son **Fritz** (b. 1923). His wife **Betty** (b. 1897) and son

Heinz-Joachim (b. 1920) had already been deported to Auschwitz in 1942.

Tati (Bertha) Kupke (1904–2003), née Lindemann, sister of **Mia Eger**, lived with her husband Willi Kupke in Pankow.

Ruth Lachotzke (b. 1924), fiancée of *Fritz Goldberg*, survived, and in 1951, under her married name of Bornstein, emigrated to Sydney, Australia, with her two sons.

Mia (Mia) Lindemann see *Herbert Eger*.

Shu Ka Ling (b. 1906) came to Berlin in 1933. He was arrested in June 1942, and released from Sachsenhausen concentration camp in August 1943. He married after the Second World War, became the father of two children, and died in Bremerhaven in 1967.

Gertrud (Trude) Neuke, née **Aernecke** (b. 1907), died in 1981 in Berlin-Pankow. She was married first to **Rudolf Hubbe** (1902–1932), and second to **Julius (Jule) Neuke** (1902–1965).

Edit Rabinowitsch (b. 1904), daughter of **Ellodie Klaczko**. She, her husband and her daughter have been missing since the Second World War.

Edith Rödelsheimer (b. 1909) survived the Nazi era and emigrated to the USA after the Second World War.

Liesbeth (Lieschen) Sabbarth (b. 1913) died in the USA in 1993.

Doris Schapiro (1855–1932), née **Wolkowyski**, great-aunt of Marie Jalowicz.

Karoline (Karola or **Rola) Schenk** (b. 1903), née Münichshofer, died in Mannheim in 1989.

Irene Scherhey (b. 1920) emigrated and died in the USA in 1991.

Ernst Schindler (b. 1890), regional court judge, survived the Second World War with the support of his non-Jewish wife Erna.

Max Schulz (b. 1904), tool-setter working for Siemens, died in Berlin-Spandau in 1965.

Heinrich Simon (1921–2010), fellow student of Marie Jalowicz at the Jewish High School, emigrated to Palestine in 1939 and returned to Germany in 1947. In 1948 he married Marie Jalowicz. The children of the marriage were Bettina Simon (1952–1989) and Hermann Simon (b. 1949).

Nora (née Anna-Georgette) Schmilewicz (b. 1921) was deported to Auschwitz in 1943.

Herbert Steinbeck (b. 1907), neighbour of *Trude Neuke*, fell in the war in 1945.

Adolf Waldmann (b. 1899) emigrated to Shanghai in 1939, with his wife **Margarete**, née Hageleit, and their son **Martin**.

Ernst Wolff (b. 1892) was deported to Theresienstadt in 1942, with his parents, his sister **Thea Wolff** (b. 1904) and his aunt Ernestine Wolff (b. 1874).

Picture Credits

All photographs and documents are from the private property of Hermann Simon, with the exception of the following illustrations. The publisher thanks their originators or the possessors of the rights to them for kind permission to reproduce them here:

[p. 86], New Synagogue Foundation, Berlin – Centrum Judaicum, archive signature CJA 4 1, no. 2058; [p. 116], the family of Hans Goll; [p. 145], Neukölln Museum; [pp. 149 and 151], Archive of circus, music-hall and other artistes, Marburg; [p. 222], Hennie Burgers; [p. 332], Joachim Thurn

Thanks to the Following Institutions and Persons

Administrative Office for Citizenship and Order, Berlin, head office for affairs of inhabitants; Administrative Office for Health and Social Affairs, Berlin, medical records (Dieter Dureck); Archive of circus, music-hall and other artistes in Marburg (Karl Braun); Archives of the Berlin Traffic Services (Christian Piepert);

Archives of the Charles University, Prague (Petr Svobodny); Archives of the District Museum of Friedrichhain-Kreuzberg (Gerhard Grosche); Archives of the Humboldt University, Berlin (Winfried Schulze); Archives of the University of Vienna (Kurt Mühlberger); Berlin-Kreuzberg District Museum (Detlef Krenz); Berlin Law Society (Hans-Joachim Ehrig, Marion Petrusky); Berlin Museum of Communications (Veit Didczuneit); Berlin Provincial Archive (Kerstin Bötticher, Gisela Erler, Andreas Matschenz, Anne Rothschenk, Axel Schröder, Bianca Welzing-Bräutigam); Branden-burg Main Provincial Archive (Monika Nakath); Bundeswehr Museum of Military History in Dresden (Gerhard Bauer); Central State Archive of Bulgaria; Charlottenburg-Wilmersdorf Registry Office, Berlin (Fr. Teuchert); Dahme-Spreewald District Archive (Karin Deumer); Embassy of the Republic of Bulgaria, Berlin (Violeta Karaivanova, Radi Naidenov, Meglena Plugtschieva); Federal Archive, Berlin (Undine Beier, Heinz Fehlauer, Andreas Grunwald, Monika Kaiser); Federal Commissioner for the documents of the State Security Service of the former German Democratic Republic (BstU); Federalnoe Archivnoe Agenstvo, Moscow (Andrey N. Artizov); German Department – WASt (Bernd Gericke, Wolfgang Remmers, Hans H. Söchtig, Hans Peter

Wollny); German Railways Company History/Historical Collection (Susanne Kill); German Resistance Memorial (Johannes Tuchel; Andreas Herbst); German Technical Museum of Berlin Foundation (Alfred Gottwald); Marzahn-Hellersdorf Museum (Dorothee Ifland); Municipal and District Archive of Arnstadt (Andrea Kirchschlager); Municipal Archive of Detmold (Andreas Ruppert); International Tracing Service Bad Arolsen (Susanne Urban); Municipal Archive of Mannheim (Karen Strobel); Municipal Archive of Oranienburg (Petra Ramlow); Municipal and Provincial Archive of Vienna; Municipality of Wieselburg (Gerhard Buchegger); Neukölln Museum (Julia Dilger); New Synagogue Berlin Foundation – Centrum Judaicum (Sabine Hank, Barbara Welker, Anna Fischer, Daniela Gauding, Monika Junker, Stephan Kummer, Chana Schütz); Pankow Museum (Birgit Kirchhöfer); Parish of Wieselburg (Franz Dammerer); Political Archive of the Foreign Office (Martin Kröger, Sabine Schafferdt); Provincial Archive of Nordrhein-Westfalen, Rheinland Department (Peter Klefisch); Sachsenhausen Memorial and Museum (Monika Liebscher); Siemens Archive (Frank Wittendorfer); Spandau Museum of Municipal History, archive (Heiko Metz); Topography of Terror Foundation (Andreas Sander); Quierschied Registry Office (Irmgard Pfoser).

Monika Behrens; Inge and Josef Bornhorst; Hennie Burgers; David Dambitsch; Vladimir Danovsky; Christian Dirks; Ralf Dose; Kurt-Leo Eger; Jochen Fahlenkamp; Jochen Fleischhacker; Ernest Fontheim; Eugen Herman-Friede; Ulrich Werner Grimm; Ora Guttmann; Karen Holtmann; Akim Jah; Harald Kindermann; Dorothea Kolland; Norbert Krenzlin; Christoph Kreuzmüller; Heike Lindemann; Hans-Jürgen Lödden; Ingo Loose; Alexander Lorenz; Dick de Mildt; Frank R. Mützel; Uwe Naumann; Rainer Nitsch; Karl-Heinz Noack; Cord Pagenstecher; Andreas Pretzel; C.F. Ruter; Angelika Salomon; Deborah Simon; Christian Schölzel; Mila Zaharieva-Schmolke; Hans-Georg Schrader; Diana Schulle; Brigitte Schulz; Barbara Sauer; Rebecca Schwoch; Jürgen Sielemann; Isolde Stark; Jonny Markschiess van Trix; Sabine Wehrle; Grischa Worner.

Marie Jalowicz
Addresses 1922–1945

1 19a Prenzlauer Strasse
(now Karl-Liebknech-Str.,
road configuration changed)
parental apartment

2 47a Prenzlauer Strasse
with Waldmann

3 32 Landsberger Strasse
(now Landsberger Allee,
road configuration changed)
with Goldberg

4 9 Prenzlauer Strasse
with Ernsthal

5 26 Schmidtstrasse
with Jacobsohn

6 13 Nitzwalder Strasse
with Koch

7 4a Hiddenseestrasse
with Kupke

8 Karlstrasse
(now Reinhardstrasse)
with 'Lotte'

9 126 Schönhauser Allee
with Kahnke

10 Lychener Strasse
with Frau Schülz

11 Berlin-Kladow
with 'Captain Klaar'

12 36 Braunauer Strasse
(now Sonnenallee)
with Schenk

13 18 Schierker Strasse
with Janicke

14 5 Waldstrasse,
Zeuthen-Miesdorf
with Fiochi

15 6 Fürstenstrasse
(now Bergfriedstrasse)
with Galecki, the 'rubber director'

16 13 Schönleinstrasse
with Neuke

17 92 Planufer
with Adam

18 2 Am Oberbaum
with Blase

19 7 Binzstrasse
own apartment